Praise for Heather Covington Literary Divas

At the Harlem Book Fair's Phyllis Wheatley Awards, as Heather Covington escorted Maya Angelou from the Schomburg Stage upon her receiving a Lifetime Achievement Award..."Child, take my hand!"
—Dr. Maya Angelou, World Renown Poet & Author

Heather Covington is beating down the doors of the publishing industry with a sledgehammer. The sister continues to strive for the rise of black intelligence and creativity in her new book, Literary Divas.
—Omar Tyree, NAACP Image Award winner and *New York Times* bestselling author

A wonderful and poignant tribute to the literary work of an impressive selection of extremely talented, achieved and successful sistahs. Literary Divas is an important acknowledgement which not only highlights and **details our collective body of work,** but most importantly will inspire the up-and-coming Literary Divas and Dons to realize their potential as writers.
—Terrie M. Williams, author, *It Just Looks Like I'm Not Hurting: Depression, Hope and Healing in Black American Life* (Scribner, 2007)

Ms. Covington brings an informed, finely-crafted, and reader-friendly road map to the vast canon of American literature. Her books provide not only an excellent start point in the exploration of African black writing, but offer an insightful gender perspective on the stories and issues that black authors have shared.
—Max Rodriguez, Founder, The Harlem Book Fair and *The Quarterly Black Review* (QBR)

*What a great concept! Heather Covington provides a **valuable reference with glowing tributes to women who are making a difference.***
—Ann Burns, Associate Editor, *Library Journal*

Reading holds the keys to expanding one's mind and the writer is the person who makes those keys. Open the door to your mind with Literary Divas. Once you step in, you'll learn what it takes to be a LITERARY DIVA. A very important work has arrived!
—Double Emmy Award Journalist Bill McCreary &
Media Pr Guru Kim Fuller, McCreary & Fuller Media

Heather Covington has done an amazing job in her deeply rooted commitment to the literary world and African-Americans alike. Literary Divas is a MUST HAVE for our future brothers, sisters and the present generation.
—James M. Lisbon, Publisher and Founder of AMAG, Inc.

I am always inspired by books about African-Americans in history and sisterhood like Literary Divas. Terry McMillan has been one of my inspirations from the start.
—Janine A. Morris, Author of *Diva Diaries*;
HOT 97 Music Coordinator

Without the contributions of African-American women in literature, Black people could not have made progress as a race, a nation and throughout the universe. All praise for the Literary Divas of today, from the past and on the way! A TREASURE IS BORN!
—Lawrence Wayne—Founder of Memphis Black Writer's
Conference and Southern Film Festival

Prepare to be enlightened and entertained. Literary Divas is an insightful journey and MUST READ BOOK OF THE YEAR!
—Rachel Breton & Alicia M. Rivers, *Jolie* magazine

Literary Divas ™
The Top 100+ Most Admired African American Women in Literature

By Heather Covington

Edited by Yvonne Rose

Amber Books
(A Division of Amber Communications Group, Inc.)

Phoenix
New York   Los Angeles

Literary Divas™ : The Top 100+ Most Admired African American Women in Literature

By Heather Covington

Published by:
Amber Books
A Division of Amber Communications Group, Inc.
1334 East Chandler Boulevard, Suite 5-D67
Phoenix, Z 85048
amberbk@aol.com
WWW.AMBERBOOKS.COM

Tony Rose, Publisher/Editorial Director   Samuel P. Peabody, Associate Publisher
Yvonne Rose, Sr. Editor & Associate Publisher   Jarmell Simms, Editor
The Printed Page, Interior & Cover Design

ISBN#: 0-9767735-3-8 / 978-0-9767735-3-5

Library of Congress Control Number: 2006925676

Contents

Dedication

Literary Divas is dedicated to God for guiding my hands, mind, spirit, heart and soul to responsibly tell the story and pass on the legacy of "The Great Ones".

To the late Rosa Parks (1913- 2005)

... and Coretta Scott King (1927- 2006). May their symbolism, message of peace, epitome of grace, intelligence and influence on a nation of African-American women of literature live on forever.

To C. Covington, my loving mother and a NAACP Teacher of the Year whose words of wisdom and support inspired a village of children to dare to be more than their dreams ever imagined.

To Mr. Tony Rose & Mrs. Yvonne Rose, Publishers, Amber Communications Group, Inc., thank you for believing in me from the start and sharing the vision of being true to oneself despite much opposition and adverse conditions in the world. You are truly a "King & Queen of this Era" to be admired and respected for all you've selflessly done to help others.

To Mr. Max Rodriguez, (Founder of Harlem Book Fair) for supporting my dreams from the start, giving me the opportunity to be the publicity director of the Harlem Book Fair 2005, work with the renown members of the Harlem Book Fair Advisory, judge the Harlem Book Fair Spelling Bee at HueMan and produce the Harlem Authors' On Stage Tour. You are a hero to the African-American literary community.

To all poets out there who struggle for the intellectual rise of literature in poetical form, who make the world go round with philosophical happiness. You are No.1.

To my Alpha Kappa Alpha sisters of Tau Omega. Your guidance and support has kept me grounded, humble and always reminiscent of the hard work that is necessary to make it to the top, and I thank you.

To my students who, one day, may discover *Literary Divas* one day. Please understand that the sacrifice I made to document each and every *Literary Diva* was to preserve history so you may pass on this torch to your children someday. Never let your history die. Never let anyone dim your light. Be brave, be proud, be dignified, be YOU!

To the *Literary Divas* I have been blessed to research, read your books, browse through your web sites, speak to those who speak highly of you and most of all, document your history. May our literary sisterhood shine on for all future *Literary Divas*.

To Sheila Johnson (The Nation's First Black Billionaire and Co-Founder of BET), an inspiration to my soul who said... *"You have to remain resilient and flexible and you have to be steadfast in not letting any obstacle be a deterrent in trying to reach your goals."* You are an inspiration to my soul.

To the readers of *Literary Divas* who took the time to get to know each and every *Literary Diva*. I am honored. I hope you are inspired and motivated to tell your story one day.

To the victims of Hurricane Katrina and all disasters of the world. My prayers, deepest condolences and heart beats for you and your families.

"May this literary wave of excellence begin. It's the *Literary Divas* time to shine!"

PerSOULnal Blessings,

Heather "The Heat of the Literary World" Covington

About the Author

Heather Covington is the author of *The Disilgold Way: Countdown 101 from Writer to Self Publisher*; two negativity defying poetry books, *PerSOULnalities:*™ *Poems For Every Kind of Woman* and *PerSOULnalities:*™ *Poems For Every Kind of Man*; and an educational resource on teaching children how to read, *Li'l PerSOULnalities: A Children's Book for Parents & Teachers*.

She is an educator of kindergarten children by day, and a part time Certified Reading Specialist. When not teaching, Heather serves as the president of the YOUnity Reviewers Guild of America, editor-in-chief of *Disilgold Soul Literary Review*, and is noted as one of the nation's top media personalities and promoters of literary artists.

Heather is the publicity director of the Harlem Book Fair, New York, maintains a weekly column called the *Literary Dish* on EURweb.com, and is the producer of the YOUnity Reviewers Guild of America Annual Literary & Media Infusionary ™ Legend Awards Gala. She has also written music and movie reviews for *Jolie* magazine.

Heather's work as a poet, author, producer, publisher, promoter, educator and humanitarian has been cited on the *Michael Baisden Show*, 107.5 WBLS, WBLS.com, *Marc Medley Radio Show*, PBS, The Learning Channel, *AMAG, QBR, Black Book Review, Black Issues Book Review, Sister Divas* magazine, *The Amsterdam News, The Harlem News, The New York Beacon, Caribbean Life* and the *Daily News*, to name a few.

Heather is the winner of the Memphis Writer's Conference & Southern Film Festival "Best Online Network Award", the "Hall of Fame Award", and she received C & B Book Distribution's "Best Website of the Year" award. Her poetry has been called "Impressive Work!" by *Writer's Digest*.

As a photojournalist and historian, Heather enjoys chronicling, documenting, showcasing, honoring and immortalizing legends. Her website can be visited at www.Disilgold.com.

Acknowledgments

My heartfelt thanks goes out to the members of A YOUnity Book Club, DLNA Literary Celebrity Hangout Forum, Tony Rose (AmberBooks.com), Yvonne Rose (AmberBooks.com), Max Rodriguez (QBR.com), Deirdre Savoy (Co-op Writer's Workshop), Terrie Williams (TerrieWilliams.com), Lucille Beckles, Pamela Yvette Exum (SpiritofSisterhood.com), Carol Rogers and Brenda Piper (CBBooksDistribution.com), Shanta Covington, Brandon, Nyaja, Kim Fuller (McCreary & Fuller), Randa (107.5 WBLS) Delores Thornton(Marguerite Press.com), Donna Hill (DonnaHill.com), Heather and Aalim Elitou (www.NesheePublication.com), Renee Flagler (www.Aspicomm.com), Rel Dowdell (RelDowdell.com), Omar Tyree (Omar Tyree.com), Lettice Graham, featured in Essence as a Golden Diva, my first interviewed guest at Disilgold and featured in the book, *Queens*, Dr. Clara Burgess, Janine A. Morris (Hot 97), Charlene Skipworth Luke, Joe James (Dinkentertainment.com), Sylvia Sandridge, Yvette Thompson (Yvette Modeling Agency), E. Covington, Ron Kavanaugh (MosaicBooks.com), Francis Moorehead, Phil Andrews (PAPublic Relations), Wendy Malliet, Rosalyn Graves Baker, Arlene McLarin, Kent Kirby and Gary Williamson of Caribbean Life, Lawrence Wayne (Memphis Writer's Conference), Ruby Dee, Rosa Guy, Maya Angelou, Doris Mitchell, Dorothy Fall, Gloria Wright, Troy Johnson (AALBC.com), Charisse Marshall, The Beacon News, Amsterdam News staff, Staff, C. Virginia Fields, Wendy Malliet, Rosette M. Union (Producer), MoShines (Author and Producer of Urban Lit), Katherine Nero, Michael Baisden (for shouting me out on the radio), James Lisbon (AwarenessMagazine.com) Karen Myrie, Anissa Rochester (Beautywithintv.com), Sarah Woodson, Alicia M. Rivers and Rachel Breton (*Jolie* Magazine), Electa Rome Parks (Bestselling author), Donna Hill (Cross Talk Radio, multiple bestselling author), Steve, Kyla, Letoya, Lamont, the late Erma O'Brien, Diane Deveaux who introduced me to the renown (Frank Silvera's Writer's Workshop), DAS Productions, Candice Smith, Kashamba Williams (Precious Tymes Entertainment). The ladies of Tau Omega, Alpha Kappa Alpha, and the staff of my school. Your support since day one has been PHENOMENAL!

Many thanks to the Katrina Literary Collective,® my heroes, Tony Rose, Publisher/CEO and Yvonne Rose, Associate Publisher, Amber Communications Group, Inc. (ACGI); Bill Cox, former Publisher and Adrienne Ingrum, former Associate Publisher, *Black Issues Book Review*; Faye Childs, President, BlackBoard Bestsellers; Max Rodriguez, Publisher, QBR. QBR.com/ Founder, The Harlem Book Fair; Kassahun Checole, Publisher, Africa World Press, Inc.; Wade Hudson, President/ CEO and Cheryl Hudson, Publisher, Just Us Books; Jessica Care Moore- Poole, Publisher, Moore Black Press; Mark Anthony, Publisher, Q-Boro Books; Nancey Flowers, Publisher, Flowers in Bloom Publishing; Azania Brown, Publisher, In Time Publishing; Tonya Evans Wells, Publisher, FYOS Entertainment; Earl Cox, Publisher, Writers and Poets.com; Gina Clark, Publisher, Alight! New York Grit Books; Willie and Gwen Richardson, Co-founders, Cush-City.com; Paul Coates, Publisher, Black Classic Press; Yolanda Bridges, Publisher, LOF Publishing with Reshonda Tate Billingsley, Author / Channel 26, Fox News Reporter); Tom Joyner, BlackAmericaWeb.com Relief Fund; Dorris Ellis, Publisher, The Houston Sun; Linda Washington-Johnson, JMRC- Book Donation Fund; Carmen Pettie, Programs Manager, Metropolitan Tulsa Urban League; Sharon Haynes, Coordinator, Sisters Sippin' Tea Literary Group; Tamm E. Hunt, Woman Power Global Network; Sabra Robinson, Author; Valder Beebe, Author; and Andrea Brown, Author. (See Circle of Sisters link at www. Disilgold. com for Book Donor List).– *List complied on September 19th 2005.*

If I left out an important soul who has been part of the fabric of my existence, thank you for your support.

Heather Covington

"It was a long time ago. I have almost forgotten my dream. But it was there then, in front of me, bright like the sun— My dream.

—Langston Hughes

Introduction

Literary Divas: The Top 100+ Most Admired African American Women in Literature marks the historical turning point of a new century of African-American women in literature who have arrived.

Literary Divas also marks the birth of the "Neo-Soul Literary Renaissance" women from every urban city, suburban town and rural area within the realm of this land, including descendants and emigrants from the Caribbean, Africa, Europe and Asia to Canada, South America and indigenous countries throughout the Diaspora. These women have symbolically united in oneness to culturalize the "Black Experience" through "Our Words, Literature and Voices!"

Literary Divas are our grandparents, mothers, sisters, and daughters. *Literary Divas* are our teachers, storytellers, historians, role models, leaders and heroes. Most of all, it takes a *Literary Diva* to know a *Literary Diva,* and to recognize and appreciate those *Literary Divas* who have paved the way.

The *Literary Divas* featured have style, charisma, feminine mystique, intelligence, business savvy and most of all, they are disciplined, focused and respect the craft of writing. The *Literary Diva* may write a story every 4 years or just one story for a lifetime. The *Literary Diva* may pen 20 books or more in a decade. The *Literary Diva* may write in many genres, contribute works to anthologies, magazines and various publications.

Literary Divas are passionate about writing every day, acknowledge other *Literary Divas*, are great communicators, know what they want and go after their dreams. *Literary Divas* are history makers and the voices of the next generation. Like their African-American brothers such as Malcolm X, Dr. Martin Luther King, Jr., Nelson Mandela, W.E.B. DuBois, Langston Hughes, Wayne Dawkins, Jesse Jackson, Michael Baisden, Troy Johnson, Rel Dowdell, Herb Boyd, Lee Bailey, Tavis Smiley, Anthony Asadullah Samad, Michael Eric Dyson, Mo Kelly, Bill McAllister, Phil Andrews, James Lisbon, Omar Tyree, Lerone Bennett, Jr., Hon. Bill McCreary, Seitu Oronde,' George Fraser, Jake Brown, Kim Fuller, David Dinkins, Kevin Powell, Amiri Baraka, Haki Madhubuti, Ishmael Reed, Gil Noble, Les Brown, Ron Kavanaugh, Layding Kaliba, Marc Lacy, ShoLove Da Poetic,

Darren B. Rankins, Tony Rose, Vincent Alexandria, Ed Gordon and our dearly missed pioneers, John Johnson, Lou Rawls, Johnny Cochran, and Gordon Parks Sr.; their literary words play like a written symphony too remarkable and bright to ignore.

Literary Divas share their pain, struggles, desires, and triumphs through their written words as messengers of time and circumstance. Their triumphs and achievements to socio- political cries disguised within novels, poetry, non-fiction reference resources, children's books, romance novels, mysteries, commentaries, and today's urban books invite readers to journey through their experiences from bold love and romance to unabashed self-identity crisis and political issues to the plight of today's Black family and rise in rank all the way to the top. *Literary Divas'* stories will amaze as well as make us cry, bring joy and laughter.

Literary Divas' words encourage people of all nationalities, cultures and creed to rejoice and embrace one another. *Literary Divas'* words symbolize amazing feats never imagined. The *Literary Divas'* written words are powerful, boundless, miraculous, paranormal and the best mentor to a writer's soul. To discover each one's lives is to discover one's own greatness.

The late Billie Holiday, Shirley Chisholm, Rosa Parks, Pearl Bailey, Hallie Quinn Brown, Celia Cruz, Coretta Scott King, Octavia Butler, Sojourner Truth, Phillis Wheatley, and even Nefertitti were *Literary Divas*, as well. The newest of *celebrity Literary Divas* like Karrine Steffans, Oprah Winfrey, Yvonne Rose, Susan Taylor, Pearl Cleage, Jill Nelson, Maryse Conde, Elizabeth Nunez. Terry McMillan, Sister Souljah, Holly Robinson-Peete, Laila Ali, Whoopie Goldberg, Suzi Lori- Parks, Patti LaBelle, Tananarive Due, Delores Phillips, Yolanda Joe, Tanya R. Bates, Lynette Khalfani, and Jackie Joyner-Kersee make *Literary Divas* of today so proud. *Literary Divas'* history is a relevant and historical tool that all men and women of the literary kind must read.

Their lives will bring out the *Literary Diva* or if you are a gentleman, the *Literary Don* in you. This is only volume one. Your rise to literary excellence may be featured soon. For now, dare to rediscover what you already know to ignite your passion to be great along with the *Literary Divas.*

Volume one only begins the dream of many *Literary Divas* with unity!

Let the celebration begin! Get Ready! Get Set! Go!

Part One

Literary Divas of Excellence

Literary Divas™ Reading Group & Discussion Guide

After you have read Literary Divas, here are some questions you can answer:

1. What is your definition of a Literary Diva?

2. Which Literary Diva reminded you of someone you know?

3. Do you feel that the subject, content and genre of work published by a Literary Diva says volumes about the Literary Diva's personality?

4. Which Literary Diva's story encouraged you to purchase a book by the author as soon as you read her biography?

5. What do you think it takes to become a Literary Diva?

6. If you could rewrite a Literary Diva's life, whose life might you change because of the circumstances she endured?

7. Have you met a Literary Diva? If not, which Literary Diva would you like to meet?

8. Do you recall important facts about the Literary Divas? If so, which facts do you vividly remember?

9. If you could be one Literary Diva for a day, who would it be and why?

10. Who would you like to give Literary Divas to as a gift? Why?

11. Are you a Literary Diva? Why?

If so, email your biography, Timeline of published works and photo to Amberbk@aol.com, Disilgold@aol.com. You may very well be featured in a future edition.

Alice Walker

Born February 9, 1944 in Eatonton, Georgia, Alice Walker received the Pulitzer Prize in 1983 for her literary work, *The Color Purple*, an award considered one of the most prestigious honors for writers.

Today, Alice Walker is a worldwide literary icon, in the company of classic artists such as Dr. Maya Angelou, Toni Morrison, Terry McMillan, Nikki Giovanni, Rosa Guy, Sister Souljah, Teri Woods, Sonia Sanchez and many more shining literary stars.

Millions of people heard about the grand opening night performance of the new musical play adaptation version of *The Color Purple* in 2005, based on Alice Walker's Pulitzer Prize-winning novel and the landmark film by Steven Spielberg that earned eleven Oscar Nominations.

However, it is Alice's writing style in her book, *The Color Purple*, that captured a nation of fans, beginning with a narrative of the life of Celie, a fourteen-year-old black girl who lives with her sister Nettie, and dying mother. Celie is left at the hands of her stepfather, Alfonso, who is emotionally, physically and sexually abusive. Her narrative style and gift for telling a story is powerful.

Before her recent reclaim to fame for the adaptation of the play version of The Color Purple, Alice was already a renowned writer who took the craft of writing very seriously. Her writing work ethic is a phenomenon and to this day, she continues to out do her self with each published work.

Many people do not know that her upbringing was as challenging as her writing career. She suffered a horrific accident during her youth. Her elder brother accidentally wounded her eye with a BB gun. This ordeal caused Alice who was only 8 years old to lose complete eyesight in one of her eyes. This must have been a traumatic experience for a young budding writer like Alice.

This travesty did not stop the talented and vivacious Alice Walker who went on to excel and win top honors in high school as the valedictorian of her class. She continued her studies while attending renowned colleges, such as Spelman and Sarah Lawrence College, and successfully earned a Bachelor of Arts Degree.

Her desire to take on political issues began while in college when she traveled as an exchange student to Africa. She would give birth to her daughter, Rebecca, in 1969 upon migrating from New York to Tougaloo, Mississippi. Alice's historic migration symbolically embellished her strong stance for Civil Rights.

At the time, Coretta Scott King would lead a march on Washington in protest for a national holiday for her late husband, Civil Rights Leader Dr. Martin Luther King, Jr., who peacefully protested for equality among blacks and whites, but was assassinated in 1968. Alice would join in the struggle for the holiday, as a leading activist of the Civil Rights Movement and against Apartheid in Africa. Her activist voice became a symbol for women's rights.

In 1984, Alice founded her own publishing company, Wild Trees Press. Her company published some of the great literature and poetry works from the talented Alice Walker. Today, her writings and work are revered as the quintessential symbolism of the best modern writing of our time in African—American literature. Alice Walker's writing style set the standard for great literary works.

Alice Walker is currently the award recipient of the Lillian Smith Award from the National Endowment for the Arts, Rosenthal Award from the National Institute of Arts & Letters, Radcliffe Institute Fellowship, Merrill Fellowship, Guggenheim Fellowship; and she was nominated for the National Book Award. She also, received the Front Page Award for Best Magazine Criticism from the Newswoman's Club of New York, the Townsend Prize and the Lyndhurst Prize.

(Website: Luminarium/org/contemporary/alicew/)

Timeline of the Literary Diva's Published Work

- 2005—The Color Purple—(Stage play adaptation produced by Oprah Winfrey)
- 2004—Absolute Trust in the Goodness of Earth—(Random House)
- 2003—The Color Purple—(Harvest Books)
- 2003—A Poem Traveled Down My Arm—(Random House)
- 2003—Meridian—(Harvest Books)
- 2002—Langston Hughes: American Poet—(Amistad)
- 2001—Sent by Earth: A Message from the Grandmother Spirit After the Bombing of the World Trade Center and the Pentagon—Open Media
- 1998—Anything We Love Can Be Saved—(Ballantine Books)
- 1997—The Temple of My Familiar—(Washington Square PR)
- 1997—Possessing the Secret of Joy—(Washington Square PR)
- 1997—Anything We Love Can Be Saved: A Writer's Activism—(Washington Square PR)
- 1996—The Sane River Twice: Honoring the Difficult—(Scribner)
- 1996—The Color Purple—(Pocket Books)
- 1996—Warrior Marks—(Harvest Books)
- 1996—Banned—(Aunt Lute Books)
- 1993—The Hell With Dying—(Voyager Books)
- 1993—The Third Life of Grange Copeland—(Pocket Books)
- 1993—Her Blue Body Everything We Know: Earthling Poems—(1965-1990 Complete)
- 1991—Finding the Green Stone
- 1989—Living By the Word—(Harvest Books)
- 1998—By the Light of My Father's Smile—(Random House)
- 1986—The Color Purple—(G. K. Hall & Company; Large Print edition)
- 1986—Once—Poems—(Hartcourt & Brace)
- 1986—Horses Make a Landscape More Beautiful—(Hartcourt & Brace)
- 1986—Revolutionary Petunias and Other Poems—(Hartcourt Brace)
- 1985—In Love and Trouble: Stories of Black Woman—(Hartcourt Brace)
- 1984—Goodnight Willie Lee, I'll See YOU in the Morning—(Hartcourt & Brace)
- 1984—The Search of Our Mother's Gardens—(Hartcourt & Brace)
- 1983—The Color Purple—(Perfection Learning Pre-bound)
- 1982—You Can't Keep a Good Woman Down—(Hartcourt & Brace)Website References

Alicia Keys

It's often said, that it is easy for a vocal artist to break into the television and movie industry, but very difficult for a vocal artist to be taken seriously in the mainstream as an author of a poetry book. Alicia Keys, recorded as one of the greatest and most talented female singers of our time, daringly over stepped naysayers when she penned her first book entitled, Tears for Water: Songbook of Poems and Lyrics; Nov. 2004.

Born Alicia Augello Cook on January 25, 1980 to Terri Augello, an Italian—American, actress and paralegal, she penned the words to many of her poetical inspired songs that have gone on to become mega-top selling hits.

How would the world know the thoughts and emotions that stirred Alicia Keys to superstardom and the multi—talented woman she is today if it weren't for her poetry book?

She's a source of inspiration and proves with her top selling poetry book that simplicity and being true to oneself first, is the key to success. To date, Alicia Key's albums have sold over 10 million and by the likes of it, her first poetry book may match the success of her music career in years to come. She is a poet on the rise to watch.

(Website: AliciaKeys.com)

Timeline of the Literary Diva's Published Work

∞ 2004—Tears for Water: Songbook of Poems and Lyrics—(Putnam)

Discography:
∞ 2005—Alicia Keys: MTV Unplugged—DVD—(J Records)

- 2005—Unplugged; Cd and DVD—(Bmg, Int'l)
- 2005—So Amazing: An All-star Tribute to Luther Vandross /Contribution—So Amazing—(J Records)
- 2004—The Diary of Alicia Keys—(Hal Leonard Corporation)
- 2004—If I Ain't Got You; Cd Single—(Bmg, Int'l)
- 2004—Karma, Pt. 2; Cd and DVD—(J Records)
- 2003—Remixed & Unplugged in A Minor; Audio Cd—(Bmg, Int'l)
- 2001—Songs in a Minor; Audio Cd—(J Records)

Angel Hunter

Angel M. Hunter is an *Essence* magazine Bestselling Author. Her published titles include: *You Are Not Alone, A Dollar and A Dream, Around the Way Girl, Sister Girls* and *Fakin It*.

After moving to Greenville, South Caroline from Neptune New Jersey, Angel and her husband Tony Irby founded For the Soul. More than a bookstore, it's a place to meet and greet, motivate, educate, initiate, create and promote growth and awareness in the African American community.

Angel is also passionate about acting and dancing. The founder of Soulful Theater, Angel has written and produced her first play, and is currently writing a screenplay.

Angel and Tony are the parents of one son, Anthony Shacquille Irby, their pride and joy.

Timeline of the Literary Diva's Published Work

- 2006 - Fakin It - (Kensington Publishing)
- 2006 - Sister Girls - (Kensington Publishing)
- 2005 - A Dollar and a Dream - (Zebra Books)
- 2004 - Around the Way Girls - (Urban Books)
- 2001 – You are not Alone – (Essence Publications)

Angela Davis

Angela Yvonne Davis was born in 1944 in Birmingham, Alabama, in the midst of Jim Crow laws. Her father, a graduate of St. Augustine's College, a traditional black college in Raleigh, North Carolina, was briefly a high school history teacher.

Using their modest income, the family purchased a large home in a mixed neighborhood where Angela spent most of her youth. The neighborhood, called locally "Dynamite Hill," was marked by racial conflict.

By her junior year, at 14, she applied for and was accepted to a program of the American Friends Service Committee, which placed Black students from the South in integrated schools in the north. Angela had occasionally spent time on her uncle's farm with friends in New York City and enjoyed the change in scenery. She chose to attend high school at Elizabeth Irwin High School, also known as the Little Red School House, in Greenwich Village in New York City, a small private school favored by the radical community. There she was exposed to the study of socialism and communism and was recruited to the Communist youth group, "Advance", where she became acquainted with children of the leaders of the Communist Party including her lifelong friend, Bettina Aptheker.

Angela had political activism instilled in her by her mother, who had a very political background since her college days. As an elementary school student, Angela would accompany Salley E. Davis, whenever she would participate in sit-in protests and demonstrations.

Upon graduation from high school, Angela was awarded a full scholarship to Brandeis University in Waltham, Massachusetts, where she was one of three Black students in her freshman class.

Initially alienated by the isolation of the campus, Angela soon made friends with the foreign students on campus. She worked at part-time jobs earning money to spend her summer in Europe and attended the eighth World Festival for Youth and Students in Helsinki. Angela returned home to an FBI interview about her attendance at the Festival, which the government considered communist sponsored.

During her second year of college, Angela decided to major in French. She was accepted for the Hamilton College Junior Year in France Program and managed to talk Brandeis into extending support with her scholarship to cover the expenses. In Paris, she and other students lived with a French family. Nearing completion of her degree in French language, she realized her major interest was philosophy. In 1965 she graduated, magna cum laude, a member of Phi Beta Kappa.

Angela went on to earn a master's degree from the University of California, San Diego, returning to Germany for her Ph.D. in Philosophy from the Humboldt University of Berlin, GDR.

Angela worked as a philosophy lecturer at the University of California, Los Angeles, in the 1960s during which time she also was a radical feminist and activist, a member of the Communist Party USA and associated with theBlack Panther Party.

She was ousted as the FBI's "most wanted" and hid underground while placed on America's most-wanted list. Angela was arrested, but she was acquitted of trumped up charges in 1972.

Angela ran for Vice President on the Communist ticket in 1980 and 1984 along with Gus Hall.

She has written several books, including: *If They Come in the Morning* (1971); *Women, Race and Class* (1983), *Angela: An Autobiography* (1988); and *Women, Culture and Politics* (1989). Angela continues to write and lecture, and remains politically active.

Timeline of the Literary Diva's Published Work

∽ 1971—If They Come in the Morning: Voices of Resistance—(Signet)
∽ 1972—Frame Up: The Opening Defense Statement Made—(Signet)

〜 1976—Angela Davis: An Autobiography—(Bantam Books)
〜 1983—Women, Race and Class—(Vintage)
〜 1988—Violence Against Women and the Ongoing Challenge to Racism—(Kitchen Table/Women of Color)
〜 1989—Women, Culture and Politics—(Vintage)
〜 1999—Blues Legacies and Black Feminism: Gertrude "Ma" Rainey, Bessie Smith, and Billie Holiday (Vintage)
〜 1998—The Angela Y. Davis Reader (Blackwell Publishers)
〜 2003—Are Prisons Obsolete? (Open Media)

Anita Doreen Diggs

Anita Doreen Diggs managed to distinguish herself as one of the most versatile writers at the turn of the century. She's created works of non-fiction and fiction and has mastered both genres. Her popular fiction novels, *Meeting in the Ladies Room* and *A Mighty Love* have received critical acclaim. Anita also penned a series of dynamic guides such as *Success at Work: A Guide For African Americans, Talking Drums: An African American Quote Collection, The African American Resource Guide, Barrier Breaking Resumes and Cover Letters*, and a favorite among readers, *Staying Married: A Guide For African American Couples.*

She served as the Senior Editor for One World/Ballantine Books. Some of the literary stars she brought to the company, according to her online biography, (www.AnitaDoreenDiggs.com) are the popular Judge Greg Mathis; Elizabeth Nunez; Winner of "Book Award" and a New York Times Bestseller; and Ilyasah Shabazz, a NAACP "Image Award" nominee. At Time Warner Trade Publishing she acquired books by comedian Steve Harvey and best selling author, Terrie Williams. She was a publicist for Penguin Books USA before becoming a book editor.

"Talented," "confident" and "well—researched," Anita Doreen Diggs has lectured on many topics from how to get a job in the book publishing industry, how to obtain a literary agent, which is critical toward even being considered for a book deal by mainstream publishers these days; and how to develop a solid book proposal that can land writers a top book deal.

It's no wonder Anita was placed on "The Shapers" list for year 2000 in the Columbia Journalism Review. She is one author whose discipline and hard work have won over a nation of fans.

(Website: AnitaDoreenDiggs.com)

Timeline of the Literary Diva's Published Work

- ✎ 2005—Meeting In the Ladies Room—(Kensington)
- ✎ 2005—The Other Side of the Game—(Dafina)
- ✎ 2004—A Mighty Love—(Thomas Gale)
- ✎ 2003—A Mighty Love—(Kensington)
- ✎ 1999—Breaking the Barrier: Jumping the Hurdle of Employment and Getting a Job—(Crown Publishing Group)
- ✎ 1998—Staying Married: A Guide For African American Couples—(Kensington)
- ✎ 1996—Talking Drums: An African American Quote Collection—(St. Martin's Press)
- ✎ 1994—The African American Guide—(Barricade Books, Incorporated)

Artist C. Arthur

Artist C. Arthur a.k.a. "A.C. Arthur" debuted onto the literary scene with the novel, *Object of His Desire*, a daring, captivating and bold title for many romance readers during the early 2000's. She was inspired to write her first novel upon gazing at a handsome picture of an Italian villa which sparked the idea of creating an African-American Italian hero. Her idea turned out to be more genius than A.C. had imagined.

Born and raised in Baltimore, Maryland, her active imagination and a love for reading encouraged her to begin writing in high school and she hasn't stopped since. Determined to bring a new edge to romance, she continued to develop intriguing plots and fresh dialogue between her racy characters—thus keeping readers on their toes. Little did Artist know that she would develop a knack for writing a series of romance novels that would catch the attention of readers.

It wasn't easy for Arthur to complete her first novel. After all, as a worker in the legal field for over 13 years after 6 years from the debut of her first novel, she had seen many horrific things in her life and longed for a safe haven to escape which romance novels provided.

Her efforts and dedication to her work would finally pay off. Artist was honored as one of three finalists in the 2003 Emma Awards, which was a highlight in her writing career.

    (**Website: ACArthur.net**)

Timeline of the Literary Diva's Published Work

- ∽ 2007—Corporate Seduction—(Genesis)
- ∽ 2007—Heart of the Phoenix—(Genesis)
- ∽ 2006—Love Me Carefully—(Genesis)
- ∽ 2005—Unconditional—(Genesis)
- ∽ 2004—Office Policy—(Genesis)
- ∽ 2003—Object of His Desire—(Genesis)

Barbara A. Custer

Barbara A. Custer is the publisher of *Twilight Healer*, a mythological sci-fi thriller, featured at www.AuthorHouse.com. Her own website, BloodRedShadows.com features the debut of her latest mythological and vampire infused horror that has created quite a buzz in the literary industry. Barbara first began writing in 1990 when a college instructor encouraged her to write and as a way to process the grief over her mother's death.

A Stephen King fan, she decided to try horror fiction. Many of her horror and science fiction stories soon appeared in literary and small press magazines like *The Vampire's Crypt, The Ultimate Unknown* and *Fading Shadows*. She now edits her own thriving vampire fiction magazine, *Night to Dawn*.

Barbara, befittingly so, worked full time as a respiratory therapist. Her job provided a grist for horror and science fiction stories. In *Twilight Healer*, she brings her medical background to the printed page by blending it with supernatural horror. Her hobbies have included gardening, writing, and collecting Mylar balloons for many years. Barbara's favorite time of the year is Halloween where she prepares gift baskets with spooky items and of course, her thriller books.

(Website: Bloodredshadows.com)

Timeline of the Literary Diva's Published Work

- ∞ 2004—Night to Dawn: Anthology—(Author House)
- ∞ 2003—Twilight Healer—(Author House)

Barbara Reynolds

The Reverend Dr. Barbara A. Reynolds is an award winning journalist, author and has appeared on such major television shows as the *Oprah Winfrey Show, Politically Incorrect,* "C-Span", "CNN and Co." and is heard every weekend on XM satellite radio and WOL on her own signature show called, *Reynolds Rap.* She is president of Reynolds  News Service and her syndicated newspaper columns have reached an estimated 10 million people weekly. Barbara is also a consultant to several major universities and public officials on media strategies and a writer for *Essence Magazine.*

Barbara was hired by the *Cleveland Press* in 1968, where she covered the race riots. Hired by *Ebony* magazine in 1969, she became assistant editor and wrote the monthly food column, *A Date with a Dish.* A poet, Barbara was published in *Black World* and associated with Kuumba Theatre and the OBAC Writers Workshop. In 1969, she joined Chicago *Today* and covered the murder of Fred Hampton; and later moved to the *Chicago Tribune,* where she helped found *Dollars and Sense* magazine. Soon after, Barbara became an editorial writer, Start-Up editor and columnist for *USAToday.* The first "negro" to serve in such a role at the mainstream publication, she remained in that position for thirteen years.

Dr. Reynolds is the author of several books, including: *Jesse Jackson: America's David*, an unauthorized biography; *And Still We Rise*, interviews with 50 African-American role models; *No, I Won't Shut Up! 30 years of Telling It Like It Is!* and *Out of Hell and Living Well*, released in November 2004. She is also a mentor/professor in religion and journalism at Howard University in the School of Communications.

Born in Columbus, Ohio, Barbara received her BA in journalism from The Ohio State University, her Masters Degree from Howard University School of Divinity in 1991 and her doctorate in Ministry from the United Theological Seminary in Dayton, Ohio in 1998. She also has been awarded honorary doctorates from Shenandoah University and her alma mater, The Ohio State University. Bishop Alfred A. Owens Jr. in 1995 ordained her an elder of the Greater Mount Calvary Holy Church. In 1997 she launched a citywide deliverance ministry for female substance abusers, called Harriet's Children, headquartered at Greater Mount Calvary. Dr. Reynolds also teaches the "Black Presence in the Bible" and Pneumatology at the Calvary Bible Institute, where she serves on the board of directors.

Reverend Dr. Reynolds has preached in many churches and for many denominations across the United States. In 1997, she became one of the first African American female ministers asked to serve as Chaplain of the Week at Chautauqua Institution, a Christian resort center where presidents from Harry Truman to Bill Clinton have vacationed in that meditative spiritual setting. As a professor, Dr. Reynolds has held the Jessie Ball Dupont Chair in Journalism at Shenandoah University in Winchester, Virginia and was a Freedom Forum Scholar for the 1998 school year in journalism at Florida A&M University in Tallahassee, Florida. Currently she mentors journalism students and religion majors at the Howard University School of Communications.

Dr. Reynolds is the recipient of many honors. They include the Martin Luther King Jr. Drum Major for Justice Award, the 1999 Journalist of the Year Award from the National Association of Black Journalists, Outstanding Achievement Award from the Columbia University (Missouri) School of Journalism and she was a Nieman Fellow at Harvard University. Bishop Alfred Owens, Pastor of Greater Mt. Calvary Holy Church, named her Woman of the Year for 2004. She has recently been voted into

Leadership Washington, a powerful group of leaders in the Washington area, who as a network bring help, hope of healing to those in need. With the hand of God upon her, she plans to build a national network of healing centers for female victims of addiction and abuse. She lives in the Washington area with her son, John Eric, who is a college sophomore.

Dr. Reynolds graduated from Howard University School of Divinity in 1992 and the United Theological Seminary in Dayton, Ohio in 1998. She is an ordained minister and serves at the Greater Mount Calvary Holy Church in Washington, DC.

(Website: www.reynoldsnews.com)

Timeline of the Literary Diva's Published Work

- 1985 —Jesse Jackson: America's David —(JFJ Associates)
- 1988 —And Still We Rise —(USA Today Books)
- 1998 —No, I Won't Shut Up! 30 years of Telling It Like It Is! —(JFJ Associates)
- 2004 —Out of Hell and Living Well —(Xulon Press)

Bea Joyner

If laughter is the best medicine, then *Don't Need No Soaps, My Life Is Soap Enough!* offers a cure. It is a humorous look at life from a woman who admits she has made errors in her life but survived with her sanity intact. The humorous Beatrice Joyner looks at her life objectively and without bitterness as she shares her wisdom. Many women experience the thralls of falling in love, but Bea Joyner tells how love can make you forget your common sense. Unlike many others these days, she admits she's no expert on love.

As a single parent, Bea unlocks the mystery of parenting by revealing the *Real Parents Training Manual*. She candidly and in purest comical style, explains how ordinary routines of trying to get her children ready for school or getting reluctant children to eat a wholesome and nutritious meal can turn into the root cause of gray hair. Laugh out loud with her as she tries to convince her friends that her children will leave home and not return.

Bea reminds women to celebrate their victories as each one climb to what she calls "the mountain of life". She gives survival techniques while exploring the joys of living and willingly admits to being a pen pal with Ed McMahon in those mail order sweepstakes. She is convinced that her newfound status of being a prude has to be part of the aging process. Bea's wisdom comes across with more humor and graciousness as she helps women realize that one isn't alone on the most insane things that can go on in the world.

Bea Joyner shares her photographs and her poetry as well. Her beautiful black and white photographs display her gift for portraits and uniqueness as an author setting her own standards for comical genres. Bea Joyner is just as charismatic and entertaining as her novels in person. She gave a booksigning at Sister's Uptown Book Store that evoked side-splitting laughter and a love for her book from fans right in the heart of Harlem.

(Website: BeaJoyner.com)

Timeline of the Literary Diva's Published Work

- 1999—Don't Need No Soaps, My Life Is Soap Enough!—(Busy as Bee Productions)
- 1992-The Emotions of Me—(Busy as Bee Productions)

Bebe Moore Campbell

Bebe Moore Campbell was born and grew up in Philadelphia, Pennsylvania. Later on she obtained her Bachelor of Science degree in elementary education from the University of Pittsburgh.

Bebe exploded again onto best selling charts with *72 Hour Hold.* Her novel caught the attention of many people with mentally ill family members as well as readers who were intrigued by her candid ability to interweave sensitivity over this issue affecting millions of people. *Kirkus Reviews* stated, "Campbell's provocative fourth novel explores our culture's treatment of mental illness through the story of one mother's desperate attempts to save her manic-depressive teenaged daughter." Nancy Rawles of the *Washington Post* stated, "*72 Hour Hold* deserves a wide audience and the honest, open discussion that Campbell hopes to encourage."

Bebe's books give a platform for discussion on the rise of households with people suffering mental illness. Her books have reached the New York Times bestsellers list three times. *What You Owe Me* was voted as a LA Times "Best Book of the Year." *Me, Brothers and Sisters* and *Singing in the Comeback Choir*" continue to be among the favorites of her fans. Other notable works include the novel, *Your Blues Ain't Like Mine*, which was honored as New York Times "Notable Book of the Year" and even earned a NAACP Image Award for Literature.

Earning the NAACP Image Award literally set off Bebe Moore Campbell's career. Bebe proved that readers do enjoy well written books that span from a range of topics. Her memoir, *Sweet Summer, Growing Up With and Without My Dad*, is one of her most endearing books of all time. However, she showed her fans that she could also hold her own with her first non-fiction work and her first, *Successful Women, Angry Men: Backlash in the Two-Career Marriage.*

Bebe Moore Campbell's essays, articles and excerpts appear in many anthologies. She has remained dedicated toward writing books that stem from the issue of mental health awareness. It was the topic of mental illness that spurred Bebe's interest in creating her first children's book, *Sometimes My Mommy Gets Angry* (2003). The risks she took while creating a controversial book on this topic earned her the "National Alliance for the Mentally Ill (NAMI) Outstanding Literature Award for 2003." *Sometimes My Mommy Gets Angry* explores how a little girl copes with being raised by her mentally ill mother. Bebe did not stop at writing novels, children's books and essays about the topic, her first play, *Even with the Madness*, debuted in New York in June 2003.

People may have discovered her numerous articles as a journalist in top publications such as "The New York Times Magazine," "The Washington Post," "The Los Angeles Times," "Essence," "Ebony," "Black Enterprise," and many other publications. She has also been the regular commentator for National Public Radio's "Morning Edition."

(Website: BebeMooreCampbell.com)

Timeline of the Literary Diva's Published Work

- ✑ 2005—72 Hour Hold—(Knoph Publishing)
- ✑ 2005—Sometimes My Mom Gets Angry—(Penguin Young Reader's Group)
- ✑ 2002—What You Owe Me—(Penguin Group, USA)
- ✑ 2001—What You Owe Me—(Penguin Group)
- ✑ 2000—Successful Women, Angry Men—(Penguin Group, USA)
- ✑ 2000—Sweet Summer: Growing Up Without My Dad—(Penguin Young Reader's Group)
- ✑ 1998—Singing in the Comeback Choir—(Penguin Group, USA)
- ✑ 1998—Singing in the Comeback Choir; Audio Cassette (4 Cassettes-Audio Renaissance)
- ✑ 1995—Your Blues Ain't Like Mine—(Random House Publishing Group)
- ✑ 1995—Brothers and Sisters—(Penguin Group, USA)
- ✑ 1987—Backlash Marriage: The Two Career Family under Siege—(Random House Publishing Group)

Bernice L. McFadden

Bernice L. McFadden, "destined for success," was born and raised in Brooklyn, New York. The eldest of four children and the mother of one daughter, Bernice attended grade school at P.S. 161 in Brooklyn and Middle School at Holy Spirit, also in Brooklyn. She attended high school at St. Cyril Academy an all-girls boarding school in Danville, Pennsylvania.

In1983 she enrolled in NYC fashion college: Laboratory Institute of Merchandising. Bernice had dreams of becoming an international clothing buyer. Soon she attended LIM for two semesters. She took a position at Bloomingdale's and later with Itokin, a Japanese owned retail company. Then Bernice attended Marymount College where she received a certificate of completion in Travel and Tourism. After Bernice gave birth her daughter in 1988, she obtained a job with Rockresorts, a company then owned by the Rockefeller family. Bernice was let go when the company was sold. She remained unemployed for one year. This time period became a major turning point in Bernice McFadden's life.

Bernice had begun to dedicate time developing her writing skills. During the next nine years she held three more jobs. Her quest was to find a job that was enjoyable. Bernice enrolled at Fordham University. She took many courses that reflected upon Afro-American history and literature, as well as creative writing, poetry and journalism. Her professor's guidance and fascination with some of her favorite authors gave her the inspiration and ability to write the kind of books she is able to pen today.

One day Bernice decided to send out hundreds of query letters to agents and publishers in an attempt to sell one of her short stories or perhaps, a novel she was working on. In 1997, Bernice quit her job and dedicated seven months to re-writing her novel that would become, "SUGAR." In May of 1998, after depleting her savings, she took her last and final position within corporate America. "On Feb 9th, 1999, her daughter's eleventh birthday (and Alice Walker's birthday—one of Ms. McFadden's favorite authors) she sent a query letter to an agent who signed her two weeks later and the rest is literary history!"—(Cited from www. BerniceMcFadden.com)

Timeline of the Literary Diva's Published Work

- 2006—No Where is a Place—(Dutton Adult)
- 2004—Loving Donovan—(Plume)
- 2004—Camilla's Roses—(Thorndike Press)
- 2002—The Warmest December—(Plume)
- 2001—Sugar—(Plume)
- 2001—The Bitter Earth 12—(Plume Books)

Bertha Davis

Bertha M. Davis, a Native of Mississippi, has been a freelance writer for years. She has written two books, including several independent books of poetry. Her most compelling work, *Growing up in Mississippi*, is a compelling memoir that captures the experiences of young black women in the South before and during the Civil Rights Movement. Readers were so intrigued by the scrapbook-style book cover featuring a rare photo of Bertha, many requests for the title poured in to her website. Bertha touched upon many civil issues on her book, she had been a Chaplin volunteer at the Marion County Jail in Indianapolis, Indiana.

Growing Up In Mississippi received numerous reviews, won the "Best Book Award" in 2004 and *The Five Stars Award by the DLNA YOUnity Reviewers Worldwide* in New York. The book also won "The Joy Production Award" of WHTJ Radio Station 1690-AM. Bertha was chosen "Author of the Month" for her book *Marriage and the Family* by Marguerite Press and was featured in Artist Author's "Spotlight of the Month" by Nubian Sista's Book Club and C&B Books Distribution. Her determination to share her past has influenced many writers to create thought provoking memoirs.

A family woman, Bertha has been married for more than 40 years to Mr. RC Davis Sr., her grade school sweetheart. A dedicated Christian for over 25 years, she has always enjoyed helping others. In 1988, she fulfilled a lifelong dream as a graduate from Ivy Tech State College. As a member of renowned writing organizations such as the *YOUnity Guild, Marguerite Press Promo Writers Group, The Black Vendors Association, Indiana State Festival Association, Indy Arts,* and *PubEasy Booksellers,* Bertha receives numerous requests to perform readings in schools and universities as a workshop presenter. However, as a woman who has been in a successful marriage for so many years, she is most often requested for seminars on marriage and relationships.

Bertha's infectious personality radiates from her literature, continue to earn her new honors. She's been honored with an "In Appreciation for Outstanding Services to the Community" by Sheriff Joseph G. McAtee (1994), Honorary Deputy Sheriff Award for Unselfish Service to Marion County Sheriff's Department by Sheriff Jack L. Cottey (1996), Indiana Women's Prison Recognition Award (1988-1989), Outreach Program Service Award (1984), Woman of the Year Award, Sisterhood of Grace Church (1985), Parent of the Year Award, Boy Scouts of America (1989), and many other recognitions and Certificate of Appreciation honors for her outstanding work.

(Website: BerthasBooks.com)

Timeline of the Literary Diva's Published Work

∼ 2004—Growing Up in Mississippi—(Infinity Publishing)
∼ 2002—Marriage and the Family—(Author House)

Brenda Hampton

Brenda M. Hampton is a native of St. Louis, who has a true gift and passion for writing.

Having an entrepreneurial spirit, Hampton's ideas and motivation lead to rewarding careers in insurance, writing and Print-On-Demand publishing. She is the President/CEO of Hampton Insurance Agency, where she works as an Insurance Broker for many customers throughout the St. Louis Metropolitan area. Also, she is the founder of Voices Books & Publishing, *"The place where every voice can be heard."*

After maintaining a journal for several years, Brenda's writing career exploded in early 2002. By year's end, she completed her Memoir, *Tomorrow Never Dies*, along with two fast-selling novels, *Two's Enough Three's A Crowd* and *How Can I Be Down?* Both fiction novels were published in 2003, as her upcoming fiction novels: *My Way Or No Way, SLICK,* and *Change Don't Always Come,* were already in production.

Through Brenda's persistence and success with self-publishing, in October 2004 she earned a three book deal with Black Pearl Books, Inc. Nearly one year later, her first republished and world-wide distributed title, *SLICK*, became an *Essence* magazine best-seller. Brenda is known for being a versatile writer, and her recent and future novels include: *No Justice No Peace*, *Naughty by Nature* and *The Dirty Truth*, an erotic mystery with an expected release date in January 2007.

Quoted as being, "An Author on the Rise," "A gutsy writer," and "A writer who tells-it-like-it-is," Brenda's literary works have been noted in the *St. Louis American Newspaper, The St. Louis Post Dispatch, The Riverfront Times, Essence Magazine, Romantic Tales Online Magazine, R.A.W. Sistaz, O.O.S.A Online Bookclub, BlackExpressions 2006*, the "Platinum-Hood", the award-winning *Flipside Newszine*, and many more. Radio interviews include: *Mr. Ti-Rone* in Los Angeles, CA and Majic 104.9 *Sunday Morning Live Show* with Deneen Busby. Aside from writing, Brenda enjoys watching football, and the comfort of music and skating.

(Website: BrendamHampton.com)

Timeline of the Literary Diva's Published Work

- 2006—SLICK—(Black Pearl Books, Inc.)
- 2006—Naughty by Nature—(Black Pearl Books, Inc.)
- 2005—No Justice No Peace—(Author House)
- 2004—My Way Or No Way, Part II—(Author House)2004—Change Don't Always Come, Part III—(Author House)
- 2003—Two's Enough Three's A Crowd, Part I—(Author House)
- 2003—How Can I Be Down?—(Author House)

Brenda Thomas

"Brenda Thomas is a Philadelphia based marketing professional and sought after commentator on what really goes on behind the scenes in the world of basketball. She previously worked as a senior executive secretary for IBM and went on to establish the marketing edge of the basketball footwear and apparel company, AND 1. In addition to creating her own business, Admin Ink, she also worked as the personal assistant to NBA All-Star Stephon X. Marbury." (Cited from www. phillywriter.com).

Based on a live interview with Disilgold Soul, Brenda mentioned that upon trying to get a book deal, she was rejected by over 30 editors, but her persistence paid off when *Threesome* was picked up by Pocket Books. She managed to launch her own media debut party and over 300 people showed up from multi-industries.

Brenda's books now include, *Threesome*, *Fourplay* and *The Velvet Rope*. In a class by herself, she expresses how she reads novels by Bebe Moore Campbell and Terry McMillan in order to keep on writing with the same tenacity and passion as the bestselling authors on www. Booksthatclick. com.

This best selling author is determined to let the world know she is the "Next Philly Author". But, from the likes of her meteoric rise to success in record breaking time upon unleashing the secret underground world of sex and the NBA, she has gone international.

(Website: Phillywriter.com)

Timeline of the Literary Diva's Published Work
- 2005—The Velvet Rope—(Downtown Press)
- 2004—Fourplay: The Dance of Sensuality—(Velvet Rope)
- 2001—Threesome: Where Seduction, Power and Basketball Collide—(Pocket Books)

Camille Yarbrough

A dancer, actress, singer, teacher, television producer and activist as well as a writer, Camille Yarbrough was born in Chicago, Illinois. A lady who is a connoisseur of many talents, she lives and works in Harlem, New York. Camille's multi-talented abilities have amazed those who have come to know the children's book author as someone who can do it all.

Noted for her charismatic smile and the grace of a ballerina, Camille has penned several highly-acclaimed children's books, including *The*

Shimmershine Queens, Cornrows (a "Coretta Scott King Award" winner) and *The Little Tree Growing in the Shade.*

Camille is a successful professional dancer. As an actress, she has appeared in several stage productions as well as daytime television soap operas. Yes, the familiar smile is owned by a writer who has shown others that they can take many hobbies and turn them into life-long, simultaneous careers.

Her work has touched the hearts of many children across the nation. Most already know who Camille Yarbrough is, thanks to conscientious teachers who understand how important it is to expose today's youth to quality literature. Her most recent book, *Tamika and the Wisdom Rings*, (2006) is published under the Just Us Books imprint, SANKOF BOOKS, a leading children's book publisher. Camille continues to write stories that children want to read and generations will remember her as one of the greatest children's book writers of the century.

(Website: Justusbooks.com)

Timeline of the Literary Diva's Published Work

⁓ 2004—Tamika and the Wisdom Rings—(Just Us Books)
⁓ 1997—Cornrows—(Penguin Young Readers Group)
⁓ 1996—The Shimmershine Queens—(Penguin Young Readers Group)
⁓ 1996—Little Tree Growing in the Shade—(Penguin Group, USA)

Candice Dow

Candice Dow, a native of Baltimore, Maryland debuted her first novel, *Caught in the Mix,* on the literary scene in 2004 creating so much intrigue for her work, that her first print run effortlessly sold out at every signing. A true modern day diva, who took her career as an author to the next level by creating a meticulous media kit and book cover to match, she already had the ingredients to gain national notoriety.

Candice's claim to fame began in high school. She discovered that she had a desire to write and began a collection of short stories entitled, *College Bound.* Candice graduated from the University of Maryland Eastern

Shore and John Hopkins University, obtaining a BS and MS in Computer Science. An intelligent lady with a wicked pen, and charismatic writing style, Candice went from working as a full-time software engineer and adjunct faculty member at Morgan State University to pursuing her dream of becoming a novelist.

In 2004, Candice completed her first novel, *Caught In The Mix*. That same year, her dream was fully realized when she signed a two-book deal with Kensington Publishing. *Caught In The Mix* became available in book-stores everywhere. Her second novel, *Ain't No Sunshine* was announced on literary e-zines to be released in June 2006. She also attended *QBR: The Black Book Review* "Black History Month Launch Celebration" in 2006. While there, she introduced her book to the most important eyes in the literary industry at the Nubian Heritage in Harlem, New York, receiving monumental applause as a popular author among book clubs. Candice presently resides in both Maryland and New York.

(Website: CandiceDow.com)

Timeline of the Literary Diva's Published Work
- 2006—Ain't No Sunshine—(Kensington Publishing)
- 2004—Caught in the Mix—(Kensington Publishing)

Cassandra Darden Bell

Cassandra Darden Bell, whose original name is Cassandra Terrell Gorham, was born in Kings County Hospital in Brooklyn New York, July 12th 1969. Her family relocated to Falkland, North Carolina just a few months after her birth. Spending her early years on the farm, Cassandra said that she developed a love for two things, writing and playing basketball. She graduated from J.H. Rose High School in 1987. Through tough college semesters and long study sessions, her desire to play basketball was replaced with her need to write. Upon graduating from East Carolina University in 1992, Cassandra obtained her first job with WNCT-TV9 as a part-time Production Assistant. A cameraman and friend, Thomas Cormier, insisted that she get in front of the camera. From there she went on to be a News Reporter and News Anchor.

Cassandra left her career in news broadcasting to become a stay-at-home mom and full-time writer. In May 2002, she self-published her first book, *The Color of Love,* and completed her second manuscript, *Mississippi Blues,* a few months later. This landed her a two-book deal with BET Books, the publishing arm of Viacom, Inc. Cassandra now writes for Harlequin Enterprises, *Kimani Press Sepia* line. When she is not busy writing, Cassandra enjoys spending time with her family, playing basketball on the basketball court—her pastime desire, and "reading whatever she can get her hands on."

(Website: CassandraBellDarden.com)

Timeline of the Literary Diva's Published Work

- ∞ 2007—Unzipped—(Harlequin/Kimani Press)
- ∞ 2006 -Changing Lanes—(Harlequin/Kimani Press)
- ∞ 2005—After The Storm—(BET/ Kensington)
- ∞ 2005—After the Storm—(BET/Sepia)
- ∞ 2004—Mississippi Blues—(BET/Kensington)
- ∞ 2004—Mississippi Blues—(BET/Sepia)
- ∞ 2002—The Color of Love—(BET/Kensington)

Celise Downs

Celise Downs was born, and currently resides, in Phoenix, AZ. Her love of writing began in the seventh grade and was further encouraged by a high school English teacher. She considers her novels to be "young adult fiction" with a twist. "There's the normal things that teenagers go through like acne, peer pressure, and angst over the opposite sex," she says. "Then there's the other not-so-normal, unexpected stuff. I happen to like writing about both."

Celise is a big fan of James Bond, Betty Boop and adult series romance books. She enjoys going to the movies, reading, listening to music (especially Linkin Park), and watching her favorite TV shows: *Smallville* and *Alias*. She is a member of PMA-Online and several organizations.

(Website: GeminiMojoPress.com)

Timeline of the Literary Diva's Published Work

- 2005—Dance Jam Production; Young Adult—(Gemini Mojo Press)
- 2004—Secrets and Kisses; Young Adult—(Gemini Mojo Press)

C. F. Hawthorne

C.F. Hawthorne was raised in Texas where she diligently listened to stories told by her grandfather. C.F's fascination for her grandfather's stories inspired her to develop a longing to follow in his footsteps. Soon she discovered that she had developed a second fascination for poetry.

One day, her high school English teacher sent her to the library for being a class clown. This single incident spurred her to write more poetry. Deep down inside, C. F. hated English. Her writing suffered from what seemed to be an over use of commas, but, her *style* of writing was actually that of a poet waiting to surface. She was becoming a writer with an amazing ability to create stories that exemplified her poetical writing style. C.F. finally realized that she had a unique way of writing stories and many readers of her work agreed.

She took her new-found confidence as a poet and turned it into one of the most intriguing novels of our time. Today, C.F. Hawthorne no longer has to lash out in rebellion for having trouble with commas. She replaced the hurt, pain and humiliation she had suffered in English class with a solid well-written novel, *For Every Black Eye: Revenge: When Nothing Else Works*.

C. F. returned again with another smash hit, *Homeless Love*, and her reign as one of the most mysterious writers still continues to this date. Her characters are intelligent and daring just as intelligent and daring as she is. Her writing exudes fine development of wholesome and enriching characters, a signature trademark of her style.

(Website: CFHawthorne.com)

Timeline of the Literary Diva's Published Work

- 2004—Homeless Love—(Sloan to Sloan)
- 2002—For Every Black Eye: Revenge: When Nothing Else Works—(Dark Corner Press)

Cheryl Willis Hudson

When Cheryl Willis Hudson wrote the popular *AFRO-BETS® A B C Book*, everyone knew she was destined for publishing success. A graduate of Oberlin College in Ohio, she has more than 25 years of experience in publishing as a graphic designer, art director and publisher of children and young adult books at Just Us Books.

Cheryl's career in publishing began at Houghton Mifflin Publishing Company in Boston, Massachusetts. She worked for Macmillan Educational Publishing Company in New York and has been a design consultant for several educational publishers. She had also designed and art directed books for a number of trade and mass market publishing houses. Her talents in the publishing arena were endless, but it is Cheryl's writing that has taken the literary world by storm and her unique books that have won over the hearts of youngsters across the nation.

Cheryl Hudson's books for children and young readers included the popular *AFRO-BETS® A B C Book, AFRO-BETS® 1 2 3 Book, Bright Eyes, Brown Skin and Many Colors of Mother Goose*, all published by Just Us Books. She also wrote and edited a number of books for Scholastic, Inc. including *Good Night, Baby* and other titles in the *What-A-Baby* board book series; *Hold Christmas in Your Heart: African-American Songs, Poems and Stories for the Holidays and How Sweet the Sound: African-American Songs for Children*.

Cheryl's titles *Hands Can* and *Construction Zone* were published by Candlewick Press. A recent release, *Come By Here: Everyday Prayers for Children* was illustrated with photographs by Monica Morgan. Cheryl is currently a member of the Author's Guild, PEN America and a number of professional and community organizations. Her sense of knowing what children like has been a phenomenon. This probably is the reason that her books are a favorite among children as well as with parents and teachers.

(**Website: JustusBooks.com**)

Timeline of the Literary Diva's Published Work

- 2003—Hands On—(Candlewick Press)
- 2002—AFRO-BETS® A B C Book—(Just Us Books.com)
- 2002—1, 2, 3 Book—(Sagebrush Education Resources)
- 2002—Hold Christmas in Your Heart: African-American Songs, Poems and Stories for the Holidays—(Just Us Books)
- 2001—Come By Here: Everyday Prayers for Children—(Just Us Books)
- 2000—Many Colors of Mother Goose—(Just Us Books)
- 1997—Good Morning Baby—(Scholastic, Inc.)
- 1997—Animal Sounds for Baby (What-A-Baby Board Books/Scholastic, Inc.)
- 1997—In Praise of Our Fathers and Our Mothers—(Just Us Books)

1997—Let's Count Baby—(Scholastic, Inc.)

- 1996—Kids' Book of Wisdom: Quotes from the African American Tradition—(Just Us Books)
- 1996—How Sweet the Sound: African-American Songs for Children—(Just Us Books)
- 1990—Bright Eyes, Brown Skin and Many Colors of Mother Goose—(Just Us Books)

Cherlyn Michaels

Cherlyn Michaels began her reign to fame when she originally self-published *Counting Raindrops through a Stained Glass Window* in January 2004 through her company, Archland Books. Her original animated cover along with well-written story plot earned her the 2003 *Shades of Romance* magazine "Best New Multi-cultural Author of the Year". By 2004, Cherlyn was nominated for the "African American Literary Awards Show Open Book Award for Best Self-Published Author of the Year" for 2004. She set out on a multi-city campaign signing books in over 30 bookstores and festivals around the country.

As a youth, Cherlyn was an avid reader with a very strong desire to write. However, she put off her writing to pursue a degree in chemical engineering. Cherlyn not only hid her writing talent for many years, but also her extreme intellect and ability to take on science and math subjects.

Finally, in late 2002, she decided to put her career aside in order to pursue her dream of writing a novel. She began by reading books on writing, and taking writing classes, attending seminars, and workshops. In January 2003, she began writing her novel and self-published it. Cherlyn's novel hit bookstore shelves by January 2004. In October 2004, she accepted a 2-book publishing deal from Hyperion Books. She soon began working on her second title, *First Fridays*.

Cherlyn has inspired many writers during her journey from writer to published author. She maintained an online journal that revealed her trials and tribulations. She works with a St. Louis group of literary enthusiasts with hopes of establishing the St. Louis Writer's Studio. This non-profit organization is dedicated to supporting students (ages 8-18) with creative and expository writing skills, and helping teachers inspire their students to write.

(Website: CherlynMichaels.com)

Timeline of the Literary Diva's Published Work

∽ 2006—First Fridays—(Hyperion)
∽ 2005—Looking Through a Stained Glass Window—(Hyperion)

Christine Young Robinson

Christine Young-Robinson was raised in New York. She turned to writing as a form of relaxation. Like a flower, her first children's book, *Isra the Butterfly Gets Caught for Show and Tell*, bloomed. She was inspired by her granddaughter and decided to put her book into print to share with other children.

Christine soon earned the Carrie Allen McCray Award, "Honorable Mention" for Juvenile Fiction from by the South Carolina Workshop Conference and NEA's "Read Across America Certificate of Participation" in 2002. She participated in the African American Read-In and soon became a member of the Society of Children Writers and Illustrators and the South Carolina Writer's Workshop.

Christine's fascination for children's books would lead her to work on several children's picture books, a chapter book, *Oh no! Not Uncle Roy*, and a young adult book, *Hip-Hop and Punk Rock*. Her short story, *Miss Amy's Last Ride* was featured in the anthology, *Proverbs for the People* (June 2003). Christine now resides in Columbia, South Carolina.

(Website: ChristineYoungRobinson.com)

Timeline of the Literary Diva's Published Work

✒ 2001—Isra the Butterfly Gets Caught for Show and Tell—(Yoroson Pub)

Corey Sue Ward

Corey Sue Ward was born in Lima, Ohio. After graduating from Shawnee High School, she entered the United States Army as a Personnel Management Specialist. She exchanged her maiden name of Lawrence to Ward when she married her high school boyfriend, Dennis, in 1983. Corey and Dennis started their family after they relocated from Texas to Germany,.

When their firstborn was just eight months old, Corey and her husband were reassigned to Augusta Georgia, where she served at Fort Gordon and received an honorable discharge.

Remembering her childhood dreams and goals, Corey began her quest to obtain her bachelor's degree. The three-year plan turned into a twelve-year journey that began at Augusta State University, venturing to Paine College and ending at the Ohio State University with a major in English.

Corey's two novels, *Where's Daddy?* (May 1999) and *Lust of the Heart* (June 2001) touched on issues that affect young adults today, through fictional formats that allow the reader to follow the journey of her characters as they deal with various issues of life. These novels allow the reader to settle their own personal issues in a creative way.

The fact that Corey's father had died on Father's Day when she was a child gave her a story line that she felt passionate about. "I believe that the trauma I experienced at 11 years old with my dad's death was meant to destroy me and my dreams. However, it was a great moment when I realized that his death only prepared me for this time in history where our young people are dying on the inside from the pain of loss," says Corey who also states, "I have an assignment to help mend the hearts of our nation's teens through books, music and the spoken word while making sure that my own children are secure and ready to face life's challenges."

An ordained Minister at World Harvest Church of Columbus Ohio, Corey is the owner of Yeroc Enterprise, a management company. An advocate of volunteerism, she often volunteers with non-profit organizations such as the United Way and her hometown's St. Jude Telethon. Whether on the road, serving as a substitute teacher, learning the ropes at the Publishing Company that prints her books or spending quality time with her family and friends, Corey is ever cognizant of her assignment to the youth of America.

(Website: Yerocenterprise.com)

Timeline of the Literary Diva's Published Work

- 2004—A Woman's Guide To Spiritual Victory—(Author House)
- 1999—Where's Daddy?—(Author House)
- 2001—Lust of the Heart—(Author House)

Crystal McCrary Anthony, Esq

Crystal McCrary Anthony, Esq., became a very popular author for her work, *Homecourt Advantage*, co-written with Rita Ewing, published by Avon (1998). The work was received so favorably, it became a "Literary Guild Featured Alternate Selection" and was optioned by Sony/Screen Gem to be made into a feature film. Crystal's second published novel, *Gotham Diaries*, co-written with Terry Lewis Lee, Spike Lee's wife, made it onto the "New York Times Best-Seller List" and was the 2005 "Blackboard Fiction Book of the Year". Her novels have reached astronomical success.

A cum laude graduate of the University of Michigan, Ann Arbor, Crystal double-majored in English and Communications. She received her BA in 1991. Soon after, Crystal attended Washington College of Law at the American University and New York University School of Law earning her JD in1995. (Cited from www.Crystalmccraryanthony.com)

During this period, Crystal participated in the international law program sponsored by Tulane University and studied European Community law while living in Paris, France. Barred in the State of New York, she practiced entertainment law specializing in theatre production and publishing contracts with the New York firm of Paul, Weiss, Rifkind, Wharton and Garrison before leaving to pursue a full-time career in writing.

Crystal has written for several magazines including, *Vibe*, *Glamour*, *Savoy* and *Tastemakers NYC* and she has been featured in *Mirabella*, *Newsweek*, the New York Times, Essence, O Magazine, People and Sister-to-Sister. Crystal has also appeared on several television shows including: *Access Hollywood, Extra, Good Morning America, Tavis Smiley* and, as a regular pop culture critic, on *CNN American Morning.* Crystal has also been a legal analyst on numerous television shows including Fox News Channel, CNBC and Court TV.

(Website: CrystalMcCraryAnthony.com)

Timeline of the Literary Diva's Published Work

- 2004—Gotham Diaries—(Hyperion)
- 1998—Homecourt Advantage—(Avon)

Crystal Lacey Winslow

Crystal Lacey Winslow was born in Brooklyn, New York. She earned her BA degree in Legal Assistant Studies and worked for one of the largest law firms in the country. Crystal began writing creatively at an early age.

At eight years old, she won her first journalist contest. She realized that she had a gift for writing and continued honing her craft writing poetry/prose. Crystal published *Melodrama,* a poetry chapbook in 2000, and founded her own publishing company, Melodrama Publishing in 2001. However, at age fourteen, Crystal had already written her first unpublished novel.

A very diverse and multi-talented individual, Crystal lived in various cities like Virginia, Maryland, and Washington, D.C. before returning to her native New York City. Having lived in and traveled to many places, as well as taking on numerous hobbies, such as archery, horseback riding and playing the flute, Crystal reflected upon her personal and environmental experiences which, are the inspirations for her writings.

The result is a unique and melodramatic storytelling technique, which is evident in her deeply personal poetry book, *Up Close & Personal,* and novels like, *Life, Love & Loneliness* and *Criss Cross,* which continue to receive critical acclaim. Remarkably, she has also published other author's works and opened a bookstore.

(Website: CrystalLacyWinslow.com)

Timeline of the Literary Diva's Published Work

- 2006—Sex, Sin & Brooklyn II—(Melodrama Publishing)
- 2004—The Criss Cross—(Melodrama Publishing)
- 2003—Up Close & Personal—(Melodrama Publishing)
- 2002—Life, Love & Loneliness—(Melodrama Publishing)

Crystal Rhodes

Crystal Rhodes is a native of Indianapolis, Indiana. This is where Crystal honed her craft of writing after moving to the San Francisco Bay Area where she worked as a reporter, a reviewer, columnist and an entertainment editor. She's written hundreds of articles, profiles and interviews for both newspapers and magazines. Crystal has served as the producer and writer of a weekly cable television series, "Getting By" as well as served as the producer and hostess of her own Bay area radio show titled "Bay Arts Beat".

Crystal enjoys writing plays almost as much as writing novels. In fact, she's written twenty-one plays, nineteen of which have been produced in theatres throughout the United States. *The Trip*, has been published in two play anthologies: *Center Stage: An Anthology of 21 Contemporary Black Playwrights* (University of Illinois Press) and *Black Women's Blues: A Literary Anthology, 1934-Present* (G.K. Hall & Co.).

In 1993 Crystal was nominated for a "L.A. Dramalogue Award" as "Best Original Writer for a Comedy", for *The Trip*. In 1995, she was thrilled when her play, *Stoops*, won the "Black Theatre Alliance Award" (BTAA) for "Best Play" (an ETA Creative Arts production, Chicago, Illinois). She also won the BTAA for "Best Original Writing" for *Stoops*.

Crystal earned her BA degree in Social Work from Indiana University and a M.A. degree in Sociology from Atlanta University. She currently lives in the Midwest.

(Website: CrystalRhodes.com)

Timelineof the Literary Diva's Published Work

- 2004—Grandmother's Inc.—(Crystal Ink Pub)
- 2002—Sweet Sacrifice—(Crystal Ink Pub)

Cydney Rax

Cydney Rax is the author of the successful debut novel *My Daughter's Boyfriend*, the story of Tracey Davenport, a 34-year old single mother that becomes romantically involved with her teenage daughter's boyfriend.

She was born and raised in Detroit. A graduate of Cass Technical High School, she earned an undergraduate degree in written communications from Eastern Michigan University. Cydney has been featured in publications, including: *Publishers Weekly, Quarterly Black Review Magazine, Booking Matters Magazine,* among others.

Her debut novel received glowing reviews from *Romantic Times Book Club Magazine,* The Reading and Writing Sistaz Book Club, and *Kirkus Reviews. My Daughter's Boyfriend* is a Black Expressions Book Club best seller, and sales of the trade paperback required a second printing. *Kirkus Reviews* stated Cydney Rax's book is a "Juicy debut, capably written!" Alongside great talents, including: Terry McMillan and Walter Mosley, Cydney was a featured author at the 2005 National Book Club Conference held in Atlanta.

Cydney is an avid reader as well as creator of www.book-remarks.com, a popular website that is devoted to promoting African-American literature. She has interviewed authors such as Carl Weber, E. Lynn Harris, Eric Jerome Dickey, Kimberla Lawson Roby, and dozens of others.

(Website: CydneyRax.com)

Timeline of the Literary Diva's Published Work

∿ 2006—My Husband's Girlfriend—(Three Rivers Press)
∿ 2005—My Daughter's Boyfriend—(Three Rivers Press)
∿ 2004—My Daughter's Boyfriend (Crown Publishing Group)

Cynthia Highsmith-Hooks

The Soul of a Black Woman: From a Whisper to a Shout marks Cynthia Highsmith-Hooks' debut onto the literary scene. This poetry collection spans thirty-one of the author's first forty years and tells her story with remarkable candor and heartache.

From thousands of poets who entered Disilgold Soul's Literary Review YOUnity Guild contest, Cynthia was presented with the "Omar Tyree Poetry Circle Award". Through her poetry, she shares her innermost thoughts as she overcomes the crippling effects of fatherly rejection, the pain of first love, early pregnancy and the loss of that child, the insecurity of adolescence and the struggles of single parenthood to finally find herself and her place in the world. From beginning to end, it is a story of empowerment and triumph written during various stages of her life and told in four parts: *Little Girl Lost, Between Two Worlds, Natural Woman* and *A New Attitude, A New Direction.*

Cynthia Hooks was born Cynthia Renee Highsmith in Hempstead, New York. She discovered a talent for writing at an early age and wrote her first story when she was just six years old. After graduating from Hempstead High School in 1981, she attended Dillard University, then went into the military. She spent 5 years in the U.S. Army, traveling to Europe and Korea. She was discharged in 1989 and moved to Texas for the birth of her son, Maurice, who was born the same year. Two years later, she met Walter Hooks. They were married in 1994 and moved to San Diego, California on military orders.

Between 1994 and 2000, Cynthia worked as a Medical Laboratory Technician, a Phlebotomist and a Customs Inspector on the U.S. border with Mexico. In 2000, she fell into the field of Criminal Investigations where she currently works when she is not writing or preparing for a career in Forensic Science.

Over the years, Cynthia has probably penned more than 25 short stories and essays, over 200 poems and 2 novels. All of these were locked away until 2001 when she and her brother began brainstorming about movie projects. He asked Cynthia if she was still writing and she told her brother about the old Army footlocker full of her writings. Her brother suggested she dust off her old work and the rest is history. Her first poetry book appeared on Mosaic Books.com.

Cynthia was amazed to rediscover the writing she had stored away over the course of her life. In 2002 at the age of 39, she finally decided to self-publish some of the poetry she had been hiding. The result was *The Soul of a Black Woman: From a Whisper to a Shout*. She's working on her second poetry book and a series of other projects.

Cynthia calls out to poetry lovers to, "Come along on this emotional journey into the mind and soul of a black woman; a woman who did not find her own voice until she turned a deaf ear to the voices of others."

(Website: CHighsmithHooks.com)

Timeline of the Literary Diva's Published Work

🖋 2002—The Soul of a Black Woman: From a Whisper to A Shout—(Xlibris)

Darcel P. Williams

Darcel Patrice Williams was born in Houston, Texas, the second of five siblings. She attended school in the Houston Independent School District, completing high school with honors, and going on to attend the prestigious Texas Southern University and the world-class University of Houston. Darcel has studied creative writing with published author Bapsi Sidwa, script writing with Dr. William Hawes and while *Soaring on Clipped Wings* was in development, she took a workshop course in novel writing with Alysse Rassmussen, a romance-author.

Darcel worked full-time in the production department of *KUHT*, the public television station in Houston, while she studied film-and-television production at the School of Communications, University of Houston. Later, she assisted entrepreneurs with development of their independent production concerns in Houston.

Darcel moved to Tulsa, Oklahoma in 1990, where she became a massage therapist, worked as a community center director and organized support groups for community concerns while she planted the seeds of a youth production program. Darcel continues to reside in Tulsa, where she has completed the most revered role of her life, that of rearing her son to become the fine man and college student that he is today. Her desire is to positively impact society with writing that brings messages of hope and encouragement.

(Website: DarciWilliams.com)

Timeline of the Literary Diva's Published Work

∽ 2002—Soaring On Clipped Wings—(American Book Publishing)

Darline Dorce-Coupet

Darline Dorce-Coupet was born in Port-au-Prince Haiti but was raised in Miami, Florida, which was home for years. However, Darlene relocated to the Atlanta, Georgia area to teach for Dekalb County Schools. Teaching and writing are dual careers for her.

Darline earned an Associate degree from the University of Florida in Gainesville. While at the University of Florida, she participated in an exchange program to study abroad for a year at the Sorbonne University and American College in Paris studying French Civilization and Haute Couture Fashion. She earned a Bachelor of Arts in Communications, with a minor in French from Barry University. She studied film-making from concept to finish at the University of Miami, and earned a Masters (MAT) in Teaching English from Barry University, where she has taught Freshmen Composition and English literature courses. From time to time, Darline also takes courses in Creative Writing at Florida International University and enjoys mixing with other writers.

"I write because I have to," says Darline. "I can't and don't even try to avoid it. It's an overwhelming passion, creating characters, building worlds, ruling the universe. Writing a novel is a lot like playing God and I love it! I just sit there and the story comes pouring forth, and it's a truly sumptuous feeling—like giving birth to a child."

At thirteen, Darlene hand-wrote her first 130-page manuscript, *Growing Up*. A year later, she wrote the sequel, *Growing Up, Part II*. For years, she would write story after story, culminating with a 967-page manuscript entitled *Queen of Pain*, which she wrote after finishing college. *Embracing the Horror*, her latest venture, is a story of forbidden love.

The characters in this story literally jump off the page, they're so real, she's been told. "Arielle, Leah, Cedric and Danyel are compilations of a lot of people I've known and who have touched my life. Of course, there is a little of me thrown in here and there, but essentially, all of these characters are larger than life. They are not your run-of-the mill ordinary people, and they are not supposed to be. They're all CRAZY! But that's what makes reading about them so interesting," Darlene says. "They make you question how you live and make you want to jump up and want to have as much fun as they seem to be having. They entertain you." In 2006, she completed *Between the Devil & the Deep Blue Sea*, the sequel to *Embracing the Horror*. Her bold new novel, *Just One Night* is written under the pen name D.M. Coupet.

(Website: DarleneDorce-Coupet.com)

Timeline of the Literary Diva's Published Work

- 2006—Just One Night—(Firefly Publishing and Entertainment)
- 2006—Between the Devil and the Deep Blue Sea—(Firefly Publishing and Entertainment)
- 2004—Embracing the Horror—(Firefly Publishing and Entertainment)

Dawn Breedon

Dawn Breedon is a motivational speaker, trainer, facilitator, activist, and author of *Remember to Breathe*. In 1991 while she was five months pregnant, she was diagnosed HIV positive. Resolving to believe God's prognosis instead of the doctor's diagnosis, she eagerly awaited the arrival of her baby. A year after her son was born, a two-year custody battle with her son's father began and ended with a vicious attack on her and the murder of her son. No question, Dawn's faith and forbearance pulled her through!

Dawn gives you inspiration to do things you never thought you could, no matter how afraid you may be or how impossible it may seem. In the middle of crazed media coverage and the steady churning of her hometown's rumor mill, Dawn learned she was pregnant again. Today she is the mother of a healthy, happy son.

Determined not to allow the situations in her life to dictate her success, Dawn speaks at corporate events, churches, for women's groups and for high schools. She offers up empowering useable techniques to manage change, and to help push through gut wrenching emotional pain. Lessons learned on HIV prevention, alternatives to domestic violence and substance abuse awareness have helped Dawn to build powerful self-esteem boosting presentations.

Dawn is currently working in prisons helping repeat offenders learn how to take responsibility for their actions and make smarter choices. She works with public assistance recipients helping to raise their self-esteem and to have a larger vision for themselves.

Dawn also provides pragmatic strategies to enable people to identify dishonest and dangerous behavior in their mates. She has helped countless women to discern bisexual behavior in their partners often referred to as the *Down Low*. From the National Football League to Mary Kay Cosmetics, countless diverse audiences have benefited from Dawn's seminars.

(Website: DawnBreedon.com)

Timeline of the Literary Diva's Published Work

~ 2005—Remember to Breathe—(Ellington Publishing)

Deborah Gregory

Writer, performer and designer Deborah Gregory is the award-winning author of "The Cheetah Girls" novel series (Disney Publishing Worldwide). The 13-book series is about five talented teens, who form a singing group and make their dreams come true in the jiggy jungle. The Disney Channel original movie, which was based on the book series, stars Raven Symone and Lynn Whitfield. Deborah Gregory served as a co-producer on the film project. In 2001, the series was chosen as the "Blackboard Children's Book of the Year".

Deborah received her A.A.S. from Fashion Institute of Technology, then received a B.S. from Empire State University in 1986. She has been a contributing writer for *Essence* magazine since 1992.

Her work has also appeared in *VIBE, MORE, Heart & Soul, Entertainment Weekly,* and US magazines. Her pop culture column, *THE DIVA DIARIES,* appears in *Grace* magazine, the national fashion and lifestyle "reality" publication targeted at multi-cultural women. She is currently writing an adult novel as well as developing a one-woman show *LEOPARD LIVES,* a coming of age story about a foster child growing up in the New York City foster care system, of which Gregory is also a survivor. Deborah has performed segments of her work-in-progress one-woman show at the Women of Color Festival, winning the festival's Best Comedy Award for 2001; Dixon Place, Caroline's Comedy Club and Solo Arts Festival.

Deborah has contributed to several books including, *Men of Color: Fashion, Mission, Fundamentals,* (Artisan Publishing); *Body and Soul, SoulStyle: Black Women Redefining the Color Fashion, Essence Total Makeover Book, 50 Most Influential People,* and *Beautiful: Nudes by Marc Baptiste* (Rizzoli/Universe Publishing).

Cheetahrama, a collection of her original designs including hand crafted decoupage art cases and hair accessories, which are sold at stores nationwide, is one of Deborah's newest ventures.

Deborah currently lives in New York City with her pooch Cappuccino who poses as the Cheetah Girls mascot Toto.

(Website: Cheetahrama.com)

Timeline of the Literary Diva's Published Work

- 2005—The Cheetah Girls: Off the Hook!: Bin-Up#4—(Jump at the Sun)
- 2003—The Cheetah Girls Livin' Large: Books 1—4—(Jump at the Sun)
- 2003—The Cheetah Girls Supa-Dupa Sparkle: Books# 5-8—(Jump at the Sun)
- 2001—The Cheetah Girls: Cuchifrita Ballerina—Book #10—(Disney Press)
- 2001—The Cheetah Girls: Shop in the Name of Love—Book#2—(Disney Press)
- 2000—The Cheetah Girls: Growl Power—Book #8—(Jump at the Sun)
- 2000—The Cheetah Girls: Hey, Ho, Hollywood—Book #4—(Jump at the Sun)

✒ 2000—The Cheetah Girls: Woof, There It Is—Book #5—(Jump at the Sun)

✒ 1999—The Cheetah Girls: Who's Bout to Bounce, Baby Book#3—(Jump at the Sun)

Deborah Smith

Born the youngest of eight children to Bishop and the late Constance Smith, Deborah was raised as an active member of her family's church— Christian Pentecostal Church of Christ in Irvington, New Jersey.

For the greater part of her teenage years Deborah lived the typical life of an urban PK (preacher's kid). Little did she know that, at the tender age of seventeen, her life would take an unexpected turn for what seemed to be the worse. "This turn" for Deborah was a life-altering car accident on a busy highway, which left her severely cut and bruised. While in recovery, she mentions, " I not only prayed for the healing of my body, but also began to surrender to the arduous process of the healing of my soul."

She mentions, "As an act of obedience and exchange of her will for God's perfect will, I accepted the Lord Jesus as her personal Savior at the age of twenty." Overtime, Deborah physically recuperated and went on to college at Hampton University. Her desire for "personal, spiritual healing and a deeper understanding of the "Word of God", she says, led her to earn her undergraduate degree at United Bible College in Florida. She then went on to earn her Masters in Religious Education from Lighthouse Bible College in Beebee, Arkansas.

Deborah's life story has been one of an over comer as evidenced by her survival of many other life changing events, namely divorce, domestic abuse, countless family tragedies, several disappointing relationships and the tragic loss of her mother to diabetes." Deborah says that she "better understands that the tragic events in her life were all a part of what she calls God's master plan", each event necessary in order to receive the anointing that is currently resting upon her life. "Every tear, every heartache, every lie, every disappointment was only fuel for the fire that has unleashed the woman that God has ordained me to be today."

Deborah currently resides in a suburb of Northern New Jersey with her son and daughter. She is the author of two powerful Christian novels, *Ministers with White Collars and Black Secrets* and its newly released sequel, *Robbed Without A Gun*.

(Website: DeborahSmithOnline.com)

Timeline of the Literary Diva's Published Work

- 2005—Ministers with White Collars and Black Secrets—(DSP)
- 2005—Robbed Without A Gun—(DSP)

Debra Clayton

Born and raised in Drakes Branch, Virginia, along with her two sisters and four brothers, Debra Clayton learned at a very young age, how to escape the monotony of the every day world through her writing. A shy child, Debra learned that in her writings, she could be whoever she wanted to be and go wherever she wanted to go. Now fast-forward some twenty plus years, you'll find her still very much in love with the written word.

Debra currently resides in Pendleton, South Carolina with her three children. After earning an Associate Degree in Business Computer Programming, she started her career in the Information Technology field. Although she enjoys writing computer code, it was her life's dream to weave intricate tales of romance, drama and suspense.

In 2002, Debrah penned her first novel and after several unsuccessful attempts to get it published through traditional presses, she decided to follow in the steps of Michael Baisden, Zane and Omar Tyree and self-publish. In September 2003, she started her own publishing company, which released her debut novel *Rap Superstar* in November 2003. *Rap Superstar* is a contemporary romance novel with a bit of hip-hop "flava".

After the successful release of *Rap Superstar*, Debra inked a two-book deal with Urban Books, which is owned and operated by bestselling author, Carl Weber and an imprint of Kensington Books.

Debra's passion for writing does not end with her novels. She has completed a short screenplay entitled *The Dawg* and a full-featured screenplay called *Politically Correct*. Her ultimate goal is to pursue a career in film making where she will be able to write, produce and direct her own films. (Cited from www.DebraCalyton.com)

(Website: DebraClayton.com)

Timeline of the Literary Diva's Published Work

- 2006—Fallen Star—(Urban Books)
- 2005—Rap Superstar—(Urban Books)

Dee Freeman

Delores King-Freeman is a motivated and compelling poet, author, producer and host, who is using her love, skills and creativity to help readers enjoy words and rhythmic rhyme. She left the south during the sixties to follow her dream, which proved extremely elusive. Now, finally catching and living that dream, she happily immerses herself in her passion-writing. Delores has previously published well received books of poetry entitled *Oceans of Love: To Us From Us* and *Poetry She Wrote I: Oh, Magnify Him*.

Both have been placed in the school system and libraries around her hometown. Deborah has had a number of poems appear in magazines, anthologies and new papers where some have been recognized with awards for their inspirational, even motivational message.

During Black History Month in 2005, Deborah was presented with a commendation from the City of Lansing, Michigan and the Lansing City Council. She continues to provide the *Lansing State Journal* with an article, book review or word of inspiration on a monthly basis. She also co-hosts "poetry slams" held at various locations throughout the Greater Lansing area.

Deborah looks forward to expanding her *Poetree-N-Motion* TV program, which shares information of community events, history tidbits, book reviews and has guests with current community issues. It airs in Lansing on Comcast channel 16 -Thursday @ 3:30PM and East Lansing channel

30—WELM on Tuesday @ 7:00PM. Deborah is also a talented musical lyricist, hoping to have her work recorded in the near future.

Presently, Deborah is in the completion stage of her first fiction novel-a project in conjunction with a movie producer. This novel—*Wild, Untamed Michigan: The Way It Was*—is scheduled to hit the stores in early or mid 2006, with the second of the *Poetry, She Wrote* series, following close behind.

Deborah thoroughly enjoys writing and sharing her poetry through presentations at special annual luncheons, tributes honoring the leadership of community and churches, and other venues throughout the region. She honestly feels her words will benefit all who read them, gently touching, softly soothing, delightfully awakening, enthusiastically illuminating, and fervently healing.

As the grandmother of three grandsons, Deborah sees the need for help within the community. She volunteers for readings and events throughout the Lansing School District. Deborah also works on projects with the "Michigan Million Women Movement" that sprang out of the "Million Women March" (MWM) of 1997. She's a member of several supporting organizations, such as Delores Thornton's Marguerite Press, Disilgold Soul and Publishing and Sisterhood of The Written Word. She also sings with a 35-voice group—The Earl Nelson Singers, directed by Verna Holley—which continues to keep the Negro Spirituals alive.

An alumnus of Northwood University of Midland and former Financial Analyst for General Motors, Freeman continues to reside in Lansing, Michigan with her husband, Attorney Myron S. Freeman Sr. She is proud of her three adult children, one of whom has attained stardom as an actress on Broadway.

Timeline of the Literary Diva's Published Work

∼ 2006—Poetry She Wrote I: Oh, Magnify Him—(Author House)
∼ 2005—Oceans of Love: To Us From Us—(Author House)

Deirdre Savoy

Native New Yorker Deirdre Savoy spent her summers on the shores of Martha's Vineyard, soaking up the sun and scribbling in one of her many notebooks. It was there that she first started writing romance as a teenager. The island proved to be the perfect setting for her first novel, *Spellbound*, published by BET/Arabesque books in 1999. *Spellbound* received rave reviews and earned her the distinction of the first Rising Star author of Romance in Color and was voted their "Best New Author of 1999".
Deirdre also won the first annual Emma award for "Favorite New Author", presented at the 2001 *Romance Slam Jam* in Orlando, Florida and in 2006 she won another award for "Best Suspense Novelist".

Deirdre's second and third books, *Always* (2000) and its sequel *Once and Again* (2001), were chosen as selections for the *Black Expressions* Book Club. *Midnight Magic*, the third book in the Thorne family saga was a 2001 Holiday release.

Deirdre's fifth book, *Holding Out for a Hero*, was published in September 2002. *Holding Out for a Hero* features fictional hero, NYPD detective Adam Wexler and real-life hero firefighter Paul Haney, the winner of the 2001 "Arabesque Man Contest" on the cover. *Holding Out for a Hero*, was also selected by *Black Expressions* Book Club and was featured on the cover of their holiday 2002 brochure.

In April 2003, Deirdre's first novella, *Fairy Godfather* was published as well as her first hardcover title, *To Mom With Love*, a Mother's Day anthology. *Could it Be Magic?* Deirdre's sixth book was published in May 2003 to rave reviews, and she received the "Gold Plug Award" from "The Romance Reader's Connection".

In June 2004, Deirdre's novel, *Lady in Red*, served as the lead off title in BET's "Sizzling Sands" summer series. Other participants in the series included Donna Hill, Gwynne Forster and Sandra Kitt. In 2005, Deirdre released *Looking for Love in All the Wrong Places*, a follow-up to her popular *Could It Be Magic?* and *Body of Truth*, the first in a trilogy of books about three Bronx detective brothers.

Deirdre is the president of "Authors Supporting Authors Positively" (ASAP) and the founder of the "Writer's Co-op" writer's group. She lectures on such topics as *Getting Your Writing Career Started, Taking Your Writing to the Next Level,* and other subjects related to the craft of writing. She is listed in the *American and International Authors and Writers Who's Who,* as well as the *Dictionary of International Biography.*

Deirdre lives in Bronx, New York with her husband of 10-plus years and their two children. In her spare time she enjoys reading, dancing, calligraphy and "wicked" crossword puzzles.

(Website: DSavoy.com)

Timeline of the Literary Divas Published Work

- 2005—Looking For Love in All the Wrong Places—(BET/ Arabesque)
- 2005—Body of Truth—(Dafina)
- 2004—Lady In Red—(BET Books)
- 2003—To Mom, With Love; Anthology—(BET Books)
- 2003—Always—(BET/Arabesque)
- 2003—Not the One—(BET/ Arabesque)
- 2003—Could It Be Magic-(BET/ Arabesque)
- 2002—Holding Out For a Hero—(BET/Arabesque)
- 2001—Once and Again—(BET/ Arabesque)
- 2001—Midnight Magic—(BET/ Arabesque)
- 1999—Spellbound—(BET/Arabesque)

Delores Thornton

Delores Thornton, a lifelong Indianapolis resident, belongs to several writing organizations including her own Marguerite Press, founded in 1996; Marguerite Press Promo, founded in 2003, and Marguerite Press PR (launched 2006). She is host of the *BookNook* and *A Round 2 It,* radio shows on www.margueritepress.com . A columnist for the Indiana Herald Newspaper, and Blackrefer.com, Delores has been inducted into the "Self Publishing Hall of Fame". (www.bookmarket.com/selfpublish.html)

Delores started writing several years ago and friends encouraged her to publish her first novel, *Ida Mae,* in 1997. Her second work, *Ida Mae: The*

Saga Continues, was released in 1998; and in 2000, she released *Ida Mae—The Combined Edition*. Delores' third novel, *Babe* was also released in 2000.

In January 2003 *Anybody Seen Junebug?* was published by iUniverse.com, followed up by *Divine Appointment: A Caregiver's Guide*, August 2004; *How to Self-publish That Great Novel: Without Going Nuts!*, 2005; and *Airing Dirty Linen*, 2006.

Voted "Queen of Promotion" by C & B Books Distribution, Delores is the "Literary Expert" on Blackrefer.com. She is also a contributor to *Word Life News, NuShape Publication Newsletter, Bahiyah Woman Magazine, Black Poe 2.0, Urban Book Battles, Chaotic Dreams,* and the *Naldar Publishing Newsletter*.

Delores is a graduate of the LongRidge Writers Group of West Redding, Connecticut. She currently attends Simmons Bible College in Indianapolis, and is a volunteer mentor for the Marion County Probation Department. Whenever she has spare time, Delores likes long drives and visiting her grown children and grandchildren.

(Website: MargueritePress.com)

Timeline of the Literary Diva's Published Work

- ∞ 2006—Airing Out Dirty Linen—(iUniverse)
- ∞ 2005—How to Self-publish That Great Novel: Without Going Nuts!—(Marguerite Press)
- ∞ 2004—Divine Appointment: A Caregiver's Guide-(iUniverse)
- ∞ 2003—Anybody Seen Junebug?-(iUniverse)
- ∞ 2000—Babe—(iUniverse)
- ∞ 1998—Ida Mae: The Saga Continues—(iUniverse)

Denise Campbell

Denise Campbell has developed the imprint Universal Write Publications; and through it, she has creatively produced works, which include: *Spanish Eyes, Love Thy Sister Watch Thy Back*, and *Man Killer*. She has also published two poetry books: *Ebony Passion* and *By Faith*. Her new release, *REM Sleep*, and her children's book series, "Cheyanne's Book Series" named for her daughter Cheyanne are the next projects on her agenda. However, that's not where her passion ends. In order to meet the demands of her own works as well as helping other writers, Universal Write Publications became a corporation with a unique concept on publishing, marketing and literary services.

By teaming and networking with prolific companies and organizations, Denise hopes to utilize her company Universal Write Publications LLC (www.universalwrite.com) to promote the freedom of lyrical poets and musical artists, internationally.

Denise is striving to provide a venue for publishing works that will benefit and uplift our people, while allowing us to strive financially as individuals and promote the social support of Black owned, Black operated businesses in our community. Denise has already dedicated her life to promoting literacy for children by working with local schools. As a survivor of abuse, she is devoted to supporting and bringing attention to Rape Crisis and Domestic Violence shelters and organizations.

Denise has performed and done theatrical performances and poetry slams nationwide and will continue to do so as an advocate for the community. She has been acknowledged with accolades in newspapers such as, *The New York Daily News, The Queens Tribune, Flatbush Life, Bay News, Canarsie Digest, The University Reporter, Sankofa Literary Journal, The Indianapolis Recorder, The Black Board Review Times, New Tech Times, Power Of The Word* and *Five Borough Magazine* (where she was the former editor-in-chief).

Denise has made major radio show appearances at WWRL 1600AM with Dr. Jeff Gardere, Clinical Psychologist, WPSC 88.7FM with Marc Medley, and several other online radio stations. Her spoken words have been recorded by Blue Note Records for Lonnie Plaxico's CD entitled "Short Takes".

(**Website: UniversalWrite.com**)

Timeline of the Literary Diva's Published Work

- 2006—By Faith—(Universal Write)
- 2003—Love They Sister, Watch Thy back—(Universal Write)
- 2000—ManKiller—(Universal Write)
- 2000—Spanish Eyes—(Universal Write)
- 2000—Ebony Passion—(Universal Write)

Denise Turney

Denise Turney is a mother and a Human Resources Specialist. She is an entrepreneur, a businesswoman and a civic and community volunteer. Denise is one of the founding members of Bucks County Pennsylvania's first African American owned and operated drug and alcohol intervention program, No Longer Bound. She is also a former volunteer in Big Brothers/Big Sisters. Her memberships include: Sigma Gamma Rho Sorority, Incorporated, The National Women's Executive Association, Black Women Entrepreneurs, The Philadelphia Writer's Organization, The International Black Writer's Organization, and The International Women's Writing Guild.

Denise attended South-Young High School in Knoxville, Tennessee, where the faculty voted her to be one of four students to attend Girls' State in Nashville. An outdoors, nature and sports lover, Denise was one of Tennessee's top high school milers. She was also one of the city of Knoxville's leading cross-country runners. After high school, Denise attended The University of Tennessee at Chattanooga and Knoxville. She served in the United States Navy from 1984—1988 and earned two Navy Achievement Medals.

As a professional author, Denise has thirty years of writing experience to her credit. She is the author of the new mystery, *Spiral* and the multi-cultural celebrity mystery, *Love Has Many Faces* She is also the author of *Portia*, the story of a successful defense attorney dealing with breast cancer. . *Love Has Many Faces, Portia* and *Spiral* are the beginning of many great works created by this exciting professional writer.

51

Denise's works have appeared in: *Today's Black Woman, Parade, Sisters In Style, Essence, Your Church Magazine, Modern Dad Magazine, KaNupepa, The Trenton Times, Family Times, The Preacher's Magazine, Black Living, Princeton, Sapphire, Bahiyah Magazine, New Jersey's Business and Entertainment Weekly—US 1, The Pittsburgh Quarterly, Pif, Q, The Trenton State College Literary Review, North Carolina University's Literary Journal, Obsidian II* and various other magazines and newspapers across the nation, including, as a contributing writer for *Proverbs For the People*, a book of stories by African American writers. *Proverbs For the People* has been praised across the nation and featured in *Ebony Magazine*.

Denise has appeared on radio and television stations across the United States. She also the host of an international radio program *Off The Shelf* at Blakeradio.com.

(Website: Chistell.com)

Timeline of the Literary Diva's Published Work

～ 2003—Spiral—(Chistell Publishing)
～ 2000—Love Has Many Faces—(Chistell Publishing)
～ 1998—Portia—(Chistell Publishing)

Donna Hill

Donna Hill began her professional career in human services in 1988, as Director of a model transitional living facility for homeless teen mothers and their babies, where she was responsible for implementing the start-up and development of the facility, programming, staffing and the daily management of the 17 bedroom apartment complex. This was followed by her tenure as Executive Director of the Brooklyn Teen Pregnancy Network a borough-wide referral and information service for at-risk adolescents, where she was responsible for grant writing, budgets and disseminating staff and information out into the community. Her book *Chances Are,* the story of a transitional residence was so highly received, that the Ray of Hope, Inc. in Lake Charles, Louisiana. asked permission to name their facility-in-progress after Ms. Hill's *Chances Are,* and she has since received the Key to the City.

Donna's writing career began in 1987. Since that time she has more than forty published titles to her credit, including full-length novels and novellas. Three of her novels have been adapted for television. She co-wrote the independent screenplay *The Return of Fire,* and served as packager and editor for five collections, two of which were nominated for awards.

Donna has been featured in *Essence,* the New York *Daily News, USA Today, Today's Black Woman,* and *Black Enterprise* among many others. She has appeared on numerous radio and television stations across the country such as B.E.T., The McCreary Report, Good Day New York, Lifetime Television, MSG Metro-At-Large; and her work has appeared on several bestseller lists. She has received several awards for her body of work as well as commendations for her community service. Donna is also head of her own business, *Imagenouveau, Inc.* which offers promotional assistance to established and aspiring authors and artists.

Donna lives in Brooklyn, NY with her family. She is represented by the Steele-Perkins Literary Agency. Her life quote is: "I'm dreaming of great things and doing them!"

(Website: www.donnahill.com)

Timeline of the Literary Diva's Published Works

Romance Novels

- 1990—Rooms of the Heart
- 1991—Indiscretions
- 1994—Temptation
- 1995—Scandalous
- 1996—Deception
- 1997—Intimate Betrayal **
- 1998—Charade
- 1998—Chances Are
- 1998—A Private Affair **
- 1998—Quiet Storm
- 1999—Pieces of Dreams
- 2000—Through the Fire
- 2001—A Scandalous Affair
- 2000—Soul to Soul
- 2001—Interlude
- 2003—Rockin' Around that Christmas Tree
- 2004—Dare to Dream
- 2005—Say Yes

Novellas

- Spirit of the Season "The Choice"
- Love Letters "Masquerade" **
- Rosie's Curl and Weave "Just Like That"
- Della's House of Style "It Could Happen to You"
- Welcome to Leo's "Eye of the Beholder" Let's Get it On "Lady in Waiting"
- Living Large "Surprise"
- Big Girls Don't Cry "Dr. Love"
- Whole Lotta Love "Over the Rainbow"
- Proverbs for the People "Rendezvous With Destiny"
- Sister Sister "Thicker than Water"
- Going to the Chapel "Distant Lover"

Erotica (short stories)

- Dark Thirst "The Touch"

- Black Silk "Mojo Lover"
- Indigo After Dark "In Between the Night"

Women's Fiction
- 2001—If I Could
- 2001—Rhythms
- 2003—An Ordinary Woman
- 2004—In My Bedroom
- 2004—Divas Inc.
- 2005—Getting Hers

Editorial Projects
- After the Vows
- Midnight Clear
- The Hot Spot
- Indecent ExposureWhere There's A Will

Upcoming Romances
- 2006—Love Becomes Her
- 2006—Long Distance Lover
- 2006—Having All My Lovin'
- 2006—Destiny's Daughters

Upcoming Fiction
- Guilty Pleasures

Special Edition Collectors Series
- Courageous Hearts
- Tis the Season

Film Credits
- The Return of Fire

*** Made for TV movies*

Dorothy Ford

Dorothy F. Ford's maternal great-grandfather was on the last known slave ship (Clotilda) to arrive in America, in a place now called Africatown (AL). She is the seventh of eleven children born to Nathan D. and Ora A. Floyd.

Dothothy the author of *The Lost Angels: Children Without Prayer,* a positive and spiritually uplifting novel that captures the essence of social turbulence in a society and demonstrates how family and community coming together can create an unbreakable bond of power.

Dorothy is a member of Zeta Phi Beta Sorority, a Life Master Bridge Player in the American Contract Bridge League, and is listed in the *1978 International Who's Who of Intellectuals, Volume III*. She was secretary of The Executive Board of the Los Angeles Metropolitan Opera Company in 1982 and President of the Los Angeles Metropolitan Opera Company in 1983. She was the Managing Director of the Africatown Folk Festival in 1986, 1987 and 1988.

A world traveler, Dorothy founded The Ora A. Floyd Foundation in the United States and Liberia, West Africa. She was a business consultant in Nigeria, West Africa, CEO of Vermont Pharmacy, Clotilda International, Pine Forge Industries and J & D Tenkerkare. Humanitarian work in Liberia and Nigeria placed her in *Who's Who in International Community Service* and *World Who's Who of Women*.

Dorothy attended Alabama State University, Xavier University; Los Angeles City College, University of California, Los Angeles; University of Wisconsin; and California Technical University. She earned Master's and Doctorate degrees in Education and a BS in Pharmacy.

(Website: TheLostAngels.com)

Timeline of the Literary Diva's Published Work

∽ 2005—The Lost Angels—(Infinity Publishing)

Dorothy Pitman Hughes

Dorothy Pitman Hughes gained notoriety in the early seventies, after joining up with feminist Gloria Steinem as public speaking partners, embarking on a national college tour. By then, she was the mother of two daughters and had another one on the way. To assure the best care for her children, she convinced her husband to allow her to turn their living room into a day care center, until she could raise the necessary funds to buy a building, which she renovated to house over 125 children while their parents worked or went to school.

In 1973, Dorothy created an alternate public school project in New York City's West Side, which resulted in Mayor John Lindsay's funding her day care and summer work programs for youth. Dorothy then proceeded to advocate for alternative to welfare legislation, better housing, jobs, job training, women's rights, civil rights, health care, social and political rights.

She soon realized that without economic empowerment there would be no social or political freedom, and as an entrepreneur, continued to rally people and organizations to join her crusade. At the suggestion of Amber Books publisher, Tony Rose, Dorothy completed her first non-fiction book *Wake Up and Smell the Dollar! Whose inner City is This Anyway! One Woman's Struggle Against Sexism, Classism, Racism, Gentrification, and the Empowerment Zone*, which was published April 2000. In the interim, Dorothy led her community in a successful mission to take back their birth town of Charles Junction (Lumpkin, Georgia) from Mead Paper Company after they had been illegally driven out by gentrification.

Dorothy began a project to enter into the economic mainstream, teaching economics 101 to thousands of people attending her seminars and lectures throughout the country. Her theme, *From Sharecropping to Shareholding* is the title of her next book, now being penned. Hughes has also purchased a shell company, in which she plans to do an IPO (Initial Public Offering), and continues to help African Americans to understand wealth creation, as opposed to making money and just spending it.

Dorothy has been written about and interviewed by hundreds of media outlets—national magazines, newspapers, radio programs and television shows, including: *Time, Ebony, US News & World Report, New York Times, New York Daily News, Harlem News, National Geographic, Black Enterprise, Kip's Business Report, People, Success, Network Journal,* the Oprah Show, the Gil Noble Show…the list goes on. She is also featured in Dominic J. Pulera's book *Sharing the Dream: White Males in Multicultural America*.

Dorothy has done major fundraising and been appointed to committees by numerous political personalities, such as: President Jimmy Carter, Reverend Jesse Jackson, Honorable Nelson Mandela, Honorable Percy Sutton, Congressman Charles Rangel, as well as hosting the opening ceremony for President Clinton's Harlem office.

Among the numerous awards Dorothy has received for her activism, she includes the 2001 "Woman of Valor" Award, which was presented by a group of corporate and professional leaders chaired by Gloria Steinem and Samuel P. Peabody.

In 2003, having had experience owning an office supply store on 125th Street in Harlem USA, before the "gentrification" of Harlem, Dorothy opened a bookstore on the campus of Edward Waters College in Jacksonville, Florida in order to continue her mission to teach economic empowerment to the people.

Hughes has returned to the south, and is currently living in Georgia and Florida. She is continuing her advocacy for economic empowerment; she is now concentrating on "Politics 2008" working with the hip hop community of 100 rappers on a national campaign to wrap up the vote.

(www.dorothypitmanhughes.com)

Timeline of the Literary Diva's Published Work

- 2000—Wake Up & Smell The Dollars!—(Amber Books)

Dorrie Williams-Wheeler

Dorrie Williams-Wheeler is the author of *The Unplanned Pregnancy Book for Teens & College Students; Be My Sorority Sister Under Pressure*; and *Sparkle Doll: Always into Something.* She was born in Champaign, Illinois where her parents attended The University of Illinois. Dorrie was raised in Illinois, Southern California and Colorado.

Dorrie has been an educator, curriculum developer and a computer specialist Intranet/Internet for the Department of Defense. Dorrie earned a BS degree and a MS degree in Education in Curriculum & Instruction (Instructional Technology) from Southern Illinois University. She then moved to New Jersey to pursue her PhD at Rutgers.

Throughout the 1990's, was a very active screenwriter and one of her scripts was considered for a major film production. In 2001, Dorrie decided to become a full time, stay-at-home mom and author.

Where some authors send out query letters in pursuit of a literary agent or major publisher, the thought never occurred to Dorrie. She mentioned, "I knew the technology was available so self publishing was my first choice." After several years as a successful self-published author, Dorrie decided to make a change.

Dorrie said, "I decided it was time to get an agent and pursue a traditional publishing deal because I just couldn't keep up with all of the book orders. It is so hard being the publisher and the author. I love to do promo, but the job of filling orders takes me away from my writing too much." Dorrie is represented by Cheryl Ferguson at the Ferguson Literary Agency.

An accomplished web designer, Dorrie has been designing web sites and maintaining a web presence since 1995. She owns and operates several high profile entertainment and business websites. She writes for numerous print and on-line publications including *Bellaonline.com, Thabiz.com, Theindustrycosign.com, Entertainmentworld.us*, and *7cities.com* (a Tribune-owned publication). The mother of two lives in Virginia with her husband Craig Wheeler.

Timeline of the Literary Diva's Published Work

- 2004—The Unplanned Pregnancy Book For Teens & College Students—(Sparkle Doll Productions)
- 2004—Be My Sorority Sister Under Pressure—(Sparkle Doll Productions)
- 2001—Sparkle Doll: Always Into Something—(Writer's Club Press)

E. Hill

Ernestine Hill is a Kansas native living in Texas. She is the author of *Die, Sweetheart, Die*, three other undisclosed novels, and is writing a fourth mystery/suspense novel.

E. Hill attended schools in Kansas City and Texas. She is the mother of three daughters and enjoys reading, and traveling. She writes mystery/suspense stories about thirty-something professional women, drawn into issues that put them in conflict with a killer. Hill pens tales of terror and suspense that keep her readers on the edge of their seats, while questioning the slightest sound, and frequently checking the locks on her doors and windows.

(Website: JeopardyPress.com)

Timeline of the Literary Diva's Published Work

🖋 2004—Die, Sweetheart Die—(Jeopardy Press)

Edith Holmes

Edith M. Holmes lives in the Deep South of Georgia. She has always enjoyed reading and writing. Edith published articles in the local newspapers in her hometown on diverse subject matters. She published her first book, 'PRESSIONS-Memoirs of a Southern Cat in 2004.

Edith is known as the person who will get things done with preparation, persistence, pride and prayer. Her creativity and ambition leads to achievement through knowledge and humor at the best of times. She has been quoted saying, "I believe that the Great Creator never created one soul without his own agenda for that soul." Writing was His agenda for Edith, says the author who earned a proclamation for the 1st YOUnity Guild Awards Show in New York for her work.

When Edith completed a matching CD for her book, the critics wrote, "A modern day spoken word star is born".

(Website: Author-me.com/edithbio.htm)

Timeline of the Literary Diva's Published Work

🖋 2004—'PRESSIONS-Memoirs of a Southern Cat—(Llumina Press)

Electa Rome Parks

Electa Rome Parks, a rising stars in contemporary fiction, is the author of the best-selling novels *The Ties That Bind* and *Loose Ends*, which were originally self-published through her own company, Novel Ideal Publishing and Editorial Services Company, a company now dedicated to quality editorial services.

Electa has been writing ever since she remembers. After years of keeping a diary, journaling, writing short stories and poems, her first novel was born in 2001. "I developed a love, respect, and appreciation for books at a very early age," states Parks. "I realized words were powerful, they could change lives, ideas, beliefs, your view of the world and yourself. Writing is my therapy. It clears out all of the clutter of everyday living."

After successfully self-publishing her debut novels, New American Library, a division of Penguin Group, bought the rights. Mrs. Parks signed a three-book deal with New American Library. Her first novel, *The Ties That Bind*, was re-released in October 2004, and *Loose Ends* was re-released in November 2004. Both books were immediately chosen as *Black Expressions Book Club* selections and embraced as *Books of the Month* by book clubs across the country. A third manuscript, *Almost Doesn't Count*, which was immediately chosen as a Main Selection for *Black Expressions Book Club* in August 2005. Parks states, "This was just the beginning of my literary journey that confirms dreams do come true; and nothing, or no one can stop the predestination that is laid out for each of us."

Recently, Electa signed her second book deal with New American Library /Penguin Group for the novel *Ladies Night Out*. Electa Rome Parks currently lives outside Atlanta, Georgia, with her husband Nelson and two children. With a BA degree in marketing and a minor in sociology, she is presently following her true passion and working on her next novel.

(Website: ElectaRomeParks.com)

Timeline of the Literary Diva's Published Work

- 2005—Almost Doesn't Count—(Nal Trade)
- 2004—The Ties That Bind—(Nal Trade)
- 2004—Loose Ends—(Nal Trade)

Elizabeth Nunez

Elizabeth Nunez was born in Trinidad. She emigrated to the United States and earned her Ph.D. and Masters degrees in English from New York University, and her B.A. degree in English from Marian College in Wisconsin. Elizabeth founded the National Black Writers Conference with John Oliver Killens, and served as the director of the conference from 1986 to 2000. The National Writer's Conference has included panelists such as: Gwendolyn Brooks, Alice Walker, Maya Angelou, Terrie McMillan, Bebe Moore Campbell, Jill Nelson, Ishmael Reed, Amiri Baraka, Walter Mosley, Marita Golden, Henry Louis Gates, Jr., Arnold Rampersad, Stanley Crouch, Mari Evans, and Maryse Condé.

Elizabeth is the author of many critical acclaimed novels including *Grace* (Ballantine, 2003), *Discretion* (Ballantine, 2002), *Bruised Hibiscus* (Seal Press, 2000), *Beyond the Limbo Silence* (Seal Press, 1998) and *When Rocks Dance* (Putnam & Ballantine, 1992). *Bruised Hibiscus* won an American Book Award in 2001. "The New York Times Book Review stated that "in its finest moments, Bruised Hibiscus leaves us with difficult lessons about the postcolonial new world order we still struggle to negotiate." *Beyond the Limbo Silence* won a 1999 IPPY Award-Independent Publishers Book Award in the Multicultural Fiction category.

Elizabeth is also the co-editor of the collection of essays *Defining Ourselves: Black Writers in the 90's* and author of several scholarly articles in professional journals. She is a CUNY Professor of English at Medgar Evers College, the City University of New York, "where she designed, developed and implemented many of the college's first major academic programs."

Timeline of the Literary Diva's Published Work

- 2006—Prosperos Daughters—(Ballantine Books)
- 2005—Blue Latitudes: Caribbean Women Writers at Home Aboard—(One World/Ballantine)
- 2003—Discretion—(One World/Ballantine)
- 2003—Bruised Hibiscus—(Seal Press)
- 2003—Grace—(One World/ Ballantine)
- 2003—Beyond the Limbo Silence—(One World/Ballantine)
- 1999—Defining Ourselves: Black Writers in the 90's Defining Ourselves: Black Writers in the 90's-
- 1987—When Rock's Dance—Ballantine Books

Erica L. Perry

Erica L. Perry is a graduate of Prairie View A&M University, where she matriculated and joined the many distinguished graduates of PVAMU with a Masters Degree in Counseling. She was born in Houston, Texas and raised on the outskirts, south west of Houston in El Campo, Texas.

At an early age Erica aspired to become a writer. Many years later her dream came to fruition. By way of a life change, emotional shift, and the need to testify that bad things can happen to good people she decided to share her heartache, disappointment, and pain with the world. All the while informing the broken-hearted they do not swim alone in the sea of infidelity.

As a counselor she knew the importance of therapy for the mind, soul, and tarnished spirit. So she took the advice she gave several times to her client's and transferred her feelings through her pen to paper. *Thank God for Unanswered Prayers*, was released in 2006. Miss Perry has been featured as the "Spotlight Author" for 3D Book Club, and *A Chocolate Affair*. Erica L. Perry resides in Houston, Texas.

(Website: EricaLPerry.com)

Timeline of the Literary Diva's Published Work

- 2006—A Lesson or a Blessing
- 2006—Thank God for Unanswered Prayers

Evelyn Palfrey

Evelyn Palfrey grew up in East Texas. She is a graduate of Southern Methodist University and the University of Texas Law School.

Evelyn is a member of Austin Writers League, the Austin Romance Writers of America, the Travis County Bar Association and the Links Inc. Her novels include middle-age heroes and heroines. She has been nominated for the "Career Achievement Award" in *Romantic Times* magazine.

(Website: Evelyn Palfrey.com)

Timeline of the Literary Diva's Published Work

- ∽ 2004—Three Perfect Men—(Moon Child Books)
- ∽ 2002—Everything In Its Place—(Atria)
- ∽ 2002—The Price of Passion—(Atria)
- ∽ 2001—Dangerous Dilemmas—(Pocket Books)

Francis Ray

"Francis Ray is a native Texan and lives in Dallas. A graduate of Texas Woman's University, she is a School Nurse Practitioner with the Dallas Independent School District. In 1999 and 2000 she was nominated for Texas Woman's University Distinguished Alumni Award.

To date, Francis has written thirty titles, many of which have been included on bestseller's lists, such as: *Blackboard* and *Essence* magazine. *Incognito*, her sixth title, was the first made-for-TV movie for BET.

Francis' awards include: "Romantic Times Career Achievement", EMMA, "The Golden Pen", and "The Atlantic Choice".

The Turning Point, her first mainstream title, was a finalist for the prestigious "HOLT Medallion Award". At the release event for *The Turning Point* in May 2001, she established The Turning Point Legal Fund to assist women of domestic violence by helping them restructure their lives.

With the release of her second mainstream title, *I Know Who Holds Tomorrow*, May 2002, Francis pledged to continue the effort. *I Know Who Holds Tomorrow* made the bestseller's list of *The Dallas Morning News*, *Blackboard*, *Black Expressions Book Club*, and *Essence* magazine. The book was one of five titles selected as "Book Club Favorites" for *Black Issues Book Review's* "Best of 2002".

Francis' third mainstream title, *Somebody's Knocking At my Door*, was released May 2003 and made bestsellers' lists across the country. *Rockin' Around That Christmas Tree*, a holiday collaboration with Donna Hill, was published in November 2003. Other books include *Someone to Love Me* (December 2003), *Trouble Don't Last Always* (January 2004), *First Touch* (February 2004), *Whole Lotta Love* (February 2004), *Love at Leo's*

(July 2004), and *The Falcon Saga* (August 2004). Francis' fourth mainstream title, *Like the First Time*, was released in May 2004 and also made the *Essence* "Bestseller's List".

January 2005 continued the *Living Large* stories, a concept of Francis Ray's fashionable and fabulous full-figured women with *Big Girls Don't Cry*. February 2005 was a major personal triumph with the release of her first Christian fiction, *Then Sings My Soul* in a trade anthology from Harlequin/Steeple Hill, *How Sweet the Sound*. March 2005 saw the release of the long-awaited continuation of The Graysons of New Mexico series with *You and No Other*. Her fifth mainstream and thirtieth title, *Any Rich Man Will Do* was published October 2005. October is National Domestic Awareness Month and, in continuing her pledge to assist women who are victims of domestic violence, Francis Ray pledged a portion of the proceeds from *Any Rich man Will Do* to The Turning Point Legal Fund. In 2005 two of Ms. Ray's titles, *Someone to Love Me* and *I Know Who Holds Tomorrow* were released in hard cover with large print by Thorndike. New releases for 2006 included: *Chocolate Kisses, Irresistible You, and In Another Man's Bed*."(Cited from FrancisRay.com).

Timeline of the Literary Diva's Published Work

- 2006—Chocolate Kisses—(NAL Trade)
- 2006—Irresistible You
- 2006—In Another Man's Bed
- 2005—Any Rich Man Will Do—(St. Martin's Griffin)
- 2005—You and No Other—(St. Martin's Paperbacks)
- 2005—Someone to Love Me
- 2005—Big Girls Don't Cry—(Signet)
- 2005—I Know Who Holds Tomorrow
- 2004—Trouble Don't Last Always—(St. Martin's Griffin)
- 2004—Whole Lotta Love—(Signet)
- 2004—Rockin' Around that Christmas Tree—(St. Martin's Press)
- 2004—The Falcon Saga—(St. Martin's Paperbacks)
- 2004—Like the First Time—(St. Martin's Griffin)
- 2003—Living Large—(Signet)
- 2003—Somebody's Knocking At My Door—(St. Martin's Griffin)
- 2003—Someone to Love Me—(St. Martin's Paperbacks)
- 2002—Gettin' Merry—(St. Martin's Paperbacks)

- 2001—The Turning Point—(St. Martin's Paperbacks)
- 2000—Welcome to Leo's—(St. Martin's)
- 1996—Only Hers—(Arabesque)
- 1994—Forever Yours—(Arabesque)

Gina Cox

Gina Cox, also known as Gina C., was born and raised in Harlem, New York. She holds a Master of Fine Arts degree in English/Creative Writing as well as a Bachelor of Arts in English and Dance. She is the author of several books, including the upcoming *Execution Style* and *Murder Capital*. Released in 2006, her critically-acclaimed, debut novel *VIGIL: You Never Know Who's Watching You* has been described as: "Arresting." by the Schomburg Center for Research in Black Culture. Her professional credits include pieces written for *African Voices* Magazine and Publishers Marketing Association; she is also featured in Speak Truth to Power!, Glimpses of the Paranormal and Time Off! The Upside to Downtime. She has ten years of experience in publishing, particularly: editorial, book production, design and marketing. Her interviews have aired on C-SPAN, ABC, NBC, CBS and BET Nightly News.

An educator in the New York City Public School System, she has completed over 300 semester hours of psychology and behavioral science-related subjects including: Educational Psychology, Abnormal Psychology, Multiple-Intelligences and Theoretical Foundations. In addition, she is trained in: Violence Prevention, Identifying Child Abuse and Maltreatment, Health Education and ESL Methodologies. Some of her writings are drawn from her life experiences in the inner-city and work with emotionally-disturbed youths; others stem from her international travels and focus on spirituality.

Her main goal as an author is to share her knowledge, enlightenment and experiences by providing information and resources within the context of her writings. Gina often includes factual information pertaining to African-Americans, both current and historical, in the fiction stories she writes. Some of her writings develop into subtle political and social commentaries. She says: "For me, reading is much more than entertainment and writing is a perfect way to teach. If I can reach people, tell them something they didn't know before, inspire them to learn more and seek the truth, then I've achieved the biggest part of my goal."

Gina is certified by the State of New York to teach English and has received numerous academic and professional awards throughout her career. She lives in New York City and currently teaches Theatre Arts to inner-city public school children. A former model and concert dancer, her hobbies include: songwriting, visual arts, antique furniture restoration and travel. She has a growing interest in community activism and is looking for ways to improve public school curriculum for African-American students. She is a member of ASCAP and The Authors Guild. More about Gina can be obtained by logging onto: www.ginacox.com

Gloria Naylor

Gloria Naylor, a native New Yorker, was graduated from Brooklyn College and Yale University. She has received distinguished honors including: Scholar-in-Residence, the University of Pennsylvania; Senior Fellow, The Society for the Humanities, Cornell University; the President's Medal, Brooklyn College; and Visiting Professor, University of Kent, Canterbury, England. Gloria is also the recipient of Guggenheim and National Endowment for the Arts fellowships for her novels and the New York Foundation for the Arts Fellowship for screenwriting.

In 1983, Gloria won the National Book Award for first fiction for *The Women of Brewster Place,* which was made into a popular television mini-series starring and produced by Oprah Winfrey. Naylor founded One Way Productions, an independent film company, and is involved in a literacy program in the Bronx. Her subsequent novels include *Linden Hills, Bailey's Café* and *Mama Day.* In addition to her novels, Naylor has written essays and screenplays for *Bailey's Café* and *The Women of Brewster Place.*

(Website: GloriaNaylor.com)

Timeline of the Literary Diva's Published Work

- 1995—Linden Hills—(Penguin)
- 1993-Bailey's Café—(Vintage)
- 1989—Mama Day—(Vintage; Reprint edition)
- 1983-Women of Brewster Place—(Penguin)

Gwynne Forster

Gwynne Forster is the national best-selling and award-winning author of four books of general mainstream fiction, seventeen romance novels and five novellas. Kensington Publishing Corp. Dafina Books released her fourth book of general fiction, *Whatever It Takes*, in August 2005, following the immensely successful *If You Walked in My Shoes*—released in December 2004.

Gwynne's second mainstream novel, *Blues From Deep Down*, was published in March 2003 to rave reviews. Her first book of general fiction, *When Twilight Comes*—an *Essence* magazine best seller and a main selection of *Black Expressions Book Club*— was published in February 2002 by Kensington/Dafina Books to excellent reviews.

Gwynne is a winner of Black Writers Alliance "2001 Gold Pen Award" for *Beyond Desire*, best romance novel. *Beyond Desire*, is a *Doubleday Book Club*, a *Literary Guild* and a *Black Expressions Club* selection. Her 2001 romance novel, *Scarlet Woman*, is also a *Black Expressions Book Club* selection.

Romance Slam Jam 2001 nominated Gwynne for three Emma Awards and for its first "Vivian Stephens Lifetime Achievement Award". *Romantic Times* nominated her first interracial romance, *Against the Wind* for its award of best ethnic romance of 1999; and they nominated Gwynne for a Lifetime Achievement award.

The "Romance In Color" internet site gave *Against the Wind* its Award Of Excellence and named Gwynne 1999 Author Of The Year. *Fools Rush In*, which BET Books published November 1999 received the *Affaire De Coeur* magazine award for best romance with an African American hero and heroine published in 1999.

Gwynne's next mainstream novel, *Whatever It Takes*, was released in August 2005 to rave reviews followed by *Love Me or Leave Me* in September. Her most recent romance novels, *Last Chance at Love*, and *After the Loving* have been top sellers, as well.

Gwynne holds bachelors and masters degrees in sociology and a master's degree in economics/demography.

(Website: GwynneForster.com)

Timeline of the Literary Diva's Published Work

- 2006—Her Secret Life—(Kimani)
- 2005—Whatever It Takes—(Dafina)
- 2005—After the Loving—(Arabesque)
- 2005—Love Me or Leave Me—(Arabesque)
- 2004—If You Walked in My Shoes—(Dafina)
- 2004—Last Chance at Love—(Arabesque)
- 2003—Blues From Down Deep—(Dafina)
- 2003—Flying High—(Arabesque)
- 2002—When Twilight Comes—(Recorded Books)
- 2002—Once in a Lifetime—(Arabesque)
- 2001—Scarlet Woman—(Arabesque)
- 2001—Going to the Chapel—(St. Martin's Press)
- 2001—Midnight Clear—(St. Martin's Press)
- 2000—Secret Desire—(Arabesque)
- 2000—Midnight Magic—(Indigo)
- 2000—Swept Away—(Arabesque)
- 1999—Against the Wind—(Genesis Press)
- 1999—Fools Rush In—(Arabesque)
- 1999—Beyond Desire—(Kensington Publishing)
- 1999—Naked Soul—(Indigo)
- 1998—Obsession—(Arabesque)
- 1998—Wedding Bells—(Arabesque)
- 1998—I Do!—(Arabesque)
- 1997—Ecstacy—(Arabesque)
- 1996—Against All Odds—(Arabesque)
- 1996—Silver Bells—(Arabesque)
- 1995—Sealed with a Kiss—(Arabesque)

Harriette Cole

Harriette wrote the best-selling bible to African American brides, *Jumping the Broom: The African-American Wedding Planner* (Henry Holt & Co.) She followed that with the companion, *Jumping the Broom Wedding Workbook* (Henry Holt & Co.) In 1999, after traveling the country and listening to myriad concerns from many voices, she penned a guide to living with grace and integrity, *How to Be* (Simon & Schuster).

In 2003, Harriette published two more books: *Choosing Truth: Living an Authentic Life* (Simon & Schuster), a general-market book designed to encourage people to pursue rigorously honest lives and *Coming Together* (Jump at the Sun/Hyperion, with photographer John Pinderhughes), an activity book for African-American children and families, created to inspire meaningful interaction. A second edition of *Jumping the Broom* (Henry Holt), along with a new wedding book focused on designing a sacred ceremony, entitled *Vows* (Simon & Schuster) were released in February. Through Profundities, Inc, Harriette uses her life coaching skills in an effort to support people seeking to attain their life dreams.

Harriette has performed life coaching and artist development duties for notable recording artists such as: Alicia Keys, Mary J. Blige, Erykah Badu, and Carl Thomas, among others. She has also coached a great many members of the general population. Her reach extends to the non-profit and educational worlds, as well, through such organizations as the National Urban League and The Links, Inc. Harriette also creates special events that celebrate the triumphs of couples as they wed, as well as individuals and organizations, as they reach significant turning points.

A Phi Beta Kappa, summa cum laude graduate of Howard University, Harriette previously served millions of readers for 11 years when she worked as lifestyle and fashion director at *Essence* magazine. Since then, she has been able to reach a broad and diverse multi-ethnic audience through her books; her advice column, "Sense and Sensitivity", in the New York *Daily News,* which is nationally syndicated; her careers column on Niaonline.com; her one-on-one work with various clients; her active work as an inspirational speaker across the country; and her interaction with the media. Cole is the editor of *American Legacy Woman,* a lifestyle magazine targeted to African American women. She also acts as editorial director for the new publication *UPTOWN,* a lifestyle magazine for Harlem and the urban elite.

Harriette recently served as the relationship expert on an ABC Family Channel reality series entitled "Perfect Match NY", launched in July 2003 and she has been a frequent contributor to the CBS "Early Show". Harriette has also appeared on many national and local television and radio programs, including several recent appearances on "The Oprah Winfrey Show," "BET," "The View," "The Today Show," "The Other Half" and NPR. (Cited from HarrietteCole.com)

(Website: HarrietteCole.com)

Timeline of the Literary Diva's Published Work

- 2004—Vows—(Simon & Schuster)
- 2004—Jumping the Broom: The African-American Wedding Planner—(Henry Holt & Co.)
- 2004—Jumping the Broom Wedding Workbook—(Henry Holt & Co.)
- 2003—Choosing Truth: Living an Authentic Life—(Simon & Schuster)
- 2003—Coming Together—Celebrations for African American Families—(Jump at the Sun/Hyperion)
- 2000—How to Be: A Guide to Contemporary Living for African Americans—(Simon & Schuster)

Ida Greene, Phd.

Dr. Ida Greene is a Motivational Speaker; licensed Marriage, Family, Child Therapist; ordained Minister; Psychiatric Nurse; Intuitive Personal Development Coach; and an Educator at San Diego Community College, Palomar College and San Diego State University. She is a Reiki Energy Balancing Practitioner, NLP Practitioner, Certified Hypnotherapist, Actor, and founder of Our Place Center of Self-Esteem, an organization that teaches: Personal Empowerment, Self-Esteem, Etiquette, Domestic Violence and Anger Management for children and adults since 1990.

Ida is the author of 13 books: *Light the Fire Within You—Are You Ready for Success?*, *Soft Power Negotiation Skills—How to Be A Success In Business*. *Self-Esteem, the Essence of You*, *How to Improve Self-Esteem In The African American Child*, *How to Improve Self-Esteem In Any Child*, *Money, How to Get It, How to Keep It*, *Say Goodbye to Your Smallness, Say Hello to Your Greatness*, *Anger Management Skills for Children*, *Anger Management Skills for Men*, and *Anger Management Skills for Women*, *Stirring Up the African American Spirit*, and *Angels Among Us, Earth Angels*, available at www.idagreeene.com.

Ida's latest offering is coaching from a spiritual perspective, Angel Readings by phone and a weekly teleclass, on "How to Connect with your Angels." She specializes in working with Attention Deficit Hyperactive children, and conducts parenting classes for parents who children have this condition.

Dr. Ida Greene was a finalist for the "2004 Women Who Mean Business" award, received the NAWBO "BRAVO" 2004 award; the "Best Humanitarian Campaign" 2005, by the Book Publicist of Southern California; and the 1st Runner Up, 2005, "Writers Notes Book" award (Home Category) for her book *Anger Management Skills for Children*.

(Website: IdaGreene.com)

Timeline of the Literary Diva's Published Work

- 2005—Say Goodbye to Your Smallness, Say Hello to Your Greatness—(People Skills Intl.)
- 2004—Are You Ready For Success?—(AUTHOR HOUSE)
- 2004—Self-Esteem, the Essence of You—(AUTHOR HOUSE)
- 1997—Soft Power Negotiation Skills—(AUTHOR HOUSE)
- 1996—Light the Fire Within You—(P.S.I. Publishers)
- 1996-How to Improve Self-Esteem In the African American Child—(People Skills Intl.)
- 1996—How to Improve Self-Esteem In Any Child—(People Skills Intl.)
- 1995—How to Be a Success in Business—(People Skills Intl.)

Iman

Since the beginning of her career, Iman is known for being one of the first to challenge and change prevailing notions of beauty. In order to have cosmetic shades and formulas that worked perfectly for her skin tone, she learned to be a good chemist. Ultimately, Iman created a make up and skin care line specifically for women of color, precisely African American women.

The daughter of an African diplomat, Iman was born in Somalia on July 25, 1955. During her early years she mastered five languages. While working toward her political science degree as an undergraduate at Nairobi University, a well-known photographer, Peter Beard, spotted her walking across campus. Thus began her incomparable career in the fashion world.

Her first modeling assignment was for *Vogue* magazine in 1976. Iman became an instant success in fashion, favored by several top fashion designers, including: Yves St. Laurent, Versace, Calvin Klein and Donna Karan. During her 14 years as a model, she also worked with many top photographers. In 1998, Iman was listed by *People Magazine* as one of the 100 most influential women of the 20th century. She was recognized for her ground-breaking achievements, which paved the way for women of color in the beauty industry.

A U.S. citizen residing in New York, Iman is married to musician/actor David Bowie and together they have a daughter, Alexandria Zahra, who was born in August of 2000. Her daughter from a previous marriage, Zulekha, is currently a college student in the United States. In addition to running a successful beauty company, Iman is actively involved in several charities including Mother's Voices, Action Against Hunger, The Children's Defense Fund and The All Children Foundation. Her first book, *I AM IMAN* (Universe, 2001), is an autobiographical sketchbook of her working life." (Cited from ImanBeauty.com)

(**Website: ImanBeauty.com**)

Timeline of the Literary Diva's Published Work

∼ 2005—The Beauty of Color—Putnam Adult
∼ 2001—I Am Iman—(Universe)

Iyanla Vanzant

Iyanla Vanzant's claim to fame has been her hard work, dedication toward motivating others and a series of books that have changed women's lives from around the nation. Her past is sad and overwhelming to hear about, but if it weren't for Iyanla openly sharing her trials and tribulations as a teenage mother on welfare, abused wife, and sexually abused and neglected child, many women's tortured upbringing may have never exposed their stories and sought help.

She attended Medgar Evers College and the City University of New York law school. Then she moved to Philadelphia with her children. There, she practiced as a public defender for three years. She soon became an ordained minister and dedicated her life to teaching and inspiring others to commit to her "principles of divine power and self-determination."

"Iyanla (pronounced Ee-Yan-La) Vanzant is currently the bestselling author of *Tapping the Power Within, Acts of Faith* (1994 BlackBoard Book of the Year), *The Value in the Valley* (1995 BlackBoard Book of the Year), *Faith in the Valley* (1996 BlackBoard Book of the Year), and two new guides to self-awareness and spiritual fulfillment: *In the Meantime: Finding Yourself and the Love You Want* (Simon & Schuster Hardcover) and *One Day My Soul Just Opened Up: 40 Days and 40 Nights Toward Spiritual Strength* (Fireside Books/A Simon & Schuster Trade Paperback Original)" and many more books.

Iyanla has won numerous awards. In 1992, Los Angeles Mayor Thomas Bradley named October 21st "Tapping the Power Within Day". In 1994, she was named "Alumni of the Year" by the National Association for Equal Opportunity in Education, an organization consisting of the presidents and administrators of the 117 predominantly Black colleges in the United States. She was also awarded an "Oni" by the International Congress of Black Women.

Today, Iyanla is the national spokesperson for Literacy Volunteers of America. As the founder and Executive Director of Inner Visions Spiritual Life Maintenance Network, she conducts workshops and lectures to thousands around the country to support communities and self-empowerment. A powerful, positive and larger-than-life force of personality, Iyanla Vanzant brings a special brand of empathy to her life coaching work on STARTING OVER. Iyanla returns for her second season with STARTING OVER to share her wisdom, compassion and enthusiasm for life, with what she calls the "sisterhood of women" who believe in the power of television.

For 24 years Vanzant studied everyone and everything that spoke to personal strength, personal growth and empowerment. She then integrated that information with her own experiences and developed a common sense approach for addressing life's challenges. Her frank, down-to-earth, and inspiring manner resulted in the publication of over a dozen books, five of which were *New York Times* best-sellers.

An immensely popular public speaker, Vanzant teaches an accessible process for discovering spiritual identity and its inherent power. Her work, she says, "Teaches people how to move beyond whatever has happened in their lives in order to do and be what we came to life to do and be."

Vanzant teaches that one cannot evolve politically, socially or economically until one evolves spiritually. She conveys this message with love, humor and humility and her approach has earned her an Honorary Doctorate of Humane Letters from Medgar Evers College of the City University of New York.

As the Chief Executive Officer of Inner Visions Worldwide, Inc. Spiritual Life Maintenance Center in Silver Spring, MD, Vanzant conducts workshops and classes and coordinates a correspondence prison ministry with more than 3,500 incarcerated members in over 150 penal institutions nationwide. In October 2000, Iyanla headed the faculty of the Inner Visions Institute for Spiritual Development, offering a two-year certification program in Spiritual Counseling and Life Coaching, based on the principles covered in her best selling books.

A powerful, positive and larger-than-life force of personality, Iyanla Vanzant has extended her counseling by bringing a special brand of empathy to her life coaching work on STARTING OVER, a daytime reality television series. She shares her wisdom, compassion and enthusiasm for life, with what she calls the "sisterhood of women" who believe in the power of television.

Iyanla is a mother of three children, grandmother of four children and lives with her husband and cat named Mr. Coco in Silver Spring, Maryland.

(Website: WWW.INNERVISIONSWORLDWIDE.COM)

Timeline of the Literary Diva's Published Work

- 2005—Living from Your Center: Guided Meditations for Creating Balance & Inner Strength (Inner Vision Series) [UNABRIDGED] (Audio CD) -Sounds True; Unabridged edition
- 2005—Giving Thanks (Inner Vision) (Audio CD) -Sounds True
- 2004—Giving to Yourself First (Inner Vision, Sounds True); Unabridged edition
- 2004—Finding Faith in Difficult Times (Inner Vision Series) (Audio CD) -Sounds True
- 2003—Acts of Faith : Daily Meditations for People of Colour (Paperback)—Simon & Schuster Ltd

- 2003—Up From Here : Reclaiming the Male Spirit: A Guide to Transforming Emotions into Power and Freedom (Paperback)—Harper San Francisco; 1st edition
- 2003—Tips For Daily Living Cards—Hay House; Cards edition
- 2002—Every Day I Pray : Prayers for Awakening to the Grace of Inner Communion (Paperback) Fireside; Reprint edition
- 2002—One Day My Soul Just Opened Up : 40 Days and 40 Nights Toward Spiritual Strength and Personal Growth (Paperback) -Simon & Schuster Ltd
- 2001—Yesterday I Cried : Celebrating The Lessons Of Living And Loving—Fireside
- 2001—Acts Of Faith : Meditations For People Of Color [ABRIDGED] (Audio CD) -Sound Ideas; Abridged edition
- 2001—Iyanla Live Gratitude (Iyanla Live!) [ABRIDGED] (Audio CD) -Sound Ideas; Abridged edition
- 2001—Iyanla Live Volume 8 Back To Basics (Iyanla Live!) (Audio CD)-Sound Ideas
- 2001—Iyanla Live! Volume 7: Transformation (Iyanla Live!) (Audio Cassette),Sound Ideas
- 2001—Iyanla Live! Forgiveness [ABRIDGED] (Audio CD)—Sound Ideas; Abridged edition
- 2001—The Iyanla Live! Collection [ABRIDGED] (Audio Cassette)—Sound Ideas; Abridged edition
- 2001—Iyanla Live! Grace (Iyanla Live!) (Audio Cassette)-Sound Ideas
- 2001—Until Today! : Daily Devotions for Spiritual Growth and Peace of Mind (Paperback)—Gardners Books
- 2001—Best Black Women's Erotica (Best Black Women's Erotica Series) (Paperback) -Cleis Press; 1st edition
- 2001—Yesterday, I Cried : Celebrating the Lessons of Living and Loving (Paperback)-Fireside
- 2001—Living Through the Meantime: Learning to Break the Patterns of the Past and Begin the Healing Process [DOWNLOAD: ADOBE READER] (Digital)-Fireside
- 2001—Living Through the Meantime : Learning to Break the Patterns of the Past and Begin the Healing Process (Hardcover)—Fireside
- 2001—Iyanla Live Peace Of Mind (Iyanla Live!) [ABRIDGED] (Audio CD)
- 2001—Until Today! : Daily Devotions for Spiritual Growth and Peace of Mind (Paperback)-Fireside
- 2000—Iyanla Live! Volume 3: Love [ABRIDGED] (Audio Cassette)-Sound Ideas; Abridged edition

- 2000—Iyanla Live! Volume 1: Self-Value, Self-Worth, Self-Love (Audio Cassette)-Sound Ideas
- 2000—Our Relationship With Money (Iyanla Live!) [ABRIDGED] (Audio Cassette)—Sound Ideas; Abridged edition
- 2000—In the Meantime: A Diary for Finding Yourself and the Love That You Want (Calendar)—Universe Publishing (Incorporated, Div. of Rizzoli; Engagement edition)
- 2000—Iyanla Live! Volume 2: Faith (Audio Cassette)-Sound Ideas
- 2000—Until Today! (Hardcover)-Simon & Schuster
- 1999—Entretanto… (in the meantime, Spanish): Descubra Su Propio Yo y el Amor que Ansia—Fireside
- 1999—Success Gems: Your Personal Motivational Success Guide (Paperback)—Quiet Time Publishing; 2nd edition
- 1999—In the Meantime: Music That Tells the Story—Harmony Records
- 1999—Don't Give It Away! : A Workbook of Self-Awareness and Self-Affirmations for Young Women (Paperback)-Fireside
- 1999—In the Meantime : Finding Yourself and the Love You Want (Paperback)-Fireside
- 1998—One Day My Soul Just Opened Up: 40 Days and 40 nights Toward Spiritual Strength and Personal Growth (Hardcover)—Fireside
- 1997-The BIG BOOK OF FAITH (Paperback) -Fireside
- 1997—The Spirit of a Man : A Vision of Transformation for Black Men and the Women Who Love Them (Paperback)—Harper San Francisco; 1st edition
- 1996—ACTS OF FAITH (Hardcover) -Simon & Schuster
- 1996—The Valley In The Valley: A Black Woman's Guide Through Life's Dilemmas—(Paperback)—Fireside
- 1996—FAITH IN THE VALLEY : Lessons for Women on the Journey to Peace (Paperback)—Fireside
- 1995-Interiors: A Black Woman's Healing in Progress (Paperback)-Writers & Readers
- 1995—Interiors (Hardcover)-Writers & Readers
- 1993—Acts Of Faith (Paperback)—Fireside
- 1992—Tapping the Power Within: A Path to Self-Empowerment for Black Women—Writers & Readers Publishing

Jada Pinkett Smith

Jada Pinkett Smith is a movie star, mother, producer and co-business owner of Carol's Daughter featuring body and bath essentials for women of color. She's also the wife of award-winning rap artist, actor and producer Will Smith. Many people remember Jada Pinkett Smith when she aired on a *Different World (1987)*, but if you're an avid supporter of Black Films, you witnessed a talented actress in movies like *Madagascar (2005)*, *Collateral (2001)*, *Enter the Matrix (2003)*, *Maniac Magee(2003)*, *Ali (2001)*, *Kingdom Come (2001)*, *Bamboozled (2000)*, *Blossoms & Veils (1998)*,*Return to Paradise (1998)*, *Woo(1998)*, *Scream 2(1997)*, *Set It Off (1996)*, *If These Walls Could Talk (1996)*, *The Nutty Professor (1996)*, *Demon Knight (1995)*, *Low Down Dirty Shame (1994)*, *Jason's Lyric (1994)*, *Ink Well (1994)*, and *Menace II Society (1993)*.

In November 2004, Jada penned a children's book, *Girls Hold Up This World (Cartwheel)* and her rise to fame is now symbolically treasured by young readers and fans who appreciate her versatility from short crop hairstyles to flowing locks and by acting in humorous movies to series flicks. She's the ultimate Renaissance Women of today who proves that African-American women can do it all and take care of their families.

Jada and her husband, Will Smith are the duo mentioned in Alicia Key's Song, *"Unbreakable."* The world got a chance to see Jada Pinkett and Will Smith on stage together as hosts of a BET Awards Show.

(Website: www.jadapinkettsmith.com)

Timeline of the Literary Diva's Published Work

∽ 2004—Girls Hold Up This World—(Cartwheel)

Janet West Sellars

Writing has been Janet's most enduring passion for as long as she can remember. The embodiment of her passion is impressively revealed in her first novel, *Quiet As It's Kept*. Janet was born in the Washington, DC area. Her creative spirit was cultivated and nurtured by her mother's love of the arts. At home, Janet would use her already polished powers of persuasion to enlist her siblings and friends as cohorts in all types of escapades. Fueled by her burgeoning imagination, even as a child, Janet has always had a natural gift for weaving a tall tale.

A Jayne-of-all-Trades, she has lived and traveled extensively throughout the United States and Europe. Janet has had careers in the armed forces, academia, and public service. She currently works for a federal government agency investigating and resolving discrimination complaints. In addition, Janet holds a Bachelor's degree in Sociology and a Master's degree in Human Relations. Janet currently resides in Virginia with her family.

(Website: JamiseLDames.com)

Timeline of the Literary Diva's Published Works

〜 2005—Quiet as It's Kept—(I Universe, Inc.)

Janine A. Morris

Janine A. Morris is the Music Coordinator of Hot 97, a Hofstra University law student and the author of *Diva Diaries*. Born and raised in Queens, New York, Janine started writing in Junior High School on the school newspaper. Continuing with High school and college newspapers and magazines, she found she truly loved expression through writing. Since college, Janine has written for *XXL, Source, Platinum Plus, Don Diva*, and more. She has also written for 98.7 Kiss FM, Hot 97, conducting several interviews, reviews, and entertainments news pieces.

Janine's debut book, *Diva Diaries*, has earned outstanding reviews from peers in her industry.

When asked about just how great Janine's first book is, Hot 97 Radio Personality Angie Martinez says, "Seriously, I could not put the book down. Every one of us knows one of these women, or we are one of these women." LA LA, an MTV VJ mentions, "I love the way the story depicts today's modern black females. We aren't holding our men down, we are holding it down for the corporate world." Grammy award winning Fat Man Scoop, (Hot 97 Radio Personality) says "It's a real story that every woman I know can relate to," and Miss INFO, a *Vibe* columnist says, "*Diva Diaries* has more juicy drama than any reality show, and is more addictive than cigarettes and coffee! Janine writes for the everyday diva in all of us." Funkmaster Flex (Spike TV Host) says "The story is as real as it gets."

Timeline of the Literary Diva's Published Works

- 2006—Diva Diaries—(Kensington)

Jel D. Lewis (Jones)

Jel D. Lewis (Jones) is a graduate of Marion College in Chicago. She also holds a diploma from the Writer's Digest School in Cincinnati, Ohio.

In 1991, Jel decided that it was time to pursue her writing career full-time and start living her dream toward becoming a best-selling author. As a young girl, she began to write short stories and poems, and as an adult, Jel took her hobby to the next level, completing her first full-length book, *The Naked Girl, a Collection of Short Love Stories.*

Jel has written and published over 100 short stories for college publications, online publications, romance and lifestyle magazines covering such topics as relationships, health, beauty, nutrition, travel and teens. She was a regular writer for *Today's Black Woman* and "*Upscale Magazine*" from 1999-2001.

A writer of both non-fiction and fiction works, Jel is the author of ten published books. In 2002, Jel came to the attention of Amber Communications Group, Inc. and subsequently had two titles released by the publishing house: *The African-American Woman's Guide to Great Sex, Happiness and Marital Bliss*—(Amber Books) and *Michael Jackson, The King Of Pop: The Big Picture, The Music! The Man! The Legend! The Interviews! An Anthology*—(Colossus Books).

Jel D. Lewis (Jones), was born and raised in Tallahatchie County in the state of Mississippi, where she attended elementary and high school. She currently makes her home in a north suburb of Chicago, Illinois.

Timeline of the Literary Diva's Published Work

- 2006—Unbreakable Love—(Publish America)
- 2005—George Walker Bush, History Maker, 911 Champion, Iraq Dismantled—(Publish America)
- 2005—Michael Jackson, The King Of Pop: The Big Picture, The Music! The Man! The Legend! The Interviews! An Anthology— (Colossus Books)
- 2003—The African-American Woman's Guide to Great Sex, Happiness and Marital Bliss – (Amber Books)
- 2002—The Naked Girl, a Collection of Short Love Stories—(Writer's Pub Services)
- 2000—True Love Is Everlasting—(Xlibris Corporation)
- 2000—One Evening In Paradise – (Xlibris Corporation)
- 1996—The Black Virgin—(Writers Pub Unlimited)
- 1994—The Perfect Lady —(Writers Unlimited Pub)

Jessica Care Moore-Poole

Jessica Care Moore-Poole is the CEO of Moore Black Press. "One of the most celebrated, published poets and public speakers of her generation, Jessica Care Moore has issued a strong, defiant, and educated voice into the literary, theatrical, publishing and music industries.

The dynamic young voice from the Motor City swept the nationally televised *It's Showtime at the Apollo's* notoriously tough audiences off their feet, winning a record five consecutive weeks with her powerful lyrics. Jessica made history on that stage and is recognized as an Apollo Legend.

Jessica is the current star, producer and writer of the new poetry and music driven show *SPOKEN!* on the Black Family Channel, operated by CEO

Robert Townsend. The show is produced in association with Moore Black Press. As CEO of Moore Black Press, Jessica was awarded a Small Press award from the African-Americans Helping Authors Organization in NYC.

An activist and lecturer, Jessica has also become a strong voice in the fight against the AIDS epidemic, recently performing and writing an original poem, *Invisible Women* during the United Nations World Aids Day Commemoration, to bring awareness to women and children living with HIV. Jessica has offered her time and voice to the "AIDS WALK" Opening Ceremonies in NYC, San Francisco, LA and Atlanta; and she is one of the organizers of the successful *Hip-Hop-A-Thon Concert*, which helped to increase AIDS education in the Black and Latino Bay Area Community.

One of the producers of the National Black Arts Festival, Jessica is also the facilitator of The Langston Hughes National Poetry Circle Project in Atlanta. She is one of the returning stars of the HBO Series *Russell Simmons presents: Def Poetry Jam* and has been featured on B.E.T.'s, *NYLA, The Ed Gordon Show, Teen Summit, NBC's Today Show*, and U.P.N.'s *Living The Dream Special.* Jessica is the author of the play *There Are No Asylums for the Real Crazy Women.* Her new theater show, *Alpha Phobia*, is a semi-autobiographical sketch about a female poet who believes the alphabet is trying to kill her. This innovative and insightful production premiered at the 14th St. Playhouse in Atlanta during the National Black Arts Festival in 2002. She is one of the featured actors/poets in the film *Hughes Dream Harlem* (STARZ), star of the award winning indie film, *His/Herstory*, and the soon to be released hip hop film, *Under Da Gun*, featuring Umi and M1 of Dead Prez.

Jessica Care Moore-Poole has performed for audiences in Toulouse, Perriguex, Paris, England, Scotland, South Africa, Berlin, and Holland. She was recently asked to be a part of the 10th anniversary of South African Democracy Celebrations and has toured in Cape Town, Joburg, and Durban, leading workshops sponsored by the American Embassy. Her words inspire, along with her innovative approach to music. A blend of funk, hip-hop, soul and rock, she is creatively influenced by artists like, Betty Davis, Janis Joplin, Prince, The Temptations, and Marvin Gaye.

Jessica's soulful, raspy voice leads the drum & bass-rock-poetry band Detroit Read. Her dynamic stage show fuses rapid-fire-heartfelt poetry with heart-pounding rock, melodic vocals, acoustic guitar, house, & electric hip-hop. As a recording artist, she has worked with platinum Columbia recording artist NaS on *Nastradamus,* Impulse recording artist Antonio Hart's *Here I Stand,* Big Cat rap artist PBT, and is featured on The Last Poets *Tribute* Album.

Jessica is also an internationally published writer, with her work being featured in several major anthologies including, *A Different Image,* (UofD Mercy Press 2004), *Abandon Automobile,* (WSU Press 2001), *Listen Up!* (Random House, 1999), *Step Into A World,* (Wiley Publishing, 2001), *Role Call* (Third World Press 2002) *Bum Rush The Page: A Def Poetry Jam* (Crown Publishing 2001), in addition to *Essence, Blaze, Source, Vibe, African Voices, Bomb, Mosaic, Good News, Savoy, One World, BE* and many other magazines." Cited from (Http://www. MooreBlackPress.com).

Timeline of the Literary Diva's Published Work

- 2004—A Different Image—(UofD Mercy Press)
- 2003—The Alphabet Versus—The Ghetto—(Moore Black Press)
- 2002—Role Call—(Third World Press)
- 2001—Bum Rush The Page: A Def Poetry Jam—(Crown Publishing)
- 2001—Step Into A World—(Wiley Publishing)
- 2001—Abandon Automobile—(WSU Press)
- 1999—Listen Up!—(Random House)
- 1997—The Words Don't Fit In My Mouth—(Moore Black Press)

Jessica Tilles

Jessica Tilles is the best-selling author, publisher, founder and CEO of Xpress Yourself Publishing, LLC, Dancing Moon Productions, LLC, Jessica Tilles Ink, and The Writer's Assistant. A native of Washington, DC, Jessica is a writer specializing in all genres of fiction with several titles in print: *Anything Goes, In My Sisters' Corner, Apple Tree* and *Sweet Revenge.*

With a literary style described as fresh, raw and over-the-edge, Jessica's name is often compared to notorious best-selling authors. While she enjoys novels by and about African-Americans, she does not limit her literary tastes and divulges in reading the works of Jackie Collins, Danielle Steele, James Patterson, Stephen King and countless others.

For 2002 through 2004, Jessica's titles graced the Karibu Books' Best Seller's List, Book-Remarks.com, as well as countless others. Recently, her newly released title, *Sweet Revenge*, spent 10 weeks on the Karibu Books' Best Seller's List.

Jessica is the recipient of the 2003 Memphis Black Writer's Conference "Rising Star" Award and The Jackson Mississippi Readers Club's "Contribution to African American Literature" Award.

Jessica has been featured in *Booking Matters Magazine, Memphis ViP magazine* and *The Clarion-Ledger* (Jackson, MS). She has appeared on Kixie 101FM and Channel 4 News at Noon, both in Jackson, MS, and with LaDawn Black on 92Q FM (Baltimore, MD).

Jessica is the brainchild and co-founder of *J.T.'s Book Corner*, featuring personal, one-on-one interviews with authors and leaders in the literary industry. You can find *J.T.'s Book Corner* at the popular Black Men In America.com (www.blackmeninamerica.com/jt.htm) web site.

For those wishing to become published, Jessica's enthusiastic advice is to "Self-publish first. This method will enable a hands-on approach into the publishing world, allowing you to fully experience every aspect of the business."

(Website: JessicaTilles.com)

Timeline of the Literary Diva's Published Work

∿ 2005—Sweet Revenge—(Xpress Yourself Pub, LLC)
∿ 2004—Apple Tree—(Xpress Yourself Pub, LLC)
∿ 2003—In My Sisters Corner—(Xpress Yourself Pub, LLC)
∿ 2002—Anything Goes—(Xpress Yourself Pub, LLC)

Jewelene Banks

Jewelene is a wife, mother and accomplished playwright. She has written numerous plays and skits that have been enthusiastically accepted in Northeastern Ohio and beyond. She was born in Dallas, Texas, raised and educated in Akron. Her imagination and creative prowess has been a part of her persona for as long as she can remember, meaning that "her talents were not learned or manufactured, but came to this planet with her through Almighty God".

Jewelene has given people of Northeastern Ohio visions that were alien to them until the advent of her plays. She is one of the most multifaceted individuals you will ever meet. She has been presented with the 2004 NAACP "Living Legend Award". Through her presentations the message to the masses is clear, "The positive cannot survive until the negativity ceases. Get the drugs, rapists and pedophiles out of our neighborhoods and give us back our children." These messages transcend color lines and economic differences, as they beg to be heard in a myriad of writing genres.

Jewelene has written plays for the University of Akron's School of Nursing Health Fair, which focused on high blood pressure, heart attacks and strokes. Amazingly her genres focused on health, while winning a battle with cancer herself, and receiving treatments at the Cleveland Clinic.

Jewelene has recently written and released her debut, mainstream novel entitled "ZEOLA". Cited from (www. Jewelboxcreations.net.)

Timeline of the Literary Diva's Published Work
2006—ZEOLA

Jewell Parker Rhodes

Jewell Parker Rhodes is a professor of Creative Writing and American Literature and former Director of the MFA Program in Creative Writing at Arizona State University. Her stories have been published in anthologies such as *Children of the Night: Best Short Stories by Black Writers*, edited by Gloria Naylor (Little Brown, 1996), and *Ancestral House: The Black Short Story in the Americas and Europe*, edited by Charles Rowell (Westview Press/Harper Collins, 1995).

Jewell's short fiction stories have has appeared in *Callaloo, Calyx, The Seattle Review, Feminist Studies, Peregrine, Hayden's Ferry Review*, and *Shooting Star Review*. Her work has been nominated twice for the "Pushcart Prize". Her scholarly and non-fiction articles have appeared in various academic journals.

Among her numerous awards are the "Yaddo Creative Writing Fellowship", the "National Endowment of the Arts Award in Fiction", and two Distinguished Teaching Awards. She also was selected as the Creative Writing Delegate for the Modern Language Association.

Jewell earned a Bachelor of Arts in Drama Criticism, a Master of Arts in English, and a Doctor of Arts in English (Creative Writing) from Carnegie-Mellon University. In 1995 she earned the Distinguished Teaching Award in the College of Liberal Arts and Sciences at Arizona State University. She lives in Scottsdale, Arizona.

(Website: Pageturner.net/jewellparkerrhodes)

Timeline of the Literary Diva's Published Work

- ∞ 2004—Proverbs for the People—(Dafina)
- ∞ 2002—The African Guide to Writing & Publishing Non-Fiction—2002
- ∞ 2002—Douglass's Women: A Novel—(Atria)
- ∞ 2000—Voodoo Season—A Marie Laveau Mystery—(Atria)
- ∞ 1999—Free Within Ourselves—Main Street
- ∞ 1998—Magic City: A Novel—(Perennial)
- ∞ 1995—Voodoo Dreams: A Novel—(Picada)

Jill Nelson

Jill Nelson was born and raised in Harlem and has been a working journalist for over twenty years. She is a graduate of the City College of New York and Columbia University's School of Journalism. Her work has appeared in numerous publications, including *The New York Times, Essence, The Washington Post, The Nation, Ms., The Chicago Tribune* and the *Village Voice.* Jill was a staff writer for the *Washington Post* magazine during its first years of existence, and was named "Washington D.C. Journalist of the Year" for her work there.

Author of the best-selling memoir, *Volunteer Slavery: My Authentic Negro Experience* (Noble Press, hardcover, 1993 and Penguin, paperback, 1994) which won an American Book Award, she is also the author of *Straight, No Chaser: How I Became A Grown-Up Black Woman* (Putnam, Fall 1997, Penguin, Winter 1999) *Sexual Healing,* (Agate, June 2003), *Finding Martha's Vineyard: African Americans at Home on an Island,* (Random House, May 2005) and editor of *Police Brutality: An Anthology* (WW Norton,

April 2000). In addition to writing, Jill worked as a professor of Journalism at the City College of New York from 1998 to 2003. Today, along with continuing to author new books, she freelances, lectures widely, writes a twice-monthly column, "On the Verge," for NiaOnline.com and is a monthly contributor to the Op Ed page of *USA Today*.

(Website: JillScott.com)

Timeline of the Literary Diva's Published Work

- 2005—Finding Martha's Vineyard: African American's at Home on an Island—(Random House)
- 2003—Sexual Healing—(Agate)
- 2000—Police Brutality—(WW Norton)
- 1999—Straight, No Chaser: How I Became A Grown-Up Black Woman—(Penguin)
- 1997-Straight, No Chaser: How I Became A Grown-Up Black Woman—(Putnam)
- 1994—Volunteer Slavery: My Authentic Negro Experience—(Penguin, paperback)
- 1993—Volunteer Slavery: My Authentic Negro Experience—(Noble Press, hardcover)

Joylynn Jossell

Joy, a native of Columbus, Ohio, after thirteen years of being a paralegal in the insurance industry, finally divorced her career and married her mistress and her passion, writing. In the year 2000 she formed her own publishing company, End of the Rainbow Projects. Her sole purpose with End of the Rainbow was to introduce to all those she encountered the quality of sharing that her grandmother had instilled in her. Joy shares what she has learned in the literary industry by instructing a workshop entitled "Self—Publishing: The Basics You Need to Get Started."

In 2004 Joy branched off into the business of literary consulting, in which she provides one-on-one consulting and literary services, such as: ghost writing, professional read-throughs, write behinds and more. Her clients consist of first time authors, national bestselling authors and entertainers.

The end result of a couple of her client's projects resulted in Joy being able to present their manuscripts to a publisher and land book deals for them.

Lately Joy's spirit has been moving in another direction. She has been working on a Christian fiction piece entitled *Me, Myself and Him* in which a woman struggles in her walk with God and His word because she's still holding onto the hand of her mate, a man who is walking in the world. Joy hopes that the following of readers she's been blessed to have earned will decide to take this spiritual journey with her as she shifts to pen what God has called her to do. She states, "How long will we continue to wait at the end of the rainbow before realizing that we, in fact, are the pot of gold? Don't just want to write a book some day...write a book TODAY!"

(Website: JoylynnJossell.com)

Timeline of the Literary Divas Published Work

- 2006—When Souls Mate—(St. Martin's Griffin)
- 2005—Girls From Da Hood 2—(Urban Books)
- 2005—If I Ruled the World—(St. Martin's Griffin)
- 2005—An All Night Man—(St. Martin's Griffin)
- 2004—The Root of All Evil—(St. Martin's Griffin)
- 2003—Dollar Bill—(Triple Crown Publications)
- 2003—The Game: Short Stories About the Life—(Triple Crown Publications)
- 2002—Twilight Moods—(Flowers In Bloom Publishing)
- 2002—World On My Shoulders—(End of the Rainbow Projects Inc.)
- 2001—Please Tell Me If The Grass Is Greener—(End of the Rainbow Projects Inc.)

Juanita Bynum

"Juanita Bynum is an internationally acclaimed Bible teacher, prophet, psalmist, media personality; Founder and President of Juanita Bynum Ministries in Waycross, Georgia. Dr. Bynum is the wife of Bishop Thomas Weeks III, who is the pastor of Global Destiny Church where she supports and assists her husband in ministry.

A gifted vocalist and entrepreneur, Dr. Bynum has established an exciting new venture, Flow Records, with the recent release of her new worship CD, *A Piece of My Passion*. Her previously recorded worship CD's, *Morning Glory I* and *Morning Glory II*, remain popular favorites.

Dr. Bynum is the *New York Times* best selling author of the book, *The Threshing Floor*. She is also the best selling author of the book, *The Matters of the Heart*, which has sold to date over 600,000 copies. Her popular writings also include her very powerful leadership book, *My Spiritual Inheritance, No More Sheets*, and many more.

Dr. Bynum is fueled by a passion to fulfill God's mandate for these turbulent times. Her thrust on character building by merging spirituality with everyday living provokes people to pursue a life of integrity. Wherever she goes, Dr. Bynum exhorts and encourages her listeners to deepen their intimacy with God and arise to their divine calling and destiny.

Not afraid to deal with hard, relevant issues, Dr. Bynum preaches in-your-face messages that have drawn thousands of women and men to her crusades and events. Her "Weapons of Power" conference, which was last held in St. Louis, Missouri in 2003, drew over 30,000 attendees and was broadcast live on the major Christian networks, including Trinity Broadcasting Network (TBN), Daystar, and The Word network. Often addressing crowds of 50,000–100,000 as a keynote speaker at international conferences and events, Dr. Bynum has preached in many of the largest, well-respected pulpits in America and around the world.

Dr. Bynum is also a frequent radio and television guest, who serves as a regular host of TBN's worldwide flagship program, PRAISE, which is viewed by over 100 million people. Within the TBN broadcast network, she is affectionately regarded as one of the leading and highest rated National PRAISE hosts and guests with Nielson Galaxy Navigator ratings consistently among the top 10 of any host or guest on their network.

In addition, Dr. Bynum has been featured in magazines such as *Essence* and *Ebony*, and has also appeared on the front cover of the leading Christian magazines, *Charisma, Ministries Today*, and *The Spirit Led Woman*. In early 2005, Dr. Bynum ministered in song to audiences across America as a featured artist, along with Yolanda Adams, Sheila E. and others during the Southwest Airlines' "Sisters In The Spirit" music tour.

In the midst of it all, Bynum has not swayed from her mission. She readily and candidly shares, "It's not about platforms; it's about people." (Cited from www.juanitabynum.com).

(Website: JuanitaBynum.com)

Timeline of the Literary Divas Published Work

- ✒ 2005—The Threshing Floor: How to Know Without a Doubt that God Hears Your Every Prayer—(Charisma House)
- ✒ 2004—My Spiritual Inheritance—(Charisma House)
- ✒ 2002—Matters of the Heart: Stop Trying to Fix the Old , Let God Give You Something New—(Charisma House)
- ✒ 2001—No More Sheets: My Accident—(Pneuma Life Publishing)
- ✒ 2000—No More Sheets : The Truth About Sex—(Pneuma Life Publishing)

Karen Ligon

Karen Ligon was born in Jamaica, West Indies. When she was three years old, her family emigrated to the United States and settled in the Bronx, a borough of New York City. She immediately had to adjust to a fast paced lifestyle. Karen's mother divorced her husband when she was seven years old, and worked hard to raise her four children alone. Karen continued with her education and attended college in New York City. She began to write poetry to mend her emotions from her past and to overcome her mother's broken relationship with her father. The result was Karen's first poetry book, *Love is a Splendorous Thing.*

Karen admits that there is always dysfunction in family units regardless if relationships are traditional or not; but, she's learned that possessing a strong bond with her sisters, mother and grandmother have created the kind of connections in her life that are unbreakable. She currently lives in Connecticut with her family and children, and is busy at work completing two more volumes of poetry.

Karen has been quoted saying, when it comes to relationships, "We can't always do the right thing all of the time. How boring this would be, but hopefully, we learn and move on!"

Timeline of the Literary Divas Published Work

- ∞ 2006—Love Without a Net—Catch Me When I Fall, Pick Me Up to Start All Over Again—(Publish America)
- ∞ 2005—Love is a Splendorous Thing With Many Assumptions—(Publish America)

Karen E. Quinones Miller

"Born and raised in Harlem, Karen E. Quinones Miller dropped out of school at the age of 13. At age 22, she joined the Navy, and after spending five years in the military, Karen married, had a child, and divorced—all within a two-year period. She moved to Philadelphia at age 29, and got a secretarial job with *The Philadelphia Daily News* but, after three years of complaining about media coverage of people of color, she enrolled at Temple University and began to work as a correspondent for *The Philadelphia New Observer*—a weekly African American newspaper. Karen graduated magna cum laude from Temple with a B.A. in journalism, confirming her belief that the only thing she missed by skipping high school was the senior prom.

In 1994, Karen started her first permanent job at *The Virginian-Pilot* in Norfolk, Virginia. Less than a year later, she left to join the staff at *The Philadelphia Inquirer*. She has also worked as a correspondent for *People Magazine*. Karen wrote "*Satin Doll*" in 1999, and after many unsuccessful attempts at finding a publisher, she decided to publish it herself. With the support of her brother, Joe Quinones, and her daughter, Camille, she started with an initial printing of 3,000 copies, most of which were housed in her living room. (There wasn't enough room for the couch and the books, so the couch wound up on the front porch, and was later stolen.)

She and Camille posted flyers all over Philadelphia promoting "*Satin Doll*," and physically visited dozens of bookstores in the area to convince them to carry her novel. A self-published book is considered successful if it sells 5,000 copies in a year, and wildly successful if it sells 10,000 copies in a year. Karen sold her initial run of 3,000 copies in six weeks, and ultimately sold 24,000 copies nationwide in a period of eight months. *Satin Doll* wound up on the *Essence Bestseller's List* for two months.

The same publishers who had rejected her in 1999 were beating down her door in February 2000 trying to purchase the rights to *Satin Doll*. Karen obtained a literary agent, and a publishing auction was held. On June 7th. Simon & Schuster won the bidding war—six figures for "Satin Doll", and a then, unnamed second novel.

In October 2000, Oshun Publishing Company, Inc., the company Karen had created to publish *Satin Doll*, published *Yo Yo Love*, by a 23-year-old Temple University student named Daimah S. Poole. *Yo Yo Love* went on to become an *Essence Bestseller*, and Kensington Publishing Company purchased the rights in 2001.

Satin Doll was released in hardcover by Simon & Schuster in July 2001, and once again hit the *Essence Bestseller's* List. Her second book, "*I'm Telling*" was published by Simon & Schuster in July 2002, and also landed on the *Essence Bestseller's* List. Her third novel, "*Using What You Got*," was published by Simon & Schuster a year later.

Karen is presently working on a coffee-table book entitled "*I've Seen Rivers*," which will profile thirty-five African-American elders who have surpassed the age of 100. She is also working on a fourth novel, *Timing The Moon*, and a biography on Harlem gangster, Ellsworth *Bumpy* Johnson. (Cited from KarenEQuinonesMiller.com)

Timeline of the Literary Divas Published Work

- 2006—Satin Nights—(Warner Books)
- 2005—Uptown Dreams—(Simon & Schuster)

- 2004—Ida B.—(Simon & Schuster)
- 2003—Using What You Got (Simon & Schuster)
- 2002—I'm Telling—(Simon & Schuster)
- 2001—Satin Doll—(Simon & Schuster)

Karen White-Owens

As Long As There Is Love was Karen White Owens' debut novel. Karen was born in Detroit, Michigan and currently resides in the Motor City. She holds a Bachelors Degree in Sociology from Wayne State University and is working toward a Masters of Library and Information Science.

In addition to writing, Karen is a Librarian at Loyola High School and devotes her free time to editing manuscripts for aspiring authors and teaching the fundamentals of creative writing to the students of the Detroit Writers Guild Young Authors Program.

As Long As There Is Love was a "Preferred Pick" for the Detroit Public Library and *To Mom, With Love* was chosen as the "Anthology of the Year" by Gwen Osborne, the book diva for *Romance in Color* website. *To Mom, With Love* received 4 1/2 stars from *Romantic Times Book Club* and was one of their "Top Picks" for May, 2003. *Circles of Love* has received 4 1/2 Gold stars from *Romantic Times Book Club* Magazine.

(Website: KarenWhiteOwens.homestead.com)

Timeline of the Literary Divas Published Work

- 2005—Love Changes Everything—(Arabesque)
- 2004—Circles of Love—(Arabesque)
- 2003—To Mom, With Love—(Arabesque)
- 2003—You are Loved—(Arabesque)
- 2003—To Mom, With Love—(Arabesque)
- 2002—As Long as There is Love—(Arabesque)

Kashamba Williams

Author, motivational speaker, mentor, entrepreneur and advocate for youth with potential, KaShamba Williams is sincerely committed to her cause. She is passionate about making a lasting impression in the lives of those that are in her company, and has a powerful testimony that will bring you to tears.

Kashamba holds a Bachelors Degree of Science in Human Services with a concentration in Criminal Justice. She's made guest appearances in Community Centers, Prisons, Challenge Programs, Group Homes, Detention Centers, Drug & Alcohol Programs... the list goes on. She is the CEO/Publisher of Precioustymes Entertainment, which publishes a Youth Series, an Adult Series and an Empowerment Series.

Kashamba's gutsy style of writing has labeled her *The Unsympathetic Villain with a Pen*. She has received several honors, including: the Sormag Readers Choice Award for "The Best Multi-Cultural Self Published Book of The Year, 2003" and *Disigold Soul* Magazine Award for "The Female Break-Out Author of The Year, 2004".

KaShamba's debut Urban Tale, *Blinded,* formally known as *If Only Eyes Knew* created a window of opportunities with the rising publication company Triple Crown Publication that houses *Essence Best Selling* authors, Vickie Stringer, Shannon Holmes, Tracy Brown, Nikki Turner, K'wan, Joylynn Jossel, TN Baker, Jason Poole, Victor Martin, Tushonda Whitaker and Keisha Ervin.

Blinded was unleashed in stores December 2003, and sold extremely well. *The Unsympathetic Villain with a Pen* came out full force, holding no punches and keeps it straight up raw! Generational curses are sure to be shattered after reading this Urban Tale. *KaShamba Williams* was recently noted as being one, of the first three, "Hip-Hop Fiction" authors for having *Blinded* (Triple Crown Publications) published in Japan!

KaShamba's sophomore title *Grimey* was released in March 2004. The third title *DRIVEN* was released in December 2005. KaShamba's stories in *Around the Ways Girls 2*, with LaJill Hunt and Thomas Long and *Girls In Da Hood 2*, with Nikki Turner and Joylynn Jossel were published by

Urban Books in 2005. KaShamba's fourth title *At The Courts Mercy* was also released in 2005, followed by her fifth title, *Mind Games* in 2006.

(Website: PreciousTymes.com)

Timeline of the Literary Diva's Published Work
- 2005—At the Courts of Mercy—(PreciousTyme Entertainment)
- 2005—Around the Way Girls—(Urban Books)
- 2005—Driven-(PreciousTyme Entertainment)
- 2004—Grimey—(PreciousTyme Entertainment)
- 2003—Blinded—(PreciousTyme Entertainment)

Kelly Kenyatta

After reporting the news for more than a decade, journalist-author-publisher Kelly Kenyatta (a.k.a. Joyce Kelly) decided to help find solutions to the social challenges she observed. The Midwest-based writer's first novel addresses real-life issues facing upwardly mobile teenagers. Titled *"The Flava Girls vs. the Principal,"* the humorous, yet powerful book is the first in the *Flava Girls* Series. It positively, creatively and realistically addresses topics of parental control, academic success, friendship, love, pregnancy, exotic dancing, AIDS, and other topics of concern for teens.

Says Kelly, "Teenagers often see media images of the impudent underachiever and the so-called cool student who, unfortunately, makes all sorts of ill-fated decisions. Conversely, *Flava Girls* highlights your basic achiever, whose life also has challenges and excitement." She adds, "These kids are often minor characters in literature or they're mocked in entertainment; but in *Flava Girls*, they rule. Here you have students who are proud of their high grade point averages. Some of the most stylish and desirable kids have chosen to remain virgins and are confident in their choice. There are college-bound guys who teach their peers about HIV and are still popular. These characters, as do many real life teenagers, defy the negative stereotypes associated with achievement. What readers will learn is that these kids live much more gratifying lives than their peers who, because of unfortunate circumstances, have become truants, bullies and substance abusers."

Kelly is the author of six paperback books about some of the most popular entertainers of our times. Her titles all on Amber Communications Group, Inc. Imprint—Busta Books, include the bestselling ""*Aaliyah: An R&B Princess in Words and Pictures* (2002)," "*Yes, Yes, Yes: The Unauthorized Biography of Destiny's Child* (2000)," "*Destiny's Child: The Complete Story* (2001)," "*You Forgot About Dre: The Unauthorized Biography of Dr. Dre & Emimem* (2002)." and "*Red Hot Halle: The Story of an American Best Actress*," on The William H. Kelly publishing Company. *Destiny's Child: The Complete Story* was also re-released as part of a compilation on Amber Communications Group, Inc. Imprint—Colossus Books title, *Alicia Keys, Ashanti, Beyonce, Destiny's Child, Jennifer Lopez & Mya— Divas of the New Millennium* (2005), co-written by Stacy Deanne, Natasha Lowery with contributing writer Kwynne Sanders.

As a journalist, Kelly has written most recently for Reuters international news agency and the *Peoria (Ill.) Journal Star*. She writes a regular column about contemporary issues for *Pure News USA* (Springfield and Chicago, Ill.). Her byline has appeared frequently in *Black Enterprise Magazine*, the *Chicago Tribune* and *Los Angeles Times*. She has been a daily, education reporter and was a general assignment reporter for the *Indianapolis Star-News*.

Kelly wrote about the Gulf War in the early 1990s. She covered Poland President Lech Walesa's visit to Chicago in the early 1990s, the premiere of the movie *Malcolm X*, and baseball great Rod Carew's daughter's struggle with leukemia. She also wrote about the Million Woman March, for the *Chicago Tribune*. In 1999, Kelly received an award for "excellent reporting" from the National Black Leadership Initiative on Cancer for her *Chicago Tribune* article that featured the group's cancer education project.

Kelly was a publicist and spokeswoman for the American Library Association from 1996-1999, where she traveled to major cities promoting literacy and reading.

She attended undergraduate school at Northern Illinois University and received her bachelor's degree in journalism and psychology. At Columbia College, Kelly studied public affairs reporting at the graduate level. She held internships at the *Chicago Tribune's* Washington, D.C. Bureau and for former U.S. Congresswoman Cardiss Collins.

In 2003, Kelly founded the Chicago-based William H. Kelly Publishing Company. The company's mission is to educate, uplift, inspire and entertain our nation's socially and racially disadvantaged adolescents and adults through positive literature with realistic and heroic characters similar to themselves.

Kelly is an avid photographer, nature lover and traveler. Her favorite destinations include the U.S. rural South, Tahiti, the Left Bank in Paris, Mexico City and the mountains and tropical rainforests of Australia. Kelly lives in Chicago and rural Wisconsin.

(Website: WHKELLYPUBLISHING.COM)

Timeline of the Literary Diva's Published Work

- ✑ 2006—The Flava Girls vs. the Principal—(The William H. Kelly publishing Company)
- ✑ 2005—Alicia Keys, Ashanti, Beyonce, Destiny's Child, Jennifer Lopez & Mya—Divas of the New Millennium (Colossus Books)
- ✑ 2003—Red Hot Halle: The Story of an American Best Actress—(The William H. Kelly Publishing Company)
- ✑ 2002—Aaliyah: An R&B Princess in Words and Pictures—(Busta Books)
- ✑ 2002—You Forgot About Dre: The Unauthorized Biography of Dr. Dre & Emimem—(Busta Books)
- ✑ 2001—Destiny's Child: The Complete Story—(Busta Books)
- ✑ 2000—"Yes, Yes, Yes: The Unauthorized Biography of Destiny's Child—(Busta Books)

Kelly Starling Lyons

Kelly Starling Lyons is an award-winning journalist who transforms every-day moments, memories and history into stories of discovery. Growing up in Pittsburgh, the muse of celebrated playwright August Wilson and author John Edgar Wideman, Lyons was surrounded by creativity. Her mother and grandparents taught her to appreciate literature and express herself through the arts.

At Syracuse University, Kelly's writing became steeped in black culture. She penned essays, poems and short stories that gave voice to struggles and celebrated heritage. Kelly earned a B.A. in African-American Studies and a M.S. in Magazine. Her professional career began as a reporter for the Syracuse Herald-Journal. She dedicated herself to finding untold feature stories that spoke to the heart. Kelly's commitment won her awards from the African-American Studies Department of Syracuse University and Syracuse Press Club.

Kelly took her writing to a national stage when she became an associate editor of *Ebony* magazine. There, she reported to legendary historian Lerone Bennett, Jr. and covered important stories such as: the "Million Woman March"; "First Black Mayor of Stone Mountain, Georgia"; and "The Issue of Black Women and Rape".

She wrote her debut children's book, *Eddie's Ordeal* (Just Us Books, 2004), while working as a family & relationships writer for The News & Observer in Raleigh, North Carolina. Book #4 in the NEATE series created by Wade Hudson, *Eddie's Ordeal* won praise for its compelling portrayal of the relationship between a 13-year-old student-athlete and his civil rights veteran father. A major plot point was inspired by Kelly's award-winning newspaper article, "From Raleigh to Selma."

Kelly, a 2002 fellow of the Casey Journalism Center, continues to devote herself to journalism and writing for children. Her story, "One Day, You'll Understand," will appear in *Chicken Soup for the African American Woman's Soul*. Her first picture book, *A Million Men and Me* (Just Us Books), is forthcoming.

Kelly is a member of the Society of Children's Book Writers and Illustrators, The Authors Guild, National Federation of Press Women, National Association of Black Journalists and Delta Sigma Theta Sorority, Inc. Her articles and essays have appeared in *Emerge, The Black Collegian, about...time, Savoy* and *Black Family Today* among other publications.

Kelly lives in North Carolina with her husband and daughter. Find out more at http://www.kellystarlinglyons.com.

Timeline of the Litekaky Diva's Published Work

🖎 2004—Eddie's Ordeal—(Just Us Books)

Kim Robinson

Kim Robinson was born and raised in Compton, one of the toughest areas in the state of California. While growing up, she developed a fascination for cooking, having learned that the best love you can give a person is a nourishing plate of food.

A gifted and talented person and the very popular author of *The Roux of Gumbo*, a critically acclaimed novel, Kim returned to the forefront with two CD's for *Sweet Satisfaction* and *Food for the Soul*. Kim had developed her love for cooking by spending time around her grandmother, who had taught he to give to others. She realized that when you give, all comes back tenfold, when you expect nothing in return.

A married women with three children, Kim is currently a tutor for a middle school students. She enjoys sewing, something she has been doing since she was 7 years old when her father, who was a tailor taught Kim the craft.

Kim admits that she lived in the fast lane for a long time and did not have a relationship with God then, but now she cannot praise him enough. She writes what comes to her in her dreams and feels that these are the words that she has been inspired to share with her readers. Kim has a fan club online called "Kim's Crew" whose members say she is a source of inspiration. Kim may have grown up in the school of hard-knocks, but she has blossomed to be a recipe guru of our time.

Kim believes that she is being used to help lift up others as she has been lifted. She mentions, "I believe that no matter what your situation is, you can always change. I am not what I was yesterday, nor am I what I will be tomorrow."

(Website: www.Kim-Robinson.com)

Timeline of the Literary Divas Published Work

~ 2005—The Roux of Gumbo—(Whiskey Creek Press)
~ 2005—Sweet Satisfaction—(Virtual E-Book from Whiskey Creek Press)
~ 2005—Food for the Soul—(Virtual E-Book from Whiskey Creek Press)

Kimberla Lawson Roby

Kimberla Lawson Roby, has written seven novels which include: *The Best Kept Secret, Too Much of a Good Thing, A Taste of Reality, It's a Thin Line, Casting the First Stone, Here and Now* and her debut novel, *Behind Closed Doors,* which was originally self-published through her own company, Lenox Press. She has completed seven national book tours and is currently speaking at expos, luncheons, writers conferences, libraries, colleges, universities and other literary events throughout the country on request.

Kimberla's novels have frequented numerous bestseller lists, including: *The New York Times, Essence Magazine, Upscale Magazine, Emerge Magazine, Barnes and Noble, Amazon.com, Wal-Mart, The Dallas Morning News,* and *The Austin Chronicle,* to name a few. Both *Behind Closed Doors* and *Casting the First Stone* were #1 "Blackboard Bestsellers" for four consecutive months in 1997 and 2000 respectively. *Behind Closed Doors* was also the #1 "Blackboard Best-selling Book for Paperback Fiction" in 1997.

In addition, Kimberla Lawson Roby's first novel was nominated for Blackboard's 1998 and 1999 "Fiction Book of the Year Award", and she received the 2001 "Blackboard Fiction Book of the Year Award" for *Casting the First Stone.* She is also the recipient of the 1998 "First-Time Author Award" from Chicago's Black History Month Book Fair and Conference. Kimberla's fifth novel, *A Taste of Reality,* was a 2004 finalist for the "Atlanta Choice Awards" sponsored by the *Atlanta Daily World,* and *Too Much of a Good Thing* received a 2004 "Patron Choice Award" from the Central Mississippi Regional Library System.

Each of Kimberla Lawson Roby's novels has dealt with very real issues—in *Behind Closed Doors*—social status, gambling addiction, and infidelity; in *Here and Now*—single motherhood, infertility, and sibling rivalry; in *Casting the First Stone*—corruption within the church; in *It's a Thin Line*—domestic violence, sexual abuse, and care-giving of a parent; in *A Taste of Reality*—racial and gender discrimination in the workplace with subplots exploring sexual harassment; and in *Too Much of a Good Thing* (a sequel to Casting the First Stone) and *The Best Kept Secret*, church issues were revisited.

Kimberla resides in Illinois with her husband, Will. Her eighth novel, *Changing Faces*, centers on overweight issues, a female illness, damaging secrets and the importance of a devoted friendship between three women. Her ninth novel, *Love and Lies*, will be released in January 2007. (Cited from www. KimberlaLawsonRoby.com)

Timeline of the Literary Diva's Published Work

(Originally self-published titles)
- 2006—Changing Faces—(William Morrow)
- 2005—The Best Kept Secret—(William Morrow)
- 2004—Too Much of a Good Thing—(William Morrow)
- 2004—A Taste of Reality—(William Morrow)
- 2000—Casting the First Stone—(Kensington)
- 1999—Here and Now—(Kensington)
- 1997—It's a Thin Line—(Black Classic Press)
- 1997—Behind Closed Doors—(Black Classic Press)

Lenaise Meyeil Williams

Originally from Chicago, Illinois, Lenaise Meyeil Williams was raised in Milwaukee, Wisconsin by a loving single parent Linda Williams. Faced with the typical peer pressure and street dreams, Lenaise fought hard not to become another statistic by continuing her education after high school and attending Lane College in Jackson, Tennessee. She later furthered her education by receiving her Masters in Human Service with a concentration in Psychology, at Springfield College, Milwaukee Campus.

But, "don't let the degree's fool you." This young woman can truly camouflage. She states, "I'm just very versatile, I adapt to my environment very well, whether it's the hood or the country club, that's just me. I'm just your average around-the-way girl, who just so happen to be educated."

Lenaise's stories invite you into her world, they're not just your average hood fables. She discovered her creative talents at the tender age of 11, while writing poems and short stories to her, then incarcerated father, Otis Moore Jr., who was doing a 10-year federal prison sentence. Although, at that time, Lenaise was writing for entertainment purposes only, she later went on to write poems and shorts stories for her college campus literary collection.

Lenaise was inspired to write her first novel, *Stiletto: 101*, after taking up reading as a pass time hobby and discovering that her writing style had similarities to authors, such as: Shannon Holmes, Sister Souljah, Nikki Turner and other Urban writers. The novel came to life when friends and family members sampled the writings, and encouraged her to send her manuscript to various publishing companies and agents with hopes of a response. After many copies, books of stamps and patience, Lenaise's prayers were answered when author/publisher, Kashamba Williams, took interest in her manuscript and signed her with Precious Tymes Entertainment.

Lenaise writes from experience and labels herself an " educated thug Misses". Her characters are so real and familiar to all in some form or fashion, that she keeps your attention to her chronicles from beginning to end. Meet the new *Princess of Literary Hip Hop* and welcome her as she takes you on an urban ride through the realms of her imagination.

Lenaise is a full-time Social Worker for a non-profit organization and a part time mentor for juvenile delinquents. She plans to continue to script her creative words with inspiration.

(Website: www.LenaiseMeyeil.com)

Timeline of Literary Diva's Published Work

∞ 2005—Stiletto 101: Don't Let the Stiletto's Fool You—(Precious Tymes Entertainment)

Leslie Esdaile Banks

Leslie Banks is a graduate of The University of Pennsylvania Wharton undergraduate program, and alumnae of Temple University's Master of Fine Arts in filmmaking program. Leslie began her career in corporate marketing for several Fortune 100 firms and worked as an executive for over a decade at Xerox, Hewlett Packard, and Digital Equipment Corporation. She subsequently evolved her veteran marketing experience into a solid entrepreneurial career as a marketing consultant within the economic development and community-based organization environment.

In 1992, Leslie added another facet to her career, entering the publishing industry. She writes under the pseudonyms: L.A. Banks, Leslie Esdaile, Leslie E. Banks, Leslie Banks, and Leslie Esdaile Banks. Leslie has won several literary awards, has penned over 22 novels, and has contributed to over 10 anthologies in genres as diverse as romance, women's fiction, crime suspense, and dark fantasy/horror. She has contributed to magazines, newspaper columns, and has written commercial fiction for five major publishers simultaneously, including: Simon & Schuster, Bet/Arabesque, Genesis Press, Kensington, and St. Martin's Press.

Leslie's writing career took a new twist in 2000, when she won the coveted contract with Paramount/Showtime in collaboration with Simon & Schuster/Pocketbooks to write a book series for the popular cable network television series, *Soul Food*.. From there, she transitioned into another hot genre, the world of vampire fiction, to pen a nine-book series for St. Martin's Press: *Minion* (June 2003), *The Awakening* (January 2004), *The Hunted* (June 2004), *The Bitten* (January 2005), *The Forbidden*

(July 2005), and *The Damned* (January 2006), with three additional titles to be added in 2006 thru 2007.

In addition, Banks was recently signed to a St. Martin's Press inspired paranormal romance anthology, entitled, *Stroke of Midnight*, contributing with Sherrilyn Kenyon, Amanda Ashley, and Lori Handeland, which hit the *New York Times Bestseller* extended list in 2004. She has also worked with other horror anthology collections, *Dark Dreams I* and *Dark Dreams II* for Kensington Publishing.

Leslie's other works include: a crime thriller with Kensington/Dafina, which was released November 2004, *Betrayal of The Trust*; the sequel, *Blind Trust*, as well as numerous romances and women's fiction works with BET/Arabesque, Kensington Publishing, and Genesis Press. Leslie also contributed her inspirational personal story of triumph over tragedy to the upcoming anthology, *Chicken Soup for the African American Soul*.

Leslie is a native West Philadelphian and an entrepreneur, who remains fervently committed to her community. She writes and lives in University City, Philadelphia, with her husband and children.

Timeline of Literary Diva's Published Work

- A Vampire Huntress Legend (9 Book Series)—Paranormal
- 2006—The Forsaken—(St. Martin's Press)
- 2006—The Damned—(St. Martin's Press)
- 2005—The Forbidden—(St. Martin's Press)
- 2005—The Bitten—(St. Martin's Press)
- 2004—The Hunted—(St. Martin's Press)
- 2004—The Awakening—(St. Martin's Press)
- 2003—Minion—(St. Martin's Press)

Crime Suspense
- 2006—Scarface: Volume 1—(DH Press)

Horror
- 2004—Stroke of Midnight—(St. Martin's Press)
- 2006—Dark Dreams II: A Collection of Horror and Suspense—(Kensington/DafinaSuspense)
- 2004—Dark Dreams: A Collection of Horror and Suspense—(Kensington/DafinaSuspense)

- 2006—Shattered Trust—(Kensington/Dafina)
- 2005—Blind Trust—(Kensington/Dafina)
- 2004—Betrayal of the Trust—(Kensington/Dafina)

Romance & Comedy
- 2006—Valentine's Day Is Killing Me—(Kensington/Dafina)
- 2006—Take Me There—(Kensington/Dafina)
- 2005—Keepin' It Real—(Kensington/Dafina)
- 2004—Sister Got Game—(Kensington/Dafina)
- 2003—The Sistahood of Shopaholics—(St. Martin's Griffin)

BET/Arabesque
- 2002—Candlelight and You—(BET/Arabesque)
- 2002—Through the Storm—(BET/Arabesque)
- 2002—Love Potions—(BET/Arabesque)
- 2001—Love Lessons—(BET/Arabesque)
- 2001—Love Notes—(BET/Arabesque)

Sensuous Love Stories
- 2002—Tomorrow's Promise—(Genesis Press)
- 2002—Still Waters Run Deep—(Genesis Press)
- 2001—Rivers of the Soul—(Genesis Press)
- 2001—After the Vows—(Genesis Press)
- 2000—Midnight Clear—(Genesis Press)
- 2000—How to Write a Romance for the New Market and Get Published—(Genesis Press)

Paranormal/Crime Thriller
- 1997—Slow Burn—(Kensington/Arabesque)

Paranormal/Romance
- 1996—Sundance-(Kensington/Arabesque)

Romance/Drama Paramount/Showtime Soul Food the Series—(Simon & Schuster)
- 2003—Through Thick and Thin—(Simon & Schuster)
- 2002—For Better, For Worse—(Simon & Schuster)

#1 NY Times Best-selling Anthology
- 2004—Chicken Soup for the African American Soul—(HCI Publishing)

Lexi Davis

Fascinated by the supernatural realm, Lexi prefers to write about the unusual, the highly improbable and the out-of-the-ordinary. At first, she wrote horror, but that ended after she scared herself a few times and ran out of the room. An editor at Simon & Schuster convinced her to leave the horror to the Stephen Kings of the world, and to play up her witty sense of humor and fresh writing style. Thus, *Pretty Evil* was born.

Though her approach is fun and light, Lexi believes that *Pretty Evil* can serve as a warning to all self-proclaimed "playas" who like to live fast, but dangerously. "You don't really know who or what you're taking home with you. One night of thrills could cost you more than you realize."

Lexi attended UCLA for their noted writing program and received her degree in English. She also attended UCLA as a graduate and received a Certificate in Screenwriting. As a writer, Lexi's greatest fear is to bore an audience. With a debut novel as racy and "out of the box" as *Pretty Evil*, she has nothing to worry about.

The youngest of four, Lexi lives near her family in Southern California. *Pretty Evil* is her first novel.

(Website: LexiDavis.com)

Timeline of the Literary Diva's Published Work
～ 2005—Pretty Evil—(Simon & Schuster)

Margie Gosa Shivers

Margie Gosa Shivers is a fresh new voice within today's budding world of contemporary African-American fiction writers. She is the 2004 winner of the "Best Self-Published Author's Award" (Mahogany Book Club of Albany, NY); the 2004 *Disilgold* "Mystery Novelist Award of Excellence" and YOUnity Reviewers Guild "Most Sought Book of the Year 2004" (Bronx, New York).

Since the age of fifteen, Margie was a storyteller with a flair for creativity. While growing up in Greenwood, Mississippi, she acquired a strong desire to entertain her parents, four sisters and brothers. During a turning point later on in her life, Margie decided to write fiction.

Writing has become, for her, a form a therapy as well as the vehicle for which to find truths, understanding and peace. In 1999, her debut novel, *Anonymity* was published with iUniverse. Less than seven months later, she decided to cancel her POD publishing contract and created MGS Publishing to re-publish the second edition now titled, *Anonymity: A Tale of Suspense, Seduction and Revenge.*

Margie seeks to entertain and touch the lives of others through writing mystery/suspense novels. An avid reader of various genres, some of her favorite writers include: Terry McMillan, E Lynn Harris, Eric Jerome Dickey, Kimberla Lawson Roby, Mary Higgins Clark, Linda Dominique Grosvenor, Sidney Sheldon and James Patterson.

Margie is a '69 graduate of MVSU University in Itta Bena, Mississippi where she earned a BA in Elementary Education. She holds much pride for her 4-year participation as a color guard in the MVSU marching band and the fact that she marched in the '67 Rose Bowl Parade in Pasadena, California. In '86, she graduated with honors from Spertus College of Judaica in Chicago, with a masters in Human Services Administration.

Prior to moving to Chicago in 1974, she had been a primary school teacher in the Meridian Public School System from 1969-1974. She currently holds an administrator's position with two senior housing corporations sponsored by Trinity United Church of Christ in Chicago. She resides in south suburban Lynwood, Illinois.

(Website: MargeGosaShivers.com)

Timeline of the Literary Diva's Published Work

- 2006—Once is Never Enough (MGS Publishing)
- 2004—Anonymity—(MGS Publishing)

Mari Evans

Mari Evans was born in 1923 in Toledo, Ohio. She studied at the University of Toledo. In 1963, upon completing and publishing her poetry works in *Phylon, Negro Digest*, and *Dialog*, she was awarded a John Hay Whitney fellowship.

Her books include *I Am a Black Woman; Where is All the Music?; Black Women Writers* (1950-1980),*A Critical Evaluation* (1984), *Nightstar: Poems From 1973-1978* (1982), *I Look at Me; Singing Black; The Day They Made Benani*; and *Jim Flying High*.

Timeline of the Literary Diva's Published Work

- 2006—Clarity as Concept—A Poet's Perspective—(Third World Press)
- 2006—I'm Late: The Story of Laneere & Moonlight and Alisha Who Did Not Have Her Own—(Just Us Books)
- 1999 & 2003—Dear Corinne, Tell Somebody-(Just Us Books)
- 1993—I am a Black Woman—(Writers & Readers)
- 1992—A Dark and Splendid Mass—Writers and Readers Publishing—(Writers & Readers Publishing)
- 1985—Black Women Writers: Arguments and Interviews—(Pluto Press)
- 1984—Black Women Writers-1950-1980—A Critical Evaluation—(Anchor)
- 1982—JD—(Doubleday)
- 1979—Jim Flying High—(Doubleday)
- 1976—Singing Black—(Just Us Books)
- 1975—I Look at Me—Night Star: 1973—1978—(University Press)
- 1973—JD
- 1968—Where is All the Music—(Just Us Books)

Marita Golden

In a professional writing career that spans more than thirty years, Marita Golden has distinguished herself as a novelist, essayist, teacher of writing and literary institution builder. Marita's fiction includes the novels *Long Distance Life*, (a best-seller, cited as a "Best Book of The Year" by *The*

Washington Post), *A Woman's Place, And Do Remember Me*, and *The Edge of Heaven*. In the genre of nonfiction, Marita Golden has edited two anthologies, *Wild Women Don't Wear No Blues: Black Women Writers on Love, Men and Sex;* and with writer Susan Shreve, *Skin Deep: Black and White Women on Race*. As a memoirist and essayist, Marita has authored *Migrations of the Heart, Saving Our Sons: Raising Black Children in a Turbulent World,* and *A Miracle Everyday: Triumph and Transformation in the Lives of Single Mothers.*

Marita has lectured on the topic of literature, women's studies, African American Studies and African American literature nationally and internationally. She has read from her work and held writer-in-residence positions at many schools, including Brandeis University, Hampton University, Simmons College, Columbia College, William and Mary, Old Dominion University and Howard University. She has also been a guest on the Oprah Winfrey Show, and has appeared on ABC's Primetime Live. Articles and essays by Marita Golden have appeared in *Essence* Magazine, *The New York Times* and *The Washington Post*. Marita Golden founded and served as the first president of the Washington DC-based African American Writers Guild. Since 1990 she has headed the Zora Neale Hurston/Richard Wright Foundation, which presents the nation's only national fiction award for college writers of African descent and an annual summer writer's workshop for Black writers, Hurston/Wright Writers' Week, as well as the Hurston/Wright Legacy Award for published Black writers.

Among the awards Marita Golden has received in recognition of her writing career and her work as a literary cultural worker are The 2002 Distinguished Service Award from the Authors Guild, The 2001 Barnes and Noble Writers for Writers Award presented by *Poets and Writers*; an honorary Doctorate from the University of Richmond; induction into the International Hall of Fame for Writers of African Descent at the Gwendolyn Brooks Center at Chicago State University; Woman of the Year Award from Zeta Phi Beta; and a Distinguished Alumni Award from American University.

Marita Golden holds a B.A. from American University in American Studies and English and a Masters Degree from the Graduate School of

Journalism at Columbia University. (cited from www.maritagolden.com)

Timeline of the Literary Diva's Published Work

- 2003—Gumbo—(Ballantine)
- 2002—Gumbo: A Celebration of African American Writers—(Harlem Moon)
- 2001—The Complete Fiction of Nella Larsen: Passing, Quicksand, and the Stories—(Anchor)
- 2001—Long Distance Life—(Ballantine)
- 1995—A Woman's Place—(Ballantine)
- 1994—Wild Women Don't Wear No Blues—(Anchor)

Marti Tucker

While growing up in Gary, Indiana, Marti Tucker learned the art of being alone. Her mother worked and Marti's part to play in the welfare of the family was to stay home alone. "Stay out of the path of danger," as her mother called playing outside when she wasn't around. "You could get shot, run over or raped."

In complying with her mother's rules, she became friends with books, especially romances and the classics. Most of her free time was spent writing thoughts of what she imagined the outside world to be. By thirteen, she was sending out poems and short stories, and magazine editors were sending notes back to her.

Later, she attended Fisk University in Nashville, Tennessee, where she majored in Theatre Arts. She married a medical school graduate in her sophomore year and moved to California, where she completed her education at California State University, Los Angeles. Having switched her major to education, she taught elementary school in the Los Angeles City School District and wrote plays and short stories under the tutelage of world-renowned writer Budd Schulberg. A political novel, *Jive Town*, followed. Soon after, Marti became a reporter and editor for local newspapers and self-published several non-fiction books.

Marti's husband ran for the Mayor of Compton and she put all of her efforts into aiding that pursuit. After he won, they traveled on diplomatic trips to Mexico, Puerto Rico, Haiti, much of the Caribbean, Russia and various other places. Her reputation as an international hostess set the stage for Marti to become a liaison to Compton's Sister City of Seoul, Korea. She was also in the thick of Compton politics and the social life of greater Los Angeles and Beverly Hills. Her love of writing had been abandoned.

The pressure of keeping Compton from becoming a drug distribution center for the West Coast hung like a heavy dark cloud over the city and her family. Marti believed, though, that there was still a way to triumph, to create a better life for African-Americans. Compton was the ideal place for it to happen.

When her husband died in office, Tucker decided to try to make sense of all the tragedies that had taken place during his tenure. She picked up a pen once again and began to write *The Mayor's Wife*, an urban thriller. It is the story of a young mayor's wife left to carry out a rare plan of economic, social and political triumph in the inner city. That move threw her in the midst of powers too great for her. All she had to bring down her foes was her woman's intuition, a curious mind and her charm.

In the meantime, Tucker helps others pursue their writing goals by story editing and shaping and publishing their works. In the last three years, she has been a full time novelist. Tucker has four successful grown children who are closely knitted in her life and she is very active in Faithful Central Bible Church. She was once told that, when she had written a million pages, she would be a good writer. She is convinced that is true. Her goal is to create a volume of good writing in the next five years.

(Website: MarthaTucker.com)

Timeline of the Literary Diva's Published Work

➤ 2005—The Mayor's Wife—(Urban Classic Books)

Mary B. Morrison

In 1999, Mary B. Morrison decided to step out on faith. She quit her near six-figure government job with the Department of Housing and Urban Development to become a writer, saying, "I'd rather die a failure, than to have lived and never known whether I would become a success."

Before Mary resigned, she laid the foundation by writing and self-publishing her first novel, *Soul Mates Dissipate,* which quickly became an *Essence* "national best-seller".

Mary has also written a non-fiction self-help book entitled *Who's Making Love,* a poetry book entitled *Justice Just Us Just Me,* and several fiction novels, including: *Never Again Once More, He's Just a Friend, Somebody's Gotta Be on Top, When Somebody Loves you Back, Nothing Has Ever Felt Like This.* She is also co-authoring a novel with *New York Times* best-selling author, Carl Weber, and has recently completed her first screenplay for *Soul Mates Dissipate.*

The SHIFT (Supporting Healthy Inner Freedom for Teens) and The RaW (Readers and Writers) Advantage are Mary's companies. The SHIFT Program is sponsoring its first publication of short stories written by the students of Mr. Lou Richie's sixth graders at St. Lawrence O'Toole. The bookfair showcasing Diverse Stories: From the Imaginations of Sixth Graders was held January 2006, at Barnes and Noble, Jack London Square in Oakland, California .

Through the RaW Advantage, Mary conducts self-publishing workshops, sharing detailed information on how to self-publish and promote literature. In 2003, Alfonzo Tucker was the winner of a $3,000 publishing package sponsored by The RaW Advantage. Proudly, Mr. Tucker is now the published author of his debut novel, *Noesis*. Mary's novel, *Somebody's Gotta Be on Top*, was the #1 National Best-seller on *Essence* for both January and February 2005.

Mary lives in Oakland with her wonderful son, Jesse Byrd, Jr., nearby playing basketball at the University of San Francisco.

(Website: MaryMorrison.com)

Timeline of the Literary Diva's Published Work

- 2006—When Somebody Loves You Back—(Kensington Publishing Corp.)
- 2005—Nothing Has Ever Felt Like This—(Dafina Books)
- 2004—Somebody's Gotta Be On Top—(Dafina)
- 2003—Just a Friend—(Kensington)
- 2003—Never Again Once More—(Dafina)
- 2002—Soulmates Dissipate—(Dafina Books)
- 2001—Who's Making Love (2001)
- 2000—Family, Friends, Lovers & Others—(Booga Bear Poetry Group)
- 2000—The Art of Finding Your Soul Mate: Five Key Elements—(Booga Bear Poetry Group)
- 1999—Justice Just Us Just Me—(Booga Bear Poetry Group)
- 1999—Kiss Me: Now Tell Me You Love Me—(Booga Bear Poetry Group)

Maxine Thompson

On April 9, 2005, Maxine Thompson received an Honorary Doctorate Degree of Humanities from Loyola Marymount University, Westchester, California, through The R.O.S.E. Ministries- Worldwide and Love is Always The Answer Organization. Called a "Renaissance Woman" by her peers, Maxine is largely self-taught in the areas of e-book publishing, book doctoring, ghostwriting, story editing, literary coaching, column writing, information marketing, and Internet radio show hosting. She earned her Bachelor's Degree with honors from Wayne State University, Detroit, Michigan, in 1973 as an English major.

Maxine is an award-winning writer. In 1989, she won $1,000 in *Ebony's* first Writing Contest for her short story, *"Valley of the Shadow."* She received a small PEN award for her novel, *The Ebony Tree*, and an International Black Writer's Association award for her short story, *"The Rainbow."* She has self-published 2 novels, *The Ebony Tree* and *No Pockets in a Shroud*, a short story collection, *A Place Called Home (2001)* and 3 e-books, *How To Promote, Market and Sell Your Book Via e-Book Publishing (2000)*, a CD e-book, *The Hush Hush Secrets of Writing Fiction That Sells (2003)*, an e-book, *The Hush Hush Secrets of Creating a Life You Love.* (2005), and her writer's group anthology, *Saturday Morning (2002)*. On August 27, 2005, Maxine received an award from the Metro Lit Detroit Writing Collective Literary Awards Dinner for Literary Spirit in Motion: Business Supporting New and Upcoming Writers.

During a three-year period, Maxine conducted more than 500 hours of live Internet radio interviews. March 5, 2005 marks her third year as a host with Voiceamerica Internet Radio for her show, *On The Same Page.* She has been a host with Artistfirst.com for one year, and launched her own Internet Radio network on March 1, 2005 at www.maxineshow.com.

In December 1998, Maxine created *On The Same Page,* her website e-zine column for new and self-published writers. She has written a monthly column on self-publishing on careermag.com. She had a published short story, *"Dance of The DNA,"* on the Moondance website in the Summer '99 issue. She had an article on *LA Woman* magazine's website. called, *"Burn Out or Divine Discontent?"* She has been featured on *Page One, Books and Authors* and on C& B Books Distribution website. In March 2004, she was interviewed and featured as *Who's Who in The Literary Society* at The Literary World website.

Maxine has also written a monthly column on www.bwip.org and a column on The BlackMarket.com, regarding self-publishing. Her book reviews were first featured on Netnoir now know as Black Voice from 1999 to 2002 and are now on the Bookreport.com. In July 2003, Maxine began writing book reviews for Africana.com. She has numerous articles being used from IdeaMarketers.com and on other e-zines.

Maxine has been featured in *LA Times, Our Times, Black Issues Reviews , Dialogue Magazine,* and *Inland Valley News.* She has been a regular guest columnist in the *International Paper* and *The Final Call.* She has been published in *The Writer, Mosaicbooks* magazine, and *Metro Exchange* magazine. Black Butterfly Press was featured in *Black Enterprise* in April 2001. In 2002, Maxine was featured in the Spring Issue of *Iris,* a Journal about women's Emerging Voices, Article: *"Cool Women to Watch For."*

A much sought-after speaker, Maxine Thompson has conducted workshops nationwide on various aspects of writing, self-publishing, Ebook publishing. She has been a seminar conductor at Black Writers on Tour (2000 to 2005), The Dallas Black Writers Reunion Conference (2001), The New York Sodus Multicultural Fair (2001), The Baltimore Book Festival (2002), and The National Book Club Conference (Atlanta, 2003, 2004).

In 2003, Maxine began writing columns on the new literary renaissance for *Booking Matters* Magazine, and she began her Literary Agency, in order to assist writers seeking book deals with New York's traditional or mid-size publishers. As a writer, herself, Maxine has had many poems, short stories, and articles published in off-line anthologies and magazines. She authored an article called *Writer's Watershed*, which was published in the national magazine, *The Writer*, in 1997. She is the Treasurer of The Saturday Morning Literary Workshop, a group of highly-talented writers, of which she has been a member since February 1992. Her biggest writing experience comes from being a former Child Protective Services Worker for 23 years in the inner cities of Detroit and Los Angeles.

In June 2003, Maxine's short story, *Valley of the Shadow*, was published in Kensington's *Proverbs for the People*. She sold an anthology called *Secrets* to Carl Weber's Urban Books, which was released in June 2006. Her novella, *Second Chances*, is one of the stories to be published in the anthology, as well as romance writer Patricia Anne Phillips' *Irresistible Flames*, and prolific writer, Michelle McGriff's *Detoured*. Under Maxine Thompson's Literary Services. She has personally edited, formatted, or ghostwritten over 170 books in the past 5 years for other authors. Recently, she has begun an editor-in-training program to assist with the ever-growing workload.

Maxine currently resides in California, where she keeps herself busy supporting artists through her non-profit, Maxine Thompson's Literary and Education Services. She is making her mark in the literary and publishing fields, opening doors once closed to black writers and bringing new emerging writers with intriguing storylines and characters with depth and texture with her.

(Website: BlackButterflyPress.com)

Timeline of the Literary Diva's Published Work

- 2005—The Hush Hush Secrets of Creating a Life You Love—(Black Butterfly Press)
- 2003—The Hush Hush Secrets of Writing Fiction That Sells-(Black Butterfly Press)
- 2002—Saturday Morning—(Black Butterfly Press)
- 2001—The Ebony Tree—(Black Butterfly Press)
- 2001—No Pockets in a Shroud—(Black Butterfly Press)
- 2000—How To Promote, Market and Sell Your Book Via eBook Publishing—(Black Butterfly Press)

Maya Angelou

Dr. Maya Angelou, was born Marguerite Johnson on April 4, 1928 in St. Louis, Missouri, just one year before the Wall Street Crash and the word, Apartheid, was used for the first time in American history to describe racial segregation in South America. Surrealism was born in Paris, Louis Armstrong had created a solo style in jazz with trumpet improvisations, Duke Ellington introduced the world to orchestral jazz and John Logie Baird had created a high speed scanning system that lead to the development of television. (Mitchell Beazley Publishers, *Random House Encyclopedia*, (New York, 1977).

Today Dr. Angelou is a multi—faceted and accomplished writer considered the "Renaissance Woman of Poetry" and one of the greatest voices of contemporary poetry who has reached international and critical acclaim as a poet, historian, educator, actress, best-selling author, playwright, Civil Rights Activist, producer, director, visionary, humanitarian and popular storyteller.

Her achievements are "phenomenal," "incredible," and "sensational" as her work continues to transcend from generation—to—generation of readers of poetry from all diverse cultures to the most discriminating readers who have discovered Maya, "a modern day queen," "heroic martyr," "dynamic speaker," and "Mother-figure of wisdom." Her classic smile radiates warmth and charismatic upturned brow as she speaks: strength, respect and dignity, all in one. When Maya speaks, the world listens, for she exemplifies the same beauty and inner light as Coretta Scott King, Ruby Dee, Rosa Guy, Nikki Giovanni and Sonia Sanchez.

To learn about the life of Maya Angelou is a history lesson in itself and a celebration that readers of her work have shared for years. Her books

continue to rank supreme on online bookstores. She touched the hearts
of many listeners as she recited her poem, *On the Pulse of Morning*, at the
request of President Clinton for his Inauguration as the 42nd President
of the United States on January 20, 1993. On October 16, 1995, Maya
delivered one of her most powerful poems, *From a Black Man to a Black
Woman* during the Million Man March in Washington, DC. Many years
before, in 1959—1960, Dr. Martin Luther King, Jr. had requested Maya to
coordinate the Southern Christian Leadership Conference.

Maya also wrote play productions such as *Cabaret Freedom* (1960), *The
Least of These* (1966), *Gettin' Up Stayed on My Mind* (1967), *Ajax* (1974),
And Still I Rise (1976), and *Moon On a Rainbow Shawl* (1988). A favorite
was her work as a contributing writer for *The Women of Brewster's Place*,
an Oprah Winfrey Series and her weekly television series, *Down in the
Delta* (1999).

What made Maya Angelou such a revered living saint to so many readers is
that she delved into an acting career adding class to every production. She
appeared on *Sister, Sisters* (NBC) in 1982, the *Tree of Life* episode on *Touched
By An Angel* in 1995 and *Moesha* on WB TV in 1999 reaching a whole new
generation of young poets. Her brief appearances in the movies, *Poetic Justice*, featuring Janet Jackson and Tyler Perry's *Madea's Family Reunion*, captured the essence, spirit and wisdom of Maya Angelou in few words.

Maya has also appeared in countless national publications such as *Essence,
Ebony Magazine, Redbook, Harper's Bazaar, Mademoiselle. In addition*, this
multi-talented woman taught modern dance at the Roman Opera House
and The Habima Theatre in Tel Aviv. Maya's editing skills landed her positions as an Associated Editor of the *Arab Observer* in 1961-1962 and a
feature Editor's position for the *African Review* in 1964-1966. She also
wrote freelance articles for *Ghanian Times* in 1964-1966 and was a
writer-in-residence for the University of Kansas in Lawrence, 1970.

A series of speaking requests ensued by Wake Forest University, Wichita
State University, California State University and many more colleges.
Maya was so much in demand that President Gerald Ford appointed her
as a member of the American Revolution Bicentennial Council in
1975-1976, and she was requested to serve on Jimmy Carter's Presidential
Commission for "International Women's Year" in 1978-1979.

In 1995, the National Academy of Recording Arts & Sciences awarded Maya, "Best Spoken Word or Non-Musical Album" for *Phenomenal Woman* and the following year, she was honored by Kweisi Mfume, Maryland Congressman, by the United States of America Congressional Record 104th Congress, House of Representatives. The Maya Angelou Institute for the Improvement of Child & Education was founded in 1998 and just four years later, Maya was awarded lifetime membership to the National Women's Hall of Fame in 2002.

Within the span of 1990 to 2000, Maya Angelou's reign as one of the most influential figures on the planet swept the nation by storm. She was nominated for: the "National Book Award" for *I Know Why the Caged Bird Sings* (1970), the Pulitzer Prize for *Just Give Me a Cool Drink of Water 'Fore I Diiie* (1972), and the Tony Award for her performance in "Look Away" (1973). She received an Emmy Award for the made-for-television movie "Roots" (1977), was voted "Top 100 Most Influential Women" (1983), "Essence Woman of the Year" (1992) and was presented with the YOUnity Guild of America's "Lifetime Achievement Award of Excellence" (2003). Maya won the Grammy for "Best Spoken Word Album" (1994), and the Presidential Medal of Arts (2000), as well as Honorary Degrees from hundreds of distinguished universities.

Fluent in many languages, such as: English, French, Spanish, Italian, Arabic and West Fanti, Maya made a guest appearance at Coretta Scott King's Celebration, wife of Dr. Martin Luther King, Jr., a Civil Rights Leader. Maya's last words for her dedication speech given from her audio feed to the nation was, *My Name is Maya Angelou.* Now teachers across the nation have adopted a special dedication ceremony to Dr. Maya Angelou for Black history month where children get to recite, *My Name Is* while on stage, but substitute other heroes names with the mention of "Dr. Maya Angelou" for the finale' along with their own names.

(Website: MayaAngelou.com)

Timeline of the Literary Diva's Published Work

- 2005—Amazing Peace: A Christmas Poem—(Random House)
- 2005—Maya Angelou Life Mosaic; Greeting Cards—(Hallmark Gold Crown Gifts)

- 2004—The Collected Autobiographies of Maya Angelou—(Modern Library)
- 2004—Hallelujah! The Welcome Table: A Lifetime of Memories with Recipes—(Random House)
- 2002—A Song Flung Up to Heaven—(Random House)
- 1997—Oh Pray My Wings Are Gonna Fit Me Well : Poems; Audio Cassette/Book—(Random House)
- 1997—Even the Stars Look Lonesome—(Random House)
- 1996—Life Doesn't Frighten Me; Children's Book—(Stewart, Tabori & Chang)
- 1995—Phenomenal Woman: Four Poems Celebrating Women—(Random House)
- 1994—The Complete Collected Poems of Maya Angelou -(Random House)
- 1994—Wouldn't Take Nothing For My Journey Now—(Bantam)
- 1994—My Painted House; Children's Book—(Knopf Books for Young Readers)
- 1994—Kofi and His Magic—(Knopf Books for Young Readers)
- 1994—Now Sheba Sings the Song—(Plume Books)
- 1993—On the Pulse of Morning—(Random House)
- 1991—All God's Children Need Traveling Shoes—(Knoph Publishing Group)
- 1985—Getting Together in My Name—(Bantam)
- 1985—Singin' and Swingin' and Gettin' Merry Like Christmas—(Bantam)
- 1983—I Know Why the Caged Bird Sings—(Bantam)
- 1983—Shaker Why Don't You Sing—(Random House)
- 1978—And Still I Rise; Audio Cassette/Book—(Random House)
- 1971—Just Give Me a Cool Drink of Water 'Fore I Diiie—(Random House)

Discography
- 2001—The Maya Angelou Poetry Collection; Audio Cd—(Random House Audio)
- 1982-The Heart of a Woman; Audio Cd—(Bantam)

Website References
- http: //www. qbr.com/dish/dish9.html
- http://www.MayaAngelou.com
- http:// www. Poets.org
- http: // empirezine.com/spotlight/maya/maya/htm
- http: // www. gale.com

Nancey Flowers

Nancey is the author of the #1 *Essence* Bestselling novel *Shattered Vessels* and *No Strings Attached*. She is editor of the recently released anthology *Morning, Noon & Night*, a contributing author in the erotica sensation *Twilight Moods*, and the anthology *Proverbs For The People*.

Nancey attended Morgan State University in Baltimore, Maryland, where she received her bachelor's degree in mass communications with a minor in journalism. She is a member of Delta Sigma Theta, Incorporated, the book editor for *Jolie* magazine, a contributor to *Black Issues Book Review*, a former Program Director for The Harlem Book Fair, and former Managing Editor of *QBR The Black Book Review*.

Nancey is co-owner of Flowers & Hayward Management, Publicity and Entertainment and the owner of Flowers In Bloom Publishing. All of her titles have been published by Flowers In Bloom Publishing with the exception of *Proverbs for the People/Anthology*, released by Kensington Publishing in 2003.

(Website: FlowersinBloompublishing.com)

Timeline of the Literary Diva's Published Works

- ∞ 2007—One Night Stand—(Flowers in Bloom)
- ∞ 2006—Morning, Noon & Night edited by Nancey Flowers—(Flowers in Bloom)
- ∞ 2006—Down In The Dirty by J.M. Benjamin—(Flowers in Bloom)
- ∞ 2005—Runnin' Game by Courtney Parker—(Flowers in Bloom)
- ∞ 2005—No Strings Attached—(Flowers in Bloom)
- ∞ 2003—Shattered Vessels—(Flowers in Bloom)
- ∞ 2002—Twilight Moods—(Flowers in Bloom)
- ∞ 2001—A Fool's Paradise—(Flowers in Bloom)

Natalie Darden

Natalie Darden is a fresh new voice within today's budding world of contemporary Afro-American fiction writers. A writer by leisure, since the tender age of eight, Natalie decided during a turning point in her career to explore her hand as a published writer. "Writing has always been a form a therapy for me," she recalls of her formative writing years. Natalie completed two young adult novels before her seventeenth birthday. "Ever since I could remember, I was always nose-deep into a book. During high school, I chose a voluntary position as a library page to keep close ties with books as a way of fulfilling my community service obligation with the National Honor Society."

Originally, Natalie wrote as a hobby. She had never actually considered seriously publishing. It wasn't until a fiery desire for writing overpowered her ordinarily diligent work habits. That urge propelled her to leave a career of seven years to fully concentrate on writing. "I'd been so sheltered with my job responsibilities, I didn't realize that the market for African-American fiction was so vast," she commented. Less than six months and many sleepless nights later, "*All About Me* was born.

Natalie seeks to entertain and touch the lives of others through her writing. An avid reader of various genres, some of her favorite writers include Eric Jerome Dickey and Donald Goines. In addition, she enjoys horror stories and Greek mythology. Darden also heralds and holds respect for great African American contemporaries such as Alice Walker, Toni Morrison, and Gloria Naylor.

Natalie is a graduate of Rutgers University, where she obtained a BA in English and Communications. A native of East Orange, New Jersey, she currently resides in northeastern Pennsylvania and is actively working on her next novel "*Single as a Dollar Bill: Love Yourself First, the Rest Is Easy.*

Timeline of the Literary Diva's Published Work

- 2002—All About Me—(Xlibris)

Nea Anna Simone

Nea Anna Simone began her first attempt at writing, following a conversation with her best friend and prayer partner Dana Nelson. Dana stated, "God wants you to write…if you'll do that *He'll* take care of everything else. So, Nea conceded and started writing her first novel *Reaching BACK* that evening.

Over time, *Reaching BACK* became a journey through the complexities of four generations of African American women struggling with a myriad of issues that centered on the myth, intrinsic in the black community, of the superiority of light vs. dark skin. Thus began her literary journey and God was true to His word…without rhyme or reason. He opened doors and placed people in her life.

BET Books signed Nea under the Sepia Imprint, and her first novel *Reaching BACK* was published as a BET/Kensington Books Trade Paperback, a first for BET with debut authors. Another first came when *Reaching BACK* was selected as an "Original Voice of Fiction" by BORDERS Bookstores and reviewed as "A great literary work." It was the first work published by BET to receive literary acclaim. Next, *Black Expressions* reviewed *Reaching BACK* as a "Notable work of Fiction…a fresh new literary voice."

On the heels of that acknowledgment, Nea was asked to attend the 8th annual BET Walk of Fame luncheon honoring Stevie Wonder and her book was selected as the gift to all attendees. In August 2003, Nea received the *Atlanta Daily World* "Reader's Choice Award for Fiction" for her debut novel *Reaching BACK*. Many book clubs and organizations have invited Nea as a guest speaker, entertaining audiences far and wide with her humorous and heart-felt anecdotes and real life words of encouragement.

Nea's sophomore novel *ReBORN* is the sequel to *Reaching BACK*. "It was the only logical step" states Nea… *Reaching BACK* was about confrontation, the next step is self-realization…that is where *ReBORN* take you. *ReBORN* has been submitted for nomination of the Hurston-Wright Legacy Award.

Timeline of Literary Diva's Published Work
~ 2002—Reaching BACK—(BET Books)
~ 2004—ReBorn—(BET Books)

Nikki Giovanni

Yolande Cornelia "Nikki" Giovanni, Jr., born in Knoxville, Tennessee, is a world-renowned poet, writer, commentator, activist, and educator. Over the past thirty years, Nikki's outspokenness, in her writing and in person, has brought the eyes of the world upon her. One of the most widely read American poets, she prides herself on being "a Black American, a daughter, a mother, a professor of English." Giovanni remains as determined and committed as ever to the fight for civil rights and equality. Always insisting on presenting the truth as she sees it, she has maintained a prominent place as a strong voice of the Black community.

Nikki's focus is on the individual, specifically, on the power one has to make a difference in oneself, and thus, in the lives of others. She has written more than two dozen books, including volumes of poetry, illustrated children's books, and three collections of essays. Her book *Racism 101* includes bold, controversial essays about the situation of Americans on all sides of various race issues. She has received 21 honorary doctorates and a host of other awards, including "Woman of the Year" awards from three different magazines as well as Governors' Awards in the Arts from both Tennessee and Virginia. Her three most recent volumes of poetry, *Love Poems, Blues: For All the Changes* and *Quilting the Black-Eyed Pea*, were winners of the NAACP Image Award, in 1998, 2000, and 2003. Since 1987, she has taught writing and literature at Virginia Tech, where she is a University Distinguished Professor.

As a devoted and passionate writer, teacher, and speaker, she inspires not only her students, but also readers and audiences nationwide. The Nikki Giovanni Poetry Collection, a spoken-word CD, was a finalist for the 2003 Grammy Award in the category of spoken word. She published

Quilting the Black-Eyed Pea: Poems and Not Quite Poems (2002). Caedmon Records released *The Nikki Giovanni Poetry Collection* (2002). She received honorary doctorates from Pace University (2002) and West Virginia University (2003). She was featured in *Foundations of Courage...A Cry to Freedom!* on BET. Then Nikki appeared in A& E television's Witness: *James Baldwin*, and was asked to be a judge for The Robert F. Kennedy Book Awards (2002). She then served on the Multimedia Advisory Panel for the Virginia Museum of Fine Arts (2002). She received the first Rosa Parks Woman of Courage Award (2002).

Inducted into Phi Beta Kappa, Delta of Tennessee Chapter, Fisk University (2003) Nikki performs a tribute to Gwendolyn Brooks with Elizabeth Alexander, Ruby Dee, and Yusef Komunyakaa. Then, she contributed to a Smithsonian special exhibition, *In the Spirit of Martin: The Living Legacy of Dr. Martin Luther King, Jr.* Chronology by Virginia C. Fowler, *The Collected Poetry of Nikki Giovanni: 1968-1998.* William Morrow, 2003. xxxi-xliii. Nikki has done it all and is well respected and admired by the literary community at large. (Cited from www. Nikki-Giovanni.com)

Timeline of the Literary Diva's Published Work

- 2005—Rosa—Henry Holt & Co.—(Henry Holt & Co.)
- 2003—The Collected Poetry of Nikki Giovanni—(1968-1998)—(William Morrow)
- 2003—Paint Me Like I Am: Teen Poems From Writers Corps—(Rebound Sage Brush)
- 2003—The Prosaic Soul of Nikki Giovanni—(Harper Perennial)
- 2002—The Nikki Giovanni Poetry Collect CD
- 2002—Quilting the Black—Eyed—(William Morrow)
- 1998—The Genie in the Jar—(Henry Holt & Co.)
- 1996—The Selected Poems of Nikki Giovanni—(1968—1995)—(William Morrow)
- 1996—Shimmy Shimmy Like My Sister Kate: Looking at the Harlem Renaissance Through Poems—(Henry Holt & Co.)
- 1995—Racism 101—(Quill)
- 1994—Grandmothers: Poem, Reminisces and Short Stories About the Keepers of Our Traditions—(Henry Holt & Co.)
- 1993—Ego-tripping & Other Poems For Young People—(Lawrence Hill Books)
- 1992—Love Poems—(William Morrow)

- 1987—Spin a Soft Black Song—(Perennial Classics)
- 1987—Spirit to Spirit—VHS—(Direct Cinema Unlimited)
- 1976—Gemini—An Extended Autobiographical Statement on My First 25 Years—(Penguin)
- 1974—Poetic Equation—(Dafina)
- 1971—Blues For All the Changes: New Poems—(Perennial)

Ntozake Shange

Ntozake Shange was born Paulette Williams in Trenton, New Jersey on October 18, 1948. In 1971 she changed her name to Ntozake Shange which means "she who comes with her own things" and "she who walks like a lion" in Xhosa, the Zulu language. Her father was an Air Force surgeon and her mother was an educator and a psychiatric social worker. The Williams were upper middle class African Americans whose love of the arts contributed to an intellectually stimulating childhood for Ntozake and her three siblings. Dizzy Gillespie, Miles Davis, Chuck Berry, and W. E. B. Du Bois were among the frequent guests at her parents' house.

In 1966 Ntozake enrolled at Barnard College and separated from her husband, a law student. After an attempted suicide, she recovered and graduated cum laude in American Studies in 1970 and, then entered the University of Southern California at Los Angeles, where She earned a master's degree in American Studies in 1973.

Her studies included African American dance. While living in California Ntozake landed a job at Sonoma Mills College in California teaching humanities and women's studies courses. Ntzoke performed around the San Francisco Area. She produced a dance drama in 1976 called *Sassafrass* and began collaborating with Paula Moss on the poetry, music, and dance that would become the play, *For Colored Girls Who Have Considered Suicide When the Rainbow is Enuf.*

Paula and Ntozake left California for New York and performed *For Colored Girls* in a Soho jazz loft and later in bars in the lower East Side until Producer Woodie King Jr. saw one of these shows. King helped director Oz Scott stage the "choreopoem" Off Broadway at the New Federal Theatre where it ran for eight months, after which, it moved to the New York Shakespeare Company's Anspacher Public Theatre, and then to the Booth Theatre This was just the beginning of an onset of plays to follow that make Ntozake Shange a queen of stage productions such as *For Colored Girls*, Spell #7; *A Photograph: Lovers in Motion* (1979), *ThreePieces* (1981), *Boogie Woogie Landscapes* (1979) all of which were originally books by Ntozake Shange.

Ntozake's list of other books include *Nappy Edges* (1978), *Sassafrass, Cypress & Indigo* (1982), *A Daughter's Geography* (1983), *From Okra to Greens* (1984), *Betsey Brown* (1985). *See No Evil: Prefaces & Accounts,* (1984). Ntozake's Betsey Brown production opened at the opened The American Music Theater Festival in Philadelphia March 25, 1989 setting off a new trend with music accompaniment.

In addition to her plays, Ntozake has written poetry, novels, and essays. She has taught at California State College, the City College of New York, the University of Houston, Rice University, Yale, Howard, and New York University. Among her many awards are an Obie, a *Los Angeles Times* Book Prize for Poetry, and a Pushcart Prize.

She graduated from Barnard College and received her master's degree from the University of Southern California.

Timeline of the Literary Diva's Published Work

- ∞ 2006—How I Come by This Cryin' Song—(St. Martin's Press)
- ∞ 2004—Ellington Was Not a Street (Coretta Scott King Illustrator Award Winner)—(Simon & Schuster)
- ∞ 2003—Daddy Says—(Simon & Schuster Children's Publishing; 1st edition)
- ∞ 2002—Float Like a Butterfly—(Jump At The Sun; 1st ed edition)
- ∞ 2002—Tenderheaded: A Comb-Bending Collection of Hair Stories-(Washington Square Press)

- 1999—I Live In Music—(Welcome Books)
- 1999—If I Can Cook/You Know God Can-(Beacon Press)
- 1998—Black Women's Writing: Quest for Identity in the Plays of Lorraine Hansberry and Ntozake Shange—(Sangum Press LTD)
- 1997—For Colored Girls Who Have Considered Suicide When the Rainbow Is Enuf—(Scribner; Reprint edition)
- 1996—Sassafrass, Cypress and Indigo : A Novel—(Picador; Reprint edition)
- 1995—Ntozake Shange: A Critical Study of The Plays—(Garland Publishing; 1 edition)
- 1995—Liliane: A Novel—(Picador)
- 1992—St. Martin's Griffin—(St. Martin's Griffin)
- 1991—Nappy edges—(St. Martin's Griffin; Reprint edition)
- 1991—A Daughter's Geography—(St. Martin's Press)
- 1990—Studies in American Drama, 1945—Present: A Celebration of Women Dramatists—(American Drama Studies)
- 1989—Beneath the Necessity of Talking-Amer Audio Prose Library Inc.
- 1988—Black Book—(St. Martin'sGriffin)
- 1985—From okra to greens: A different kinda love story : a play with music & dance—S French
- 1985—Betsy Brown—(Picador)
- 1984—See No Evil: Prefaces, Essays and Accounts, 1976-1983—(Momos Pr)
- 1984—From Okra to Greens: A Difference Love Story—(Bookslinger)
- 1982—FOR COLORED GIRLS—(Bantam)
- 1982—Some Men—(Small Press Distribution)
- 1992—The Love Space Demands: A Continuing Saga—(St. Martin's Press)
- 1981—About Atlanta—(Book People)
- 1981—For Colored Girls Consider—(Bantam)
- For Colored Girls Who Have When the Rain—(Methuen Publishing Ltd)
- 1980—For colored girls who have considered suicide, when the rainbow is enuf: a choreopoem-(Bantam)
- 1976—Sassafrass—(Shameless Hussy Press)
- 1976—Melissa and Smith—(Bookslinger Editions)

Pam Osbey

Pam Osbey is an accomplished vocalist, poet, and freelance writer. She is a powerful spoken word artist with a mission to uplift and empower women and people of color.

Pam has an extensive background in musicality and the written and spoken word. Known as "Mocha Sistah", she began singing at the early age of 8, and has performed for weddings, talent shows, and special events. As a student at Columbia College, Pam had the opportunity to perform in a black history program for Senator Julian Bond. Her major poetic influences are Maya Angelou, Nikki Giovanni, and Sonia Sanchez. Her literary influences are Terry McMillan, Alice Walker, and Eric Jerome Dickey, just to name a few.

Pam's poetry has been published online at Ebonylove.net, Sisterfriends.com, Rhapsody Publishing, and The Nubian Chronicles; as well as by the Gramblinite and the eXpressions Journal. Pam's short stories and relationship articles have been published by the Nubian Chronicles and Sisterfriends.com. She is currently a contributing writer for several literary e-zines.

Pam has just completed her 2nd published effort, *A Love Story*, a compilation of contemporary African American love stories. She was awarded 2nd Place in the 2003 Poet of the Year Contest sponsored by *Spoken Vizions* Magazine in St. Louis, Missouri and won the April 2004 Disilgold Poetry Contest with the poem, *Heal the Land*. Pam is the recent recipient of the Gwendolyn Brooks Award and the "Most Popular Female Poet of the Year" by Disilgold and the YOUnity Literary Guild in New York City.

She has appeared on ArtistFirst.com, has been featured on Power Talk FM, Hiyaah Ground (Wisconsin Public Radio), on Zane's Literary Cruise (April 05), at the "Too Sexy For You Writers Conference" (in Detroit, MI), and also at the Los Angeles Black Book Expo (June 2005). Pam recently finished work on two novels *Cause I Can* and *When Rainbows Ain't Enough*, as well as *Rivers of My Life* (available at www.lulu.com) and *Black Orchids* (available at www.iuniverse.com), all published in 2005. Pam's poem, *Unresolved* has been published in *My Soul To His Spirit*, a compilation of daughters' thoughts about their fathers, which was highlighted in the June 2005 Issue of *Ebony* Magazine.

Pam has completed a book of poetry, *Tears of a Woman, The Light Within*, scheduled for publishing through www.lulu.com/mochasistah.

(Website: Mochahsistah.com)

Timeline of the Literary Diva's Published Work

- 2005—Cause I Can and When Rainbows Ain't Enough—(Lulu Press)
- 2005—Rivers of My Life—(Lulu Press)
- 2005—Black Orchids—(Lulu Press)
- 2005—Tears of a Woman, The Light Within—(Lulu Press)
- 2003—Musings of Mocha Sistah—(Writers Club Press)

Pamela deLeon-Lewis

Pamela deLeon-Lewis has been writing since childhood. She had her first poem published when she was eleven years old, and her first short story published a year later. At the age of twelve, she received an academic scholarship for Essay Writing to a very prestigious private boarding school; years later, she became the Editor-in-Chief of her college newspaper.

Pamela was the Sr. Associate Editor of a Caribbean entertainment magazine—*CalypSoca Beat*. Her poetry was featured in four anthologies and she was nominated -*Poet of the Year from—2002-2005*. Two of Pamela's poems, *Oh Happy Day* and *Thoughts* received Editors Choice Awards from The International Library of Poets. Pamela is also a lyricist and she composes music.

In November 2005, Pamela was *the Person of the Week* on LTH Weekly, a web radio weekly broadcast and *Smiling Thru the Tears—a Breast Cancer Survivor Odyssey* was "Book of the Month". The Montgomery Book Club Readers and the Birmingham Literary Ladies Book Club also chose *Smiling Thru the Tears* as their "Book of the Month" for November and December 2005.

In 2006, *I Fought the Fight* and *My Conversation With Breast Cancer* were nominated "Poem of the Year" on *Muses Review* Poetry Contest, and Pamela was nominated "Poet of Month" by the Brooklyn Public Library for Poetry.

A Legislative Ambassador for the American Cancer Society, Pamela deLeon-Lewis is committed to using her gift of poetry and her speaking abilities to spread her positive messages of hope and survival nationally and internationally.

As a Motivational Speaker and a first-time Author, Pamela appeared at the Marriott Hotel, Hofstra University, The College of New Rochelle, Brooklyn Public Library, Newark Public Library, Charles Otterlie Renaissance Center. She has been spreading her messages to Junior High/High School students, Churches, Hospitals, Book Clubs, Literary and Women's Groups, and the Mahogany Sisters Network. She has made television appearances and has been interviewed on several occasions on both traditional and XM Radio Shows. Pamela took her Motivational Speaking/Book Promotion Tour to Georgia and Alabama, in the summer of 2005 where she wowed her "standing-room-only" audiences for ten days,

Pamela also advocates in online cancer support chat rooms and via telephone. She publishes an online newsletter, "Metamorphosis" for breast cancer survivors and reads her motivational/inspirational poetry at Open Mics, Spoken Word, and Health and Wellness events. She now hosts Water Cooler Sessions-PoeTree and weekly Open Mic on Saturday evenings.

Pamela is a two-year Breast Cancer Survivor. She penned her first book: *Smiling Thru the Tears—a Breast Cancer Survivor Odyssey,* which has been getting rave reviews since its release in June 2005. An optimist and a very proactive individual, Pamela has been spreading her positive messages of empowerment over this dreaded disease. She has also written a second book about the rigors and challenges she faces daily, such as living as a survivor with side-effects of Chemotherapy.

(Website: AuthorsDen.com/Pameladeleonlewis.com)

Timeline of the Literary Diva's Published Work

∽ 2005—Smiling Thru the Tears: A Breast Cancer Survivor Odyssey—(Publish America)

Pat G'Orge-Walker

Pat G'Orge-Walker, the creator and author of the hilarious gospel comedy series entitled, *Ain't Nobody Else Right But Us—All Others Goin' To Hell,* a forerunner for her books such as, *Sister Betty! God's Calling You!,* *Sister Connie Fuse Makes a Grave Mistake,* and Kensington Publishers latest release, *Sister Betty! God's Calling You Again!,* a hardcover novel.

Pat has sung, acted, and performed Stand Up comedy for many years. Her venues have included—"The Improv" and Radio City Music Hall in Manhattan, New York, Universal Amphitheatre in Los Angeles, California, as well as Reno, Nevada. She has also written monologues, music, and skits for former TV show, "PM Magazine" and for Adelco Award Winner actress/singer Sandra Reaves and several others.

In addition to being a standup comedian, author, actress, singer, and successful entrepreneur, she is also a former member of R&B's Legendary girl group, "Arlene Smith & the Chantels," the Gospel Groups "The Spiritualettes" and "The Heavenly Two.

In addition to being a part of the montage in *Black Expressions* new television campaign, *Sister Betty! God's Calling You Again!* was given a separate shot along with two other books that represented the best in Christian Fiction. "*Mother Eternal Ann Everlastin's Dead,*" was published through Kensington, Dafina Books. (Cited from www. SisterBetty.com)

Timeline of the Literary Diva's Published Work

- ᴥ 2005—Mother Eternal Ann Everlastin's Dead—(Dafina)
- ᴥ 2004—Sister Betty! God's Calling You Again—(Dafina)
- ᴥ 2003—Sister Betty! God's Calling You—(Dafina)
- ᴥ 1999—Sister Connie Fuse Makes a Grave Mistake—(Word for Word Publishing Company)

Renee Daniel Flagler

Renee Daniel Flagler has been in marketing, promotions and events for over ten years. Professionally she has written numerous, articles as well as copy for ads, brochures, websites and sales & media kits, many of which have been featured in various trade, business and consumer magazines.

Since she was a young girl, Renee has always treasured the art of writing and expressed her delight in the form of short stories, poetry, lyrics and screenplays. Her first published work was a poem featured in her high school yearbook. In 2004 she took her love of creative writing seriously and self-published her first novel, *Mountain High, Valley Low,* under her company, Aspicomm Media. The book has been featured in *Ebony* Magazine, *The New York Amsterdam News* and the *Columbus Post.*

Under the divisions of Aspicomm Media, Renee has been able to marry the things she enjoys the most—marketing, events and writing—into one fulfilling personal career. She continues to consult clients with innovative marketing support, produce and coordinate captivating events and plans to publish several more titles of her own, as well as the works of other aspiring authors.

In addition to being President & CEO of Aspicomm Media, Flagler is also a Co-Founder of *SETA.*(Sisters Empowering Tomorrow's Achievers), a non-profit organization dedicated to mentoring at risk teenage girls by helping them build confidence and realize their potential in an effort to create brighter futures.

Renee is a graduate of New School University with a Masters in Media Art and a graduate of St. Johns University with a Bachelor of Science in Communications. She is a member of the National Black MBA Association, National Association of Female Executives and Publishers Marketing Association. Currently, Renee resides in Long Island, New York with her husband and two children.

(Website: www.Aspicomm.com)

Timeline of the Literary Diva's Published Work

- 2006—MisGuided—(Aspicomm)
- 2004—Mountain High, Valley Low—(Aspicomm)

Reshonda Tate Billingsley

ReShonda Tate Billingsley is a general assignment reporter for KRIV-TV, the Fox affiliate in Houston, Texas. She is a graduate of The University of Texas at Austin. The award-winning journalist has also worked for TV stations in Beaumont and Oklahoma City. The former Langston University professor also has a background in radio and newspaper, including a stint as a reporter with *The National Enquirer.*

ReShonda is a member of The National Association of Black Journalists and Alpha Kappa Alpha Sorority, Inc. An avid reader, she enjoys writing poetry and motivational speaking. Her love for the written word began before she could walk. As a child, she carried books everywhere she went. As an adult, she decided to parlay that love into a project of her own.

After successfully self-publishing her debut novel, *My Brother's Keeper*, Simon & Schuster/Pocket Books bought the rights and re-released the book in Oct. 2003. They also published her second novel, *Let the Church Say Amen*, which hit #1 on the *Essence* Bestsellers list. ReShonda is a contributor to the *Essence* Bestselling anthology, *Four Degrees of Heat* and the author of a *Something to Say: Poetry to motivate the mind, body and spirit.*

ReShonda 's other projects include: *Help! I' ve Turned into My Mother* (Dec. 2005); *I Know I' ve Been Changed* (Feb. 2006); *Have a Little Faith* (July 2006); *Everybody Say Amen* (Fall 2006); *The Good Girls Club* (Fall 2006). (ReshondaTateBillingsley.com)

(Website: ReshondaTateBillingsley.com)

Timeline of the Literary Diva's Published Work

- 2006—I Know I've Been Changed—(Pocket)
- 2006—Have a Little Faith—(Pocket)
- 2005—Help! I've Turned into My Mother—(Strebor Books)
- 2004—Let the Church Say Amen—(Pocket)
- 2006—Four Degrees of Heat—(Pocket)
- 2003—My Brother's Keeper—(Pocket Books)
- Something to Say: Poetry to Motivate the Mind, Body and Spirit

Rewa Marie Fyles

Rewa's passion for writing has been deep in her heart for many years. Her creative tenacity would not die, as she persevered through college, receiving her BBA in Management. She braved through Corporate America, successfully landing premier positions with reputable firms, all while her desire to be a writer sat patiently waiting.

After an unexpected lay-off, Rewa recognized the opportunity and self-published her first book, *Feeling Poetic—A Book of Poetry*. The opportunity to share her poetry has been fulfilling, as her poems are close to her heart. She looks forward to sharing her second book of poetry

Rewa has read at various poetry venues in and outside of Houston, as well as radio interviews and in-store signings promoting her book.

Currently, Rewa is working on her first novel. Her many writing aspirations include short stories, plays, and screenplays. Her ultimate goal is to be a screenwriter.

Rewa, born and raised in Houston, is a graduate of the University of Houston-Downtown and a member of Alpha Kappa Alpha Sorority, Inc. (www. RewaMarieFyles.com)

(Website: RewaMarieFyles.com)

Timeline of the Literary Diva's Published Work

∼ 2003—Feeling Poetic: A Book of Poetry—(iUniverse)

Rita Dove

In 1993 Rita Dove was appointed Poet Laureate of the United States and Consultant in Poetry at the Library of Congress, making her the youngest person—and the first African-American—to receive this highest official honor in American letters. She held the position for two years. In 1999 she was reappointed Special Consultant in Poetry for 1999/2000, the Library of Congress's bicentennial year, and in 2004 Virginia governor Mark Warner appointed her as Poet Laureate of the Commonwealth of Virginia.

Rita has received numerous literary and academic honors, among them the 1987 Pulitzer Prize in Poetry and, more recently, the 2003 Emily Couric Leadership Award, the 2001 Duke Ellington Lifetime Achievement Award, the 1997 Sara Lee Frontrunner Award, the 1997 Barnes & Noble Writers for Writers Award, the 1996 Heinz Award in the Arts and Humanities and the 1996 National Humanities Medal. In 2006 Rita received the coveted Common Wealth Award of Distinguished Service.

Rita was born in Akron, Ohio in 1952. A 1970 Presidential Scholar, she received her B.A. *summa cum laude* from Miami University of Ohio and her M.F.A. from the University of Iowa. She also held a Fulbright scholarship at the Universität Tübingen in Germany.

Rita's published poetry collections include: *The Yellow House on the Corner* (1980), *Museum (1983), Thomas and Beulah* (1986), *Grace Notes* (1989), *Selected Poems* (1993), *Mother Love* (1995), *On the Bus with Rosa Parks* (1999), a book of short stories, *Fifth Sunday* (1985), the novel *Through the Ivory Gate* (1992), essays under the title *The Poet's World* (1995), and the play *The Darker Face of the Earth*, which had its world premiere in 1996 at the Oregon Shakespeare Festival and was subsequently produced at the Kennedy Center in Washington, D.C., the Royal National Theatre in London, and other theatres. *Seven for Luck*, a song cycle for soprano and orchestra with music by John Williams, was premiered by the Boston Symphony Orchestra at Tanglewood in 1998.

For "America's Millennium", the White House's 1999/2000 New Year's celebration, Rita contributed—in a live reading at the Lincoln Memorial, accompanied by John Williams's music a poem to Steven Spielberg's documentary *The Unfinished Journey*. She is the editor of *Best American Poetry 2000, and from January 2000 to January 2002 she wrote a weekly column, "Poet's Choice", for The Washington Post*. Her new poetry collection, *American Smooth*, was published by W.W. Norton & Company in September 2004.

Rita Dove is Commonwealth Professor of English at the University of Virginia in Charlottesville, where she lives with her husband, the writer Fred Viebahn. They have a grown daughter, Aviva Dove-Viebahn.

Timeline of the Literary Diva's Published Work

- 2006—American Smooth: Poems—(W.W. Norton & Company)
- 2005—The Best American Poetry—(Washington University Press)
- 2004—American Smooth Poems—(W.W. Norton, Reprint)
- 2003—Conversations With Rita Dove—(University Press of Mississippi)
- 2001—Meditation: On the Bus With Rosa Parks—(University of Georgia)
- 2000—Darker Face of the Earth—(Story Line Press)
- 1996—Mother Love Poems
- 1995—The Poet's World—(Library of Congress)
- 1995—The Unite States Poetry—(Washington Square Films)
- 1993—Lady Freedom Among Us—(Janus Press)
- 1993—Through the Ivory Gate—(Vintage Contemporary)
- 1993—Lady Freedom Among Us—(University of Virginia)
- 1993—Selected Poems—(Vintage)
- 1993—Grace Notes: Poems—(W.W. Norton & Company)
- 1990—Ploughshares Spring 1990 Stories and Poems—(Ploughshares)
- 1990—Fifth Sunday: Stories (Callaloo Fiction)—(University of Virginia)
- 1989—The Yellow House on the Corner—(Carnegie Mellon University Press)
- 1986—Thomas & Beulah—(Carnegie Mellon University)
- 1986—Persephone—(Wesleyan University Press)
- 1986—Thomas & Beulah—(Carnegie Mellon University Press)
- 1983—Museum—(Carmichael & Carmichael)

Rita Ewing

Rita Ewing aka Rita Williams prior to her marriage to NBA All-Star Patrick Ewing, did not start out as a writer. After graduating from LaReine Senior High School in Suitland, Maryland, Rita accepted a four-year National Merit Scholarship to attend Howard University in Washington, DC. Starting out with a major in chemical engineering, Rita quickly decided by the end of her freshman year that she had no burning desire to pursue a career in engineering and switched over to the College of Nursing, with the intent to prepare for a future in medicine.

It was during her tenure at Howard that Rita met her future husband, Patrick Ewing, who at that time was a student at Georgetown University. While working as a summer mail clerk and receptionist for Senator Bill Bradley, Rita had to accept packages from the likes of Ewing, who worked as a summer intern for the Senate Finance Committee. What began as lunch breaks blossomed into seven years of dating until the two decided to tie the knot.

Upon completion of the four-year nursing program and with a bachelor of science degree in hand, Rita began a career in critical care nursing at Howard University Hospital. After two years of working on various medical, surgical, and cardiac intensive care wards, while at the same time trying to assist her fiance' with his newfound fame and responsibilities, Rita decided to put her nursing career on hold and go back to school. Georgetown University Law Center welcomed her into the JD/MBA program with open arms. In December 1992 Rita proudly tossed her tassel to the side and walked across the podium with a Juris Docturum in law.

Admitted to the Pennsylvania Bar Association in June 1993, Rita turned her entrepreneurial dreams into a reality. Through her first start-up venture, One on One Management, Inc., Rita was able to provide home office management techniques and consulting services to professional athletes. Working with the athletes, including her own husband at the time, Rita was privy to the nuances of the world of professional basketball and the relationships that play a major role both on and off the court. She decided to put pen to paper.

Rita created the children's book series Patrick's Pals, which was based on Patrick Ewing, Alonzo Mourning, and Dikembe Mutombo's real-life friendships portrayed by childhood friends growing up in the hood. Her next penned venture and first published novel was *Homecourt Advantage*, which Rita coauthored with Crystal McCrary Anthony, coauthor of *Gotham Diaries*. Rita and Crystal sold the film rights to *Homecourt Advantage* and still have hopes of bringing their story to the silver screen.

In 2002, Rita helped bring the nation's largest African American-owned bookstore to Harlem, New York. She is co-owner of the Hue-Man Bookstore and is proud to be able to bring renowned authors to the Harlem community. It was in Harlem, where Rita conceived her most recent novel, *Brickhouse*. She wrote *Brickhouse* while living in New Jersey with her three daughters, Randi, Corey and Kyla. Rita credits her ex-husband, Patrick, for her juicy NBA experiences.

Timeline of the Literary Diva's Published Work

∞ 2005—Brickhouse—(Avon Trade)
∞ 1998—Homecourt Advantage—(Avon Books)

Rosa Guy

Rosa Guy was born Sept. 1, 1925 in Trinidad, West Indies. In 1932 her parents could only afford to send two of their three children to America, so at age seven, Rosa and her sister traveled by boat to the Westside of New York City. Her mother died four years later and shortly thereafter, when Rosa was fourteen years old, her father passed away, leaving her as an orphan to be raised by her older sister. Rosa met a young man, got married and relocated to Connecticut, leaving her, newlywed sister behind in New York.

Rosa's husband joined the military, and after he returned from World War II, the couple broke up leaving her with a young son. Rosa moved back to New York, where she met people in the Arts and became interested in theater, dance, art and photography. She joined the American Negro Theatre and met Ruby Dee, Sidney Poitier and Alice Childress. Ruby began reading other artist's works like John Killen's. It was difficult for her to raise her son and develop her talents in the arts, but her mentors kept her motivated. She soon penned the novel, *Bird at my Window*, which was published in 1966. She, then began helping other authors to get published.

Rosa's blessings paid off very soon, but in the meanwhile, she took an interest in becoming involved with countries in Africa, where she traveled to Gambia. Her involvement with the Harlem Writer's Guild inspired Rosa to hold on to her pride as a West Indian, Black American Writer. Many people began to join the Harlem Writer's Guild like Sarah Wright and Louise Merriwether. The plight of the Congo in Africa provoked even poets like Maya Angelou to meet with Malcolm X. Rosa's deep bond with Harlem, which fascinated her as a town where Blacks all stuck together and got a along, heralded her to continue writing more books. Her full name,

Rosa Cuthbert Guy, symbolizes an African-American writer whose fiction for young adults focuses on family conflicts and the realities of life in the urban American ghetto, as well as life in the West Indies.

Rosa has since written more than a dozen other published works, many of which are rooted in experiences from her own childhood. Much of her writing for young adults also deals with family and family members' responsibility to care and love one another. Rosa's later works include *A Measure of Time* (1983); *Paris, Pee Wee and Big Dog* (1984); and *The Music of Summer* (1992). A novel for adults, titled *The Sun, The Sea, A Touch of Wind*, was published in 1985; it focuses on an American artist who re-examines her troubled past while living in Haiti.

Rosa's book *The Friends* earned the American Library Association's Notable Book Award, and *My Love, My Love* is the basis for the award-winning musical *Once on This Island*. Rosa is the recipient of the Coretta Scott King Award and the *New York Times* Outstanding "Book of the Year" citation. In July 2005, Rosa was honored for her great body of literary work with the Phyllis Wheatley Award, given by the Harlem Book Fair. She lives in New York. She currently lives in New York.

(Website: JustUsBooks.com)

Timeline of the Literary Diva's Published Work

- 2005—The Friends—(Laurel Leaf; Reissue edition)
- 2003—Rosa Guy's " The Friends:" A Study Guide from Gale's "Literature of Developing Nation's for Students" Volume 01—(Laurel Leaf)
- 2002—My Love, My Love: The Peasant Girl—(Coffee House Press)
- 2002—My Love, My Love: The Peasant—(Coffee House Press)
- 2001—Bird At My Window—(Coffee House Press; 1 edition)
- 2001—Bird at My Window—(Coffee House Press ; 1 edition) (May 1, 2001)
- 1998—Presenting Rosa Guy—(Twayne's United States Authors Series)
- 1998—And I Heard/ Bird Sin—(Laurel Leaf; Reprint edition)
- 1997—New Windmills: The Friends (Heinemann Educational Books)
- 1996—The Sun, The Sea and a Touch of Wind—(Plume)
- 1992—The Music of Summer—(Delacorte Books)
- 1992—The Disappearance—(Laurel Leaf Books)
- 1992—Billy The Great—(Dell Picture Yearling)
- 1992—The Ups and Downs of Carl Davis III—(Yearling; Reprint Edition)

- 1986—A Measure of Time (Bantam Books)
- 1984—Paris, Pee Wee and the Big Dog (Yearling)
- 1983—New Guys Around the Block—(Delacorte Press)

Sammie Ward

Sammie Ward is a fiction and nonfiction writer, born and raised in North Little Rock, Arkansas, and now living in Maryland. She began writing short stories on the advice of a friend. Her first short story was sold to Black Romance in November 2000. With newfound confidence she wrote and sold a total of over twenty short stories before turning her attention back to her first love, writing novels.

Sammie has written for *Black Romance, Black Confessions, Black Secrets, Bronze Thrills, Jive, True Black Experience,* and *True Confessions.* Her short stories have also appeared on Nubian Chronicles, NubianMindz, and Timbooktu. *A Line In The Sand, Bait, Love By Regulations, Toi,* and *What Are Girlfriends For?*" have captivated readers throughout the country. In April 2005, Sammie was voted, "Best New Fiction & Drama Writer of the Year" by the Disilgold Literary National Association for her debut novel, *In the Name of Love.* Also a contributing health writer, Sammie's health articles have appeared on DOENetwork, W3 Lifestyle, and Health Net website. They have also been featured in *Amag, Family Digest,* and *Jive* Magazines.

Frustrated with traditional publishing houses, determining the standard for readers, Sammie formed Lady Leo Publishing in September 2004. *In The Name Of Love,* is the debut novel from her publishing company, followed by, *Love To Behold,* a novella and the military-mystery, *"Seven Days".* Her latest novel, *It's In The Rhythm* was released in February 2006.

(Website: www.LadyLeoPublishing.com)

Timeline of the Literary Diva's Published Work
- 2006—It's in the Rhythm—(Lady Leo Publishing)
- 2005—Love to Behold—(Lady Leo Publishing)
- 2003—Seven Days—(Lady Leo Publishing)
- 2003—In Name of Love—(Lady Leo Publishing)

Sheila Goss

Although Sheila M. Goss earned a Bachelor of Science degree in Engineering, her first love has always been writing.

Both Sheila's novels, *My Invisible Husband* and *Roses are thorns, Violets are true* have been on various bestsellers' lists including: *Essence* magazine and the *Dallas Morning News,* several times. She is the recipient of three *Shades of Romance* magazine "Reader's Choice Multi-Cultural Awards" and the 2004 Oneswan Productions "Female Author of the Year".

Sheila's short stories and poetry have appeared in national magazines such as *Black Romance* Magazine and she was featured in a special issue of *Writer's Digest.* Her novel, *My Invisible Husband,* was honorably mentioned in a *New York Times* article in the summer of 2005.

Besides writing fiction, Shelia is a freelance writer and interviews celebrities such as: *Mary J Blige* and *Lisa Marie Presley* for various online and print magazines. Urban Soul, a women's fiction line of Urban Books/Kensington, will re-release both of her novels. The first, *My Invisible Husband* is tentatively scheduled for a December 2006 release. (www.SheilaGoss.com)

(Website: SheilaGoss.com)

Timeline of the Literary Diva's Published Work

- 2004—My Invisible Husband—(4allseasons Publishing)
- 2003—Roses are Thorns, Violets are True—(4allseasons Publishing)

Shelley Parris

"Do you take a chance to realize a dream, or do you realize that a dream is just too much to chance?" This is a quote from Shelley Parris' poem, *Do You Take a Chance?* It is the question that Shelly Parris, a native New Yorker, has dared to answer. She realized her dreams of becoming a published author. Her journey began in 1999 when she began frequenting open mic forums throughout Miami-Dade and Broward counties in

Miami, Florida. She successfully shared her poetic pieces under the stage name "Black Beauty". The lasting impressions and connections made with her audiences motivated Shelley to assemble a collection of her writings which she self-published in November 1999, entitled *In the Company of My Spirit.*

Shelley put her creative, entrepreneurial spirit to work by creating, promoting, and producing a cutting edge open mic forum, *Urban Sweets*, in Fort Lauderdale, Florida. Enthusiastic patrons crowded in on Thursday nights just to be a part of the artistic exchange! As stated by Shelley, "I combined the successes of my self-published book, *Urban Sweets*, and sheer determination that resulted from discovery that only Jesus Christ can conquer any and all personal battles, and writing soon became my ministry."

As a result, in December 2002, Shelley established her own publishing company, Infinite Possibilities Publishing Group, Inc. (IP), based in Orlando, Florida. IP released Shelley's debut novel, *In the Eyes of Truth*, in May 2003. Shelley Parris' evident love affair with words embodies the vast depth and richness of her conscious writing style. Her keen business sense has served to put IP on the publishing map.

Since the release of its second title in July 2003, IP Publishing Group continues to thrive with the addition of more than eight new authors and the release of over ten new titles. The subject matter ranges from inspirational fiction, motivational and financial self-help books to poetry and business models for individuals taking that great leap of faith into entrepreneurship. These powerful messages whether captured on DVDs, CDs or in books are shaping the lives of many nationwide and abroad. This emergent company steps into the competitive ring of publishing, needing no formal introduction! The projects speak for themselves. As Shelley simply puts it, "We're Overcoming the World One Verse at a Time." Shelley currently resides with her family in Central Florida.

(Website: Ippublishingonline.com)

Timeline of the Literary Diva's Published Work

🖊 2003—In the Eyes of Truth—(IP Publishing Group)

Sonia Sanchez

Sonia (Benita) Sanchez was born Wilsonia Driver September 9, 1934 in Birmingham, Alabama. She is well known as a poet, playwright, and educator, and noted for her black activism. People say that Sonia's work best describes the "Black Experience". She was actually the teacher of Max Rodriguez, founder of the Harlem Book Fair.

When Sonia was just an infant, her mother died. She moved to Harlem with her siblings at age nine. Sonia went on to receive a B.A. in political science from Hunter College in Manhattan (1955) and briefly studied writing at New York University.

Sonia soon joined other activists in promoting black studies in schools, and fighting for better rights of Africans. From 1966 she taught in various universities. In 1975 Sonia landed a permanent position at Temple University.

In the 1960s Sonia published poetry in journals such as: *The Liberator, the Journal of Black Poetry, Black Dialogue*, and *Negro Digest*. Sonia's first book, *Homecoming* (1969), focused on the "neoslavery" of blacks. Her style became a template for poetical activism.

Some of Sonia's later works like *homegirls & handgrenades* (1984), won an American Book Award. As the years progressed, her work became more prolific. Sonia is now considered a living legend and a pioneer of works, depicting the Black struggle for equality in America and around the world.

(Website: SoniaSanchez.com)

Timeline of the Literary Diva's Published Work

∞ 2005—Somewhere Else—(Coffee House Press)

- 2004—Full Moon of Sonia—(Via International Artists)
- 2004—We be word sorcerers—(Bantam Books)
- 2001—Bum Rush the Page: A Def Poetry Jam—(Three Rivers Press)
- 2000—Shake Loose My Skin : New and Selected Poems—(Beacon Press)
- 1998—Does Your House Have Lions?—(Beacon Press)
- 1997—Wounded in the House of a Friend—(Beacon Press)
- 1994—Autumn Blues: New Poems—(Africa World Pr)
- 1994—Continuous Fire: A Collection of Poetry—(Inbook)
- 1993—Like the Singing Coming Off the Drums (Bluestreak Series)—(Beacon Press)
- 1991—Wear the New Day Well—(Acorn Media Publishing)
- 1987—Under a Soprano Sky—(Africa World Press)
- 1986—Generations: Selected Poetry, 1969-1985—(Red Sea Press)
- 1985—I've Been a Woman: New and Selected Poems—(Third Pr Review of Books)
- 1984—Homegirls and Handgrenades—(Thunder's Mouth Press)
- 1982—We a Baddddd People—(Broadside Pr; 1st edition)
- 1980—Sound Investment: Short Stories for Young Readers—(Third World Press)
- 1975—Love Poems—(Third Pr Review of Books)
- 1973—The Adventures of Fathead, Smallhead, and Squarehead—(Third Pr Review of Books)
- 1973—A Blues Book for Blue Black Magical Women—(Broadside Pr;1st ed.)
- 1971—It's a New Day: Poems for Young Brothas and Sistuhs—(Broadside Pr; 1st ed.)
- B Ma: Sonia Sanchez Literary Review

Stacy-Deanne Reed

Stacy-Deanne Reed was born on February 5, 1978 in Houston, Texas. Growing up as an only child in a two-parent, upper-middle class household, Stacy never wanted for anything except the company of siblings. It was Stacy's childhood desire, wanting brothers and sisters that formed her vibrant imagination. As means of escaping, Stacy endlessly turned to her imagination, which became key in her writing career years later.

Stacy attended Hobby Elementary and Lanier Middle School. She graduated from Jeff Davis High School in 1996. Stacy made many dear friends in high school, but sadly lost touch with all after graduation. While growing up, she always found positive situations out of negative ones. by the time she reached the tenth grade, Stacy was always the tallest person in her class (sometimes taller than the teachers). Being 5'11" in school would have embarrassed many teen girls, but not Stacy, who always used her height and presence to shine. Through that confidence, she decided to pursue a writing career.

Stacy seeks refuge in an incredibly large family. Her mother is one of nine children and her father is one of ten. Despite being loved by a huge family, Stacy considers herself the ultimate loner. While others concentrate on the usual thrills of everyday living, she finds happiness and fulfillment in her writing. Since she began writing professionally she's come to grips with a lot of tragedies and family issues that could have caused her to give up. It was facing these struggles that truly put things in perspective. Stacy realized she was a born fighter and would forever work to achieve her goals. She wishes the same for everyone else.

Stacy-Deanne is a writer of fiction and the author of several celebrity biographies. In 2005, her Stories about Ashanti, Jennifer Lopez and Mya were included in a compilation on Amber Communications Group, Inc. Imprint—Colossus Books, *Alicia Keys, Ashanti, Beyonce, Destiny's Child, Jennifer Lopez & Mya—Divas of the New Millennium*, co-written by Kelly Kenyatta and Natasha Lowery, with contributing writer Kwynne Sanders.

Being a successful writer is not the only part of her future plans. Stacy plans to publish a book of her photographs one-day and to have her own clothing line geared towards tall women because as she humorously states, " It's murder for them to find decent pants." She also plans to start her own magazine. She also plans to start two foundations: one for Cancer Research and another for low-income families, and she's interested in adopting a few children.

Stacy is also certified in Editing. She resides in Houston, Texas. Over the last few years, Stacy has realized that life is short; and she has made a promise to make a supreme difference with the time she's given.

(Website: www.Stacy-Deanne.com)

Timeline of the Literary Diva's Published Work

🍌 2005—Divas of the New Millennium—(Colossus Books)

Star Jones

Star Jones Reynolds was born in Badin, North Carolina. She earned a B.A. at American University and got her law degree at the University of Houston. As soon as she passed the New York Bar, she went straight to the Brooklyn District Attorney's office. After three years in general trials, she moved to the Homicide Bureau, where her work earned her a promotion to Senior Assistant District Attorney in 1991.

Star Jones is one of the most talked about authors to date. She married her husband in November 2004. Her marriage made headline news and resulted in a sponsored televised wedding. She is a lawyer and former pros- ecutor, but is known for her television appearances as a co-host of *The View*, produced by Barbara Walters. Her appearance on the show along with her co-hosts, earned the show a 2003 Daytime Emmy Award for "Outstanding Talk Show". Star started on television's *Court TV* and soon appeared as a NBC legal correspondent for *Today* and *Nightly News*, cov- ering the latest developments in the Mike Tyson rape case and the Rodney King police brutality trial.

She soon acquired her own show, *Jones & Jury*. By 1995, Star was named a senior correspondent and chief legal analyst for *Inside Edition* and assigned the O.J. Simpson criminal and civil trials. She was the only news correspon- dent to obtain an exclusive interview with Mr. Simpson during the civil trial.

In 2001, Star and her fellow co-hosts were awarded the "Safe Horizon Champion Award" for their continued efforts to raise awareness on issues of importance to girls and women.

Star has graced the cover of numerous magazines including *Newsweek, TV Guide, People, Ebony, Essence, Black Enterprise, Life and Style* and *New York*.

Timeline of the Literary Diva's Published Works

∼ 1988—You Have to Stand for Something, or You'll Fall for Anything—(Bantam)

∼ 2006—Shine—(Harper Collins)

Tajuana "T. J." Butler

Tajuana "T. J." Butler was born in Indianapolis, Indiana, and grew up in Hopkinsville, Kentucky. In 1989, T.J. attended the University of Louisville, where she majored in English and minored in Political Science and then joined the Alpha Kappa Alpha, Inc. Sorority. After completing her education, she moved to Atlanta, Georgia and landed a job with a trade publication, and did freelance writing and graphic design on the side.

One night, T. J. couldn't sleep. She had imagined five characters that she had to etch out on paper. She continued to develop these five characters, and after several months of concentrating on her outline, *Sorority Sisters* was born. Soon after, T.J. began writing poetry and at age 26, she founded Lavelle Publishing. In 1997, she published, *The Desires of A Woman: Poems Celebrating Womanhood*. Finally, in 1998, her first novel *Sorority Sisters* was released. T. J. went on a national tour visiting universities and many events, including the "Zora Neale Festival" and the "*Essence* Festival".

While attending the Book Expo America in 1999, T.J. was approached by Random House's Associate Publisher, Mary Bahr. In 2001, *Sorority Sisters* was re-released and by 2001, *Hand-Me-Down-A-Heartache* was released. T. J. currently lives in Los Angeles, California. She completed her novel, *The Night Before Thirty* in May 2005. She is now developing her skills as an actor and director." Cited from (Website: www.TJButler.com)

Timeline of the Literary Diva's Published Work

- 2005—Just My Luck—(One World/Striver's Row)
- 2005—The Night Before Thirty—(One World/Striver's Row)
- 2003—Hand-me-Down-Heartache—(Villard Books)
- 2001—Sorority Sisters—Random House—(Villard Books)
- 1997—The Desires of A Woman: Poems Celebrating Womanhood—
  (Lavelle Publishing)

Takesha D. Powell

Takesha Powell is an author of three books, founder and CEO of TDP Literary Agency, and a certified Public Notary in The State of New Jersey. She is the former Managing Editor of *Black Elegance/ Belle magazine, as well as former Editor-In-Chief of Jive/Intimacy* magazines.

As the published author of three titles—*The Goode Sisters* (iuniverse.com), *Tender Headed: Poems For Nappy Thoughts I Left Uncombed* (*iuniverse.com) Her latest hit, The African American Writer's Guide To Successful Self-Publishing: Marketing, Distribution, Publicity, The Internet... Crafting and Selling Your Book (Amber Books) was an Ebony* magazine "Bookshelf Pick", a *Black Expressions Book Club* selection, *Black Issues Book Review* recommended reading and has been hailed as fresh and relevant by *BlackExpressions.com*.

Born on Aug. 23, 1973, Powell was raised in Suffern, New York and later moved to Paterson, New Jersey where she spent most of her childhood. An army brat of a Vietnam Veteran, Powell credits her father's entrepreneurial savvy and her mother's generous church missionary careers with shaping her strong belief in family.

As a child at Woodland Middle School in Plainfield, New Jersey, she discovered her love of Writing, after having won a county-wide playwriting contest, winning first place amongst every participating school in Union County.

In the spring of 1993, Takesha became a distinguished member of both Alpha Kappa Alpha Sorority, Inc. and Alpha Kappa Psi, professional business fraternity. In 1995, she graduated Cum Laude from Bloomfield

College in Bloomfield, New Jersey. A few years after receiving her bachelor's degree, Takesha returned to school while a new mother, to receive her Master's degree in Adult Education and Distance Learning from The University of Phoenix. Takesha and her husband Calvin reside in New Jersey. They have one child.

(Website: WWW.TakeshaPowell.com)

Timeline of the Literary Diva's Published Work

- 2002—The Goode Sisters (iuniverse.com)
- 2002—Tender Headed: Poems For Nappy Thoughts I Left Uncombed (iuniverse.com)
- 2004—The African American Writer's Guide To Successful Self-Publishing—(Amber Books)

Terrie Williams

The phenomenal and inspirational success story of Terrie Williams began as the tale of a caring and shy young woman who "wanted to save the world." The early chapters of her life will chronicle that she was a social worker by training that earned a Masters in Social Work from Columbia University. But it was her venture into the entrepreneurial world—as the founder of The Terrie Williams Agency, one of the country's most successful public relations and communications firms—that made an enduring mark in the archives of business history.

Since its launch in 1988, with superstar Eddie Murphy and jazz legend Miles Davis as her first clients, the Agency has handled some of the biggest names in entertainment, sports, business and politics. The likes of Janet Jackson, Russell Simmons, Sean "P. Diddy" Combs, Johnnie Cochran, the Rev. Al Sharpton, Jackie Joyner-Kersee, Sally Jessy Raphael, Time Warner, HBO, AT&T and Essence Communications Partners have retained the services of her company. Today her Agency is a division of Players Govern Players Communications (of which she is Vice-Chair), a multi-media firm that develops cause-related campaigns for personalities, products and entities.

As an author Terrie has written three successful books. Her first, *The Personal Touch: What You Really Need to Succeed in Today's Fast-paced Business World* (1994, Warner Books), is a perennial business bestseller. Her second book, *Stay Strong: Simple Life Lessons for Teens* (Scholastic, Inc., 2001), has been utilized in school curricula and was the catalyst to launch The Stay Strong Foundation, a national non-profit for youth. Her third book, *A Plentiful Harvest: Creating Balance and Harmony Through The Seven Living Virtues* (Warner Books, 2002), is her undertaking to help other achieve balance in their daily lives, reconnect with their heritage, and identify the needs of their souls.

Terrie is one of the country's most highly sought-after speakers, and has shared her unique brand of success and personal development strategies with numerous Fortune 500 companies and countless organizations, including the New York University Continuing Education Program, The New School for Social Research, The National Football League, The National Basketball Association and the National Hockey League.

Her success story has been featured in dozens of publications including *The Washington Post, The Boston Globe, Crain's New York Business, The New York Daily News* and *People, Adweek, Essence* and *Savoy* magazines. The Agency's accomplishments have been used as the basis for public relations seminars and college classes, and Terry is quoted and featured in college textbooks, industry newsletters and even novels. A sampling includes: *Public Relations: A \Values-Driven Approach* (by David Guth and Charles Marsch); *Basic Media Writing* (a college text by Melvin Mencher that has featured Terrie in every edition since 1989); *Rogers' Rules for Businesswomen* (by Henry C. Rogers); *Any Way The Wind Blows* (by E. Lynn Harris); *Keys to Positive Thinking* (by Napoleon Hill of Think & Grown Rich fame); and *Show & Tell* (by Nelson George).

Terrie's early career path—one designed to help others—lies at the very core of who she is, and is continually reflected in her work and community service. That driving force today is based in the efforts of The Stay Strong Foundation, a 501(c)(3) organization geared to support America's youth. The Foundation encourages corporate and individual responsibility, develops educational resources for youth and youth organizations, provides and coordinates internships, sets up mentoring opportunities, and facilitates visits by prominent individuals and business professionals to schools, libraries, youth organizations and group homes.

Other programs of the Foundation, which has been honored by The National Center for Black Philanthropy with its Special Achievement in Philanthropy Award, include: Terrie "Plus One," an "outside the office" opportunity for young people to join Terrie and other professionals who are recruited at black-tie fundraiser's, corporate and private dinners, movie premiers, sports events, awards shows, speaking engagements and special events; the Please…Listen! National tour series of youth speak out sessions that raise awareness of teen issues and engage young people in the solution process; and Project Believe, a life skills and leadership training and development initiative to help young people see their dreams manifest and become leaders in their schools, in their communities, and within various organizations.

Awards and honors Terrie has received over the years include "The New York Women in Communications Matrix Award in Public Relations" (she was the first and only woman of color to be so honored in the 30-year history of the award); the "PRSA New York Chapter's PhillipDorf Mentoring Award"; and "The Citizen's Committee for the New York Marietta Tree Award for Public Service". In 1996 Terrie was the first person of color honored with the Vernon C. Schranz Distinguished Lectureship at Ball State University in Muncie, Indiana. Established in 1979, the Lectureship is recognized as one of the most preeminent in public relations.

In 1998, to commemorate the 10th anniversary of The Terrie Williams Agency, Terrie donated her collection of business and personal papers to Howard University's Moorland-Spingarn Research Center. The donation was the center's first gift of material specific to the public relations field. Moorland-Spingarn Research Center is the world's largest, most comprehensive repository of information and materials about and by people of African descent, housing works by such legendary figures as Phillis Wheatley, Frederick Douglass, W.E.D. DuBois, Alice Walker, James Baldwin and Toni Morrison.

Terrie's is a success story that has been built on a foundation of the countless contacts, friends, mentors and business associates that have helped her rise to the pinnacle of her profession. "I have been blessed," Terrie says. "And I know that the best way to say thank you to all those who have done so much for me is to give something back and pass it on to those who will follow us. I always wanted to save the world," she says with a laugh. "I can't do that, of course. But I can do my part, and encourage others to do the same."

Terrie's latest title, scheduled for release in 2007, *It Just Looks Like I'm Not Hurting: Depression, Hope, and Healing in Black American Life* tells of Terrie's chronic and then crippling depression, which she kept hidden under her "game face," a story first written about in her article for *Essence* magazine—which received their largest reader response in 2005. In her book, Terrie also tells the untold story of depression among African Americans—stories from celebrities, as well as ordinary people and psychologists who want to help break the taboo that has veiled the issue and explore the centuries of trauma that have contributed to this underlying condition among so many.

(Website: TerrieWilliams.com)

Timeline of the Literary Diva's Published Work

- 2007—It Just Looks Like I Am Not Hurting: Depression, Hope, and Healing in Black American Life—(Scribner)
- 2002—A Plentiful Harvest: Balance and Harmony Through the Seven Living Virtues—(Warner Books)
- 2001—Stay Strong—Simple Lessons For Success in Life—(Scholastic)
- 1994—The Personal Touch: What You Really Need to Succeed in Today's Fast Paced Business World—(Warner Books)

Terry McMillan

Popular writer Terry McMillan was born on October 18, 1951 to Madeline Washington Tillman and Edward McMillan. Terry grew up in Port Huron, Michigan. Her parents divorced when she was thirteen and her father died three years later. Terry's mother supported her family by working nights at a factory.

As a child, Terry had little interest in literature; but she discovered the joy of reading as a teenager while working at a library shelving books. She attended the University of California, Berkeley, graduating with a bachelor's degree in journalism. At this time, she also immersed herself in African American literature. While attending Berkeley, Terry wrote and published her first short story, *The End*. After graduating, she moved to New York to study film at Columbia University, where she earned a master's degree.

Terry's first book, *Mama*, was published in 1987. She took control of the book's publicity when the publisher failed to do so, writing 3,000 letters to bookstores, black organizations and universities, asking them to promote her book. This unique marketing approach proved highly successful; Terry received several offers for book readings and six weeks after *Mama* was published it went into its third printing.

Terry continues to find much success as a novelist. *Disappearing Acts*, her second novel, was published in 1989. Her third novel, *Waiting to Exhale*, spent months on the *New York Times* bestseller list and sold nearly 4 million copies. Terry's work tapped a market that had been long ignored by the publishing industry: young, educated black women. *Waiting to Exhale* was adapted into a successful film starring Whitney Houston,

Angela Bassett, Loretta Devine and Lela Rochon. Terry followed this accomplishment with the novel *How Stella Got Her Groove Back*, an instant bestseller, which was made into a hit film starring Angela Bassett, Whoopi Goldberg and Taye Diggs. Not limiting herself to writing, Terry served as the editor of *Breaking Ice: An Anthology of Contemporary African-American Fiction*. She lives in Northern California with her husband, Jonathan Plummer, and son, Solomon. Terry's most recent novel is *A Day Late and a Dollar Short*." Cited from (The HistoryMakers.com)

(Website: TerryMcMillan.com)

Timeline of the Literary Diva's Published Work

- 2005—The Interruption of Everything—(Penguin)
- 2001—McMillan, Terry. A Day Late and a Dollar Short—(Viking)
- 1996—How Stella got Her Groove Back—(Viking)
- 1992—Waiting to Exhale—(Viking)
- 1990—Breaking Ice: An Anthology of Contemporary African-American Fiction—(Viking)
- 1989—Disappearing Acts—(Viking)
- 1987—Mama—(Houghton)

Terry a. O'Neal

Best Selling Author, Terry a. O'Neal was born and raised in Stockton, California, where her inspiration for lyrics, prose, and literature was born. Her poetry has been published in numerous magazines, journals and newspapers. Previous publications include two volumes of poetry, *Motion Sickness* and *The Poet Speaks In Black;* two children's books, *Ev'ry Little Soul* and *My Jazz Shoes;* and the award-winning family fiction novel, *Sweet Lavender*. Terry's third volume of poetry, *Good Mornin' Glory,* was released in February 2006.

Terry a O'Neal is the editor of the annual youth poetry anthology, *Make Some Noise!* an anthology by inspired youth from all around the United States, Canada and Australia. In addition to her writing accomplishments, she is the Founder and Executive Director of the non-profit organization, Lend Your Hand, Inc. Educating the World's Children.

Terry's upcoming works include the children's book, *My Jazz Shoes*, a celebration of be-bop and jazz; the non-fiction novel, *Making Mo*, a moving story of a young boy's remarkable journey from a world of tragedy to triumph; and a volume of poetry based on her own life entitled *In a World of My Own*.

Currently, Terry *a* O' Neal is residing in the county of Sacramento, with her husband and three children; working full-time as an OT at the California State Prison of Sacramento.

(Website: www. Terryoneal.com)
~ Timeline of the Literary Diva's Published Work
~ 2005—Make Some Noise—(Motion Publishing)
~ 2006—Good' Morning Glory—(Motion Publishing)
~ 2003—Sweet Lavender—(Motion Publishing)
~ 2002—Ev 'ry Little Soul—(Motion Publishing)
~ 2002—The Poet Speaks in Black—(Motion Publishing)
~ 2000—Motion Sickness—(Motion Publishing)

Toni Morrison

Toni Morrison's original name was Chloe Anthony Wofford. She was born on February 18, 1931 in Lorain, Ohio after her family had left the south to escape racism. While growing up, Toni heard many tales from her parents about their Southern heritage, which inspired her to develop a unique gift of writing the greatest stories of all time.

What was also unique about Toni was that she attended an integrated school as the first Black student in her class, and the only one who could read. She graduated with honors from Lorain High School in 1949.

Toni then attended Howard University in Washington, D.C., where she majored in English with a minor in Classics. Since many people couldn't pronounce her first name correctly, she changed it to Toni, a shortened version of her middle name. Now Toni Wofford, she was graduated from Howard University in 1953 with a B.A. in English. She then attended Cornell University in Ithaca, New York, and received a master's degree (1955).

After graduating, Toni Wofford taught English at Texas Southern University in Houston. In 1957 she returned to Howard University as a member of faculty, and a year later, met her husband, Harold Morrison, a Jamaican. During this time, she had met many people involved in the struggle of the civil rights movement, such as a poet named LeRoi Jones known today as Amiri Baraka and Andrew Young. One of her students, Stokely Carmichael, became a leader of the Student Nonviolent Coordinating Committee (SNCC), and another of her students, Claude Brown, wrote *Manchild in the Promised Land* (1965).

Toni Morrison gave birth to her first son, Harold Ford, in 1961. She continued teaching while helping to take care of her family, but she longed for the company of other people who appreciated literature as much as she did. Later, she divorced her husband and returned to her parents' house in Lorain along with her two sons.

In the fall of 1964 Toni obtained a job with Random House in Syracuse, New York as an associate editor. She decided to dig out a story that she had written for the writer's group and decided to make it into a novel.

In 1967 Toni became a senior editor at Random House. While editing books by prominent black Americans like Muhammad Ali, Andrew Young and Angela Davis, she also sent her own novel to various publishers. *The Bluest Eye* (1970) is a novel of initiation concerning a victimized adolescent black girl who is obsessed by white standards of beauty and longs to have blue eyes. The book received enormous critical acclaim.

From 1971-1972 Tony was an associate professor of English at the State University of New York at Purchase, while she continued working at Random House. She soon started writing her second novel where she focused on a friendship between two adult black women. As a result, *Sula* was born in 1973. Toni went on to be featured in numerous publications and was nominated for "National Book Award in fiction" in 1975.

In 1977, Toni began writing a novel called *Song of Solomon* as told by a male narrator in search of his own identity. It won the "National Book Critic's Circle Award" and the "American Academy and Institute of Arts and Letters Award". In 1981 she published her fourth novel, *Tar Baby*, set on a Caribbean island; it explored interaction between black and white characters. After having earned appointment by President Jimmy Carter to the National Council on the Arts, Toni Morrison appeared on the cover of the March 30, 1981 issue of *Newsweek* magazine

In 1983, Toni left her position at Random House after 20 years of service. In 1984 she started writing her first play, *Dreaming Emmett,* based on the true story of Emmett Till, a black teenager killed by racist whites in 1955 after being accused of whistling at a white woman. Her hard work resulted in a debut showing of the play on January 4, 1986 at the Marketplace Theater in Albany, New York.

Toni's next novel, *Beloved,* about a slave named Margaret Garner who escaped with her master in Kentucky in 1851 and fled to Ohio, was published in 1987. *Beloved* became a bestseller and in 1988 won the Pulitzer Prize for fiction. In 1987, Toni Morrison was named the Robert F. Goheen Professor in the Council of Humanities at Princeton University becoming the first blackwoman writer to hold a named chair at an Ivy League University.

By 1992, she started another novel, *Jazz.* In 1993, Toni Morrison received the Nobel Prize in Literature. She was the eighth woman and the first black woman to do so. Her seventh novel, *Paradise,* was published early in 1998. Cited from (Math.buffalo.edu)

(Website: ToniMorrison.com)

Timeline of the Literary Diva's Published Works

- 2005—Love—(Vintage)
- 2004—Remember: The Journey to School Integration (BCCB Award)— Houghton Mifflin
- 2004—Beloved—(Vintage International)
- 2002—Sula—(Plume Books)
- 2000—The Bluest Eye—(Plume Books)
- 1999—Paradise—(Plume Books)
- 1994—Conversations with Toni Morrison: Literary Conversations— (University Press)
- 1993—Jazz—(Plume Books)
- 1993—Whiteness and the Literary Imagination—(Vintage)
- 1987—Song of Solomon—(Plume Books)
- 1987—Tar Baby—(Plume Books)

Tonya Lewis Lee

Tonya Lewis Lee's upbringing was quite conservative. Her father was a corporate executive, her mother a schoolteacher. Tonya was steered to pursue a reliable career path. A graduate of Sarah Lawrence College and the University of Virginia law school, Lee turned to writing and TV production after specializing for several years in First Amendment issues with a major Washington, D.C. law firm. Since 1998, Tonya has produced Black History Month spots for Nickelodeon and Nick at Nite featuring various celebrities including Gregory Hines, Savion Glover, Whoopi Goldberg and Queen Latifah.

Tonya had become a concert-level pianist; and when she met Spike Lee, he inspired her to unleash her more creative side. After the couple got married, Tonya gave up practicing law, and poured her energy into creating a prototype for a magazine on black entertainment and fashion; she also started writing. "I think I've always been creative;' she says. "I was what they call a shadow artist. Plus I've learned a lot from watching Spike and how he works. The first thing you write doesn't have to be award-winning. I've come to understand and trust the process."

Tonya's early writing efforts were geared to a young audience. In 2002, she and Spike wrote a children's book called *Please Baby Please,* which followers of his movies will recognize as the signature line of the character he played in his breakout film *She's Gotta Have It.*

With a new novel out in 2005, Tonya stepped into her own light. Tonya and Crystal McCrary Anthony had met and bonded at a New York Knicks game years ago. They quickly discovered they had more in common than basketball, both were lawyers and both harbored a desire to write. Several years into their friendship, Tonya invited Crystal to accompany her to the Cannes Film Festival, since Spike's schedule would be packed with press junkets. Breathing the heady, creative air that is common at film festivals, Tonya and Crystal resolved to start writing together.

The two women, Upper East Side neighbors and friends, wrote *Gotham Diaries*, an award winning best-selling novel that portrays the intersecting lives, ambitions, foibles and betrayals of members of Manhattan's black upper crust. It's a world that has been largely absent on the literary landscape. Tonya figured that she and Crystal had already seen the world of *Sex and the City,* but they now it was time to show this world that they both knew.

A New York City-based children's advocate, Tonya has also written and produced thought provoking television documentaries for young people. Among her many production accomplishments are a series of Black History Month spots for the Nickelodeon and Nick at Nite networks. She also served as executive producer for the 2005 television mini-series "Miracle's Boys," that aired on Noggin/The N and the documentary film, *I Sit Where I Want: The Legacy of Brown v. Board of Education* honoring the fiftieth anniversary of Brown V. Board of Education.

In addition to her professional activities, Tonya serves on the boards of the NAACP Legal Defense and Educational Fund and Children for Children Foundation. With TV projects, two flourishing school-age children, a chic, luxurious and comfortable Upper East Side townhouse, and more social invitations than she can possibly attend, Lee is very much a woman in her prime. Tanya is currently working on her second novel with Crystal.

(Website: www.TonyaLewisLee.com)

Timeline of the Literary Diva's Published Work

∾ 2005—Gotham Diaries—(Hyperion)

Tracy Price-Thompson

Tracy Price-Thompson is the national bestselling author of the novels, *Black Coffee, Chocolate Sangria, A Woman's Worth* and *Knockin' Boots*. A highly decorated Desert Storm veteran, she was graduated from the Army's Infantry Officer Candidate School after more than ten years as an enlisted soldier. A Brooklyn, New York native who has traveled extensively and lived in amazing places around the world, Tracy is a retired Army Engineer officer and Ralph Bunche graduate Fellow who holds a bachelor's degree in Business Administration and a master's degree in Social Work.

Tracy is a firm believer in satisfying her muse, and takes pride in penning novels that both challenge the range of her creativity, and embrace the expanse of the human experience. A maverick at heart, Tracy feeds her muse first and all others second. She writes whatever pleases her and doesn't require anyone's permission to do so. Tracy supports and applauds emerging writers who are dipping their innovative spoons into creative wells, and mentors several new authors each year.

A dedicated wordsmith who diligently studies the art and craft of fiction writing, Tracy is also the co-editor of the anthology *Proverbs For The People*, and composes professional literary reviews based on established elements of writing for several print sources.

Tracy lives in Hawaii with her wonderfully supportive husband and several of their six bright, beautiful, incredible children. She is currently at work on her next novel.

(Website: www.TracyPriceThompson.com)

Timeline of the Literary Diva's Published Work

- 2005—Knockin' Boots—(One World/ Ballantine)
- 2004—A Woman's Worth—(Strivers Row)
- 2004—Chocolate Sangria—(One World/ Strivers Row)
- 2002—Black Coffee—(Villard)

Tyra Banks

Tyra Banks is the founder of T ZONE and famous for knocking down barriers with a long list of "firsts." As a groundbreaking, international fashion icon, Tyra became the first African-American model to *simultaneously* grace the covers of *GQ* (for which she was also named "Woman of the Year—2000") and *Sports Illustrated's* swimsuit issue. She was the first African-American model to be featured on the cover of the famed Victoria's Secret catalog and to hold a prestigious modeling contract with the company. Tyra is also the recipient of the prestigious Michael Award for "Supermodel of the Year," the fashion industry's equivalent to the Academy Award." (Cited from the TyrasShow.com)

Tyra is the executive producer of the hugely successful reality television series "America's Next Top Model", which has become the network's most watched show. She is also the president of Bankable Productions.

Tyra first co-starred with Will Smith in the hit television comedy series, "The Fresh Prince of Bel-Air." As an actress, she starred in John Singleton's critically-acclaimed film, *Higher Learning*, and in the Jerry Bruckheimer-produced *Coyote Ugly*.

Tyra acquired a deal with Telepictures Productions to host her own syndicated talk show during the fall of 2005 called the Tyra Banks Show. Some of her most watched shows were her interviews with long time past rival, Naomi Campbell, who called a truce that led to the forgiveness of misconstrued actions and words by both of the super models. Tyra hung up her modeling career in 2006, but she has so many projects underway, her reign as a Super Woman will continue to live on her dreams.

A humanitarian, Tyra's efforts to help young girls with their struggle toward self-esteem is widely known and respected. After writing *Tyra's Beauty Inside & Out* (HarperCollins), Tyra "realized that the trials she overcame as a teen allowed her to genuinely connect with girls of all backgrounds. She then created TZONE as a summer camp experience where girls are encouraged to leave their negative pasts behind and focus on inner beauty and sisterhood. Tyra's dream is to take TZONE nationwide."

Tyra is the ultimate IT girl of our time. She does it all, but gives back to so many. While her show is not even compared to the success of the "Oprah Winfrey Show" and in a class of its own, people can appreciate both Oprah and Tyra who air back to back. Oprah blessed television audiences by giving Tyra a big break to host on the Oprah show, and as a result, not only are people proud of Tyra, but they now make Oprah and Tyra two must-see daily television programs.

(Website: www.TyraShow.com)

Timeline of the Literary Diva's Published Work

⌁ 1998—Tyra's Beauty Inside & Out—(Perennial / Harper Collins)

Vickie Stringer

Vickie Stringer single handedly launched a company that supported authors who write titles dealing with street life, and earned the title "Hip-Hop Queen" by C&B Books. Vickie is the CEO of Triple Crown Publications, the world leader of urban literature publishing, and the author of the best selling books *Let That Be The Reason* and the sequel *Imagine This*.

It was through the many trials Vickie Stringer encountered during a seven-year stint in prison that instilled in her the resolve and insight to launch Triple Crown Publications, now based in the suburban business district of Columbus, Ohio. The first publication under her fledgling company was her self-published novel, *Let That Be the Reason*, a story about the choices one woman makes and how her decisions would be her emancipation from street life or her destruction.

Vickie Stringer's novel earned her instant success, and the voice and soul of Triple Crown Publications was born. The name was based on a group Ms. Stringer associated with called the "Triple Crown Posse." It honors the positive impact the group had on her life and serves as a reminder that loyalty and dedication are the only ways to achieve lasting success .

The company has grown from a one-woman operation to an establishment with nine full-time employees, distributing over one million books to bookstores and libraries throughout the United States and abroad.

In 2002, Vickie joined forces with a silent partner to stake a claim in the publishing game. Along with their plan to introduce emerging talented authors, the company's vision is longevity, integrity, gripping unforgettable tales, and prosperity.

(Website: www.TripleCrownPublications.com)

Timeline of the Literary Diva's Published Work

- 2006—Dirty Red: A Novel—(Triple Crown Publications)
- 2005—How to Succeed in the Publishing Game—(Triple Crown Publications)
- 2002—Let that Be the Reason—(Triple Crown Publications)

Victoria Christopher Murray

Victoria Christopher Murray always knew she would become an author, even as she was taking quite an unlikely path to that destination. A native of Queens, New York, Victoria first left her hometown to attend Hampton Institute in Virginia where she majored in Communication Disorders. After graduating in 1977, Victoria attended New York University where she received her Master of Business Administration in 1979.

Victoria spent ten years in Corporate America before she decided to test her entrepreneurial spirit. She opened a Financial Services Agency for Aegon, USA where she managed the number one division for nine consecutive years. However, Victoria never lost the dream to write and when the "bug" hit her again in 1997, she answered the call.

Victoria originally self published *Temptation* in 1997. "I wanted to write a book as entertaining and compelling as any of the books on the market, put God in the middle, and have the book still be a page-turner. I wasn't writing to any particular genre—I didn't' t even know Christian fiction existed. I just wanted to write about people I knew and characters I could relate to."

In 2000, Walk Worthy Press/Warner Books published *Temptation*. " It was a long road before my agent was able to find a publisher. However, it has truly been a blessing and now I know that it was all in God's perfect timing. He has certainly opened up the floodgates. " Temptation made numerous best sellers lists including *Emerge* and *The Dallas Morning News*. It remained on the *Essence* bestsellers list for nine consecutive months and was nominated in 2001 for an "NAACP Image Award in Outstanding Literature".

JOY, Victoria 's second novel was released in October 2001. "This is a story about having to make tough decisions when you' re pulled between what you may want and what God definitely wants. *JOY* reveals how one word from God will change your whole life. " *JOY* has also been an *Essence* bestseller and won the 2002 "Gold Pen Award for Best Inspirational Fiction".

Victoria is a Regional Director with *Black Issues Book Review* and a contributor to *Quarterly BlackReview.com*. She lives in Inglewood, California and attends Bible Enrichment Fellowship International Church under the spiritual tutelage of Dr. Beverly " BAM" Crawford. She is also a member of the Long Beach Chapter of Delta Sigma Theta Sorority.

(Website: VictoriaChristopherMurray.com)

Timeline of the Literary Diva's Published Work

- 2005—Grown Folks Business: A Novel—(Touchstone)
- 2006—A Sin and a Shame: A Novel—(Touchstone)
- 2006—Truth Be Told—(Touchstone)
- 2002—Joy—(Walk Worthy Press)
- 2001—Temptation—(Walk Worthy Press)
- 2004—Let the Church Say Amen—(Pocket)

Wendy Williams

Wendy Williams has managed to carve her own niche in the publishing industry with gossip revealing books. She grew up in the Wayside area of Ocean Township, New Jersey. Williams earned a Bachelor's Degree in Communications from Northeastern University in Boston, Massachusetts.

Often called the "Queen of Radio", Wendy's radio career has included interning at Kiss 108 in Boston on the Matt Siegel morning show. She's also worked for WVIS, WOL-AM, WQHT Hot 103.5FM, WPLJ 95.5 FM, WRKS 98.7 KISS-FM, WQHT-FM, Hot 97, New York and WUSL-FM, Power 99. In 2001 Wendy returned to New York to work for her current employer, WBLS-FM with her nationally syndicated radio show "The Wendy Williams Experience."

Many people do not know that some of the jobs Wendy held down were so time consuming and required so much traveling that she would have to sleep in her car between gigs to be on time for work. Her tenacity to endure in a volatile industry as a woman, has won over a nation of fans who tune into her show daily and religiously. Her listeners have developed an appreciation for all she had been through and the hard work it took to make it to the top of her career.

Wendy Williams is the recipient of the "Radio Personality of the Year" award from *Billboard* magazine, *Black Radio Exclusive* and *Radio & Records* magazine. Her literary contributions include, *Wendy's Got The Heat*—published August, 2003 with Karen Hunter who has won a Pulitzer prize for her work, *The Wendy Williams Experience* and *Drama Is Her Middle Name: The Ritz Harper Chronicles Vol. 1* (with Karen Hunter—

Harlem Moon). Wendy Williams has also hosted a series of interview specials on VH1's "Wendy Williams is on Fire".

(Website: The WendyWilliamsExperience.com)

Timeline of the Literary Diva's Published Work

- 2006—Drama Is Her Middle Name : The Ritz Harper Chronicles Vol. 1 (Paperback)—Harlem Moon
- 2003—Wendy's Got the Heat—(Atria; 1st Atria edition)
- 2004—The Wendy William's Experience—(Dutton Adult)

Yolanda Y. Joe

Yolanda Joe is a Chicago native, raised on the south side by her maternal grandparents. Her working class family was influential in pushing her to achieve her goals of being a journalist and a novelist.

Yolanda was accepted at Yale University receiving a four-year academic scholarship. She graduated with a B plus average in 1984 with a B.A. in English Literature. During her stint at Yale, she studied under well-known scholar Henry Louis Gates. She also received a fellowship to study British Literature at Oxford in England, and continued on to receive a M.S. in Broadcasting from the Columbia School of Journalism.

Yolanda returned home to Chicago and began work at WBBM-AM, an all news radio station. She worked as a production assistant, a producer, and part time writer. She transferred from radio to television and worked as a writer and producer for Channel 2, the CBS-owned station.

As a published author, Yolanda's first book, *Falling Leaves of Ivy*, Longmeadow Press 1992…was about four college friends who share a secret that could ruin their lives. Set in the fast-paced-have-it-all-80's, it is about inter-racial relationships…racism in the work place…betrayal… and murder. The book made the *Blackboard* "best seller" list in 1993.

Doubleday published Yolanda's second novel, *He Say, She Say* in January 1997. It is about how African-Americans relate to one another through friendship, family, and romance. The novel made the *Blackboard* and *Chicago Tribune* "best seller" lists. In February of 1998, Warner books released the paperback. The novel is also available in German and is proving to be a big success in the foreign market.

Yolanda's next work of commercial fiction, *Bebe's By Golly Wow*, was published in 1998 by Doubleday. It was selected by the Literary Guild and is a *Blackboard* best seller. Her fourth novel, *This Just In...* was published in April of 2000. It is about five friends in the television news business and focuses on racism and sexism in that cutthroat industry. The novel has been selected by the Doubleday, Literary Guild and *Black Expression* Book Club. An excerpt is featured in the July 2000 issue of *Essence* magazine.

Yolanda has also written a mystery series under the pen name, Ardella Garland. The first novel, *Details at Ten*, was published by Simon and Schuster in October 2000. It debuted the sassy, smart television investigative reporter Georgia Barnett——her passion for news and love for Chicago are the driving forces behind the series. The novel is a Literary Guild, Mystery Guild, and *Black Expression* Book Club selection. The second novel in the mystery series *Hit Time,* was published in 2002 and received excellent reviews. Yolanda's next two works of fiction were *The Hatwearer's Lesson* and *My Fine Lady*, published in 2003 and 2004 respectively. The most recent title under the mystery series, *Video Cowboys,* was published in June of 2005, making the *Essence* "Best Seller" list in May of 2006.

Yolanda also plans to stretch her talents by writing a non-fiction book, as well as editing an anthology. She is also a freelance journalist and has written articles for the *Washington Post, The Chicago Tribune*, and the *New York Times*. She writes and resides in her hometown of Chicago.

Timeline of the Literary Diva's Published Work

- 2005—Video Cowboys—(Simon & Schuster)
- 2004—My Fine Lady: A Novel -(Dutton Adult)
- 2003—Hit Time: A Mystery—(Pocket Star)
- 2003—The Hatwearer's Lesson—(Dutton Adult)
- 2002—Details at Ten (Georgia Barnett Mysteries; Paperback, Pocket)

~ 2001—This Just In—(One World, Ballantine)
~ 1999—Bebe's By Golly Wow—(Dell)
~ 1998—He Say, She Say—(Warner Books; Reissue edition)
~ 1992—Falling Leaves of Ivy—(Longmeadow Pr; 1st ed edition)

Yolantha Pace

Yolantha Pace is a performance arts specialist, "dance-poet" for the Kentucky Arts Council. As one of the first female African-American missionaries to Ronquitte, Haiti, Yolantha she uses her creativity to tell others about God's blessings and miracles in her life. She is the founder and facilitator for V.O.I.C.E. (Voices of Influence Creating Encouragement) and S.P.E.A.K.!!! (Stop, Please End Abuse to Kids!!!) Workshops in which she shares her story with victims, civil servants, community leaders, colleges, universities, churches, and anywhere there is a need to educate about the horrendous hate crime—domestic abuse.

Yolantha Harrison-Pace is a dedicated wife and the mother of two daughters, Erin and Diamond, and is currently married. She has won many awards, including the "2004 YOUnity Guild Award Humanitarian of Year", the "2004 Urban Spectrum Poetry Book of the Year Award" and was the First Place winner of "Letstalkhonestly.com Poetry, 2004".

In 2004, Yolantha made a Harlem Book Fair Performance to a standing ovation. She's been featured on Herspace.com, 2003; Mommytoo.com, 2004; Doenetwork.com; Centre College-performance, 2004; Lexington—Fayette Urban County, 2004 and Nubiansistas.com, 2004. One of her most poignant interviews have included *The Advocate Messenger*, 2004 and most notable speaking appearances have included, Centre College: Panhellenic Society, Empowerment; Berea College: Life Writing, Writers on Writing, Women in Literature, Women's issues; Union College: A Survivor Speaks, (first response teams, policemen, health care professionals) and Georgetown University: A Survivor Speaks for students.

(Website: www.nesheepublication.com)

Timeline of the Literary Diva's Published Work
🌿 2004—Wing Plucked Butterfly—(Neshee Publication)

Zane

Zane is the *New York Times* Bestselling Author of several titles: *Addicted, The Sex Chronicles: Shattering the Myth, Skyscraper, Nervous, Gettin" Buck Wild: The Sex Chronicles 2, The Sisters of APF, Shame on it All,* and *The Heat Seekers.* She has been published in several different languages including Japanese, Swedish, and Greek. Zane self-published three titles in 2000 and went on to sell more than 250,000 copies; virtually by word of mouth alone.

Having signed with Simon and Schuster in June 2001, Zane contracted fifteen books to a single publisher in less than three years, with all of them set being published by Spring 2005. She has been on the Essence Magazine bestsellers list consistently since she began her publishing career and currently holds the number one and number two positions in the hardcover fiction section. Zane is the only author to ever have three out of five of the top fiction sellers in one month, and she accomplished the feat for several months in a row. Zane held down seven of the top fifteen African American fiction titles at Waldenbooks Nationwide including the first, second and third positions. She has sold more than two million books since April 2000.

She is also the editor of *Chocolate Flava*, which sold nearly 100,000 copies during its first month of publication (January 2004) and it recently went into its ninth printing. *Caramel Flava* is the follow-up.

In addition to being an author, Zane is the Publisher of Strebor Books International LLC (www.streborbooks.com). She has twenty-eight authors signed to her house and the titles are distributed through Simon and Schuster. Zane is also the executive producer of "Sock it to Me": a DVD based on one of the stories in *The Sex Chronicles: Shattering the Myth.*

Zane's Endeavors Books and Gifts, her newest venture, opened its doors for business in April 2004 in the historic Fell's Point area of Baltimore.

In the near future she plans to direct her first movie and is in serious talks for several major motion pictures and numerous plays. Zane is one of the most exciting authors to date, and people are discovering she is more than an author, but an icon who has broken down doors and is leading the way." Cited from Troy Johnson's—(Cited from Troy Johnson's www. AALBC.com)

(Website: SteborBooks.com)

Timeline of the Literary Diva's Published Work

- 2002—Black Gentleman.com—(Strebor Books)
- 2005—Afterburn—(Strebor Books)
- 2004—Chocolate Flava -(Strebor Books)
- 2004—Breaking the Cycle—(Strebor Books)
- 2003—Skyscraper—(Strebor Books)
- 2003—The Sisters of APF—(Strebor Books)
- 2003—Nervous—(Strebor Books)
- 2003—The Heat Seekers—(Strebor Books)
- 2003—Sex Chronicles: Shattering the Myth—(Strebor Books)
- 2003—Sex Chronicles: Getting Buckwild—(Strebor Books)
- 2003—Shame On It All—(Strebor Books)
- 2001—Addicted—(Strebor Books)
- Erotica Noir. com Anthology—(Strebor Books)

Part Two

Editorial Divas
Keeping the Works of Literary Divas at the Forefront of the Publishing Industry

Adrienne Ingrum

Just a few of Adrienne Ingrum's many accomplishments have been noted, but her experience as publisher, editor, writer, project manager, and publishing consultant, as well as her expertise in new business development and book creation, make Adrienne a renaissance woman in publishing.

Adrienne has 27 years of experience in book publishing. She has served in VP editorial positions at G.P. Putnam's Sons (now part of Penguin Putnam), Waldenbooks, and Crown Publishers, a division of Random House. She has worked with scores of authors and published more than 500 fiction, nonfiction and sideline titles. Adrienne is proudest of having developed the instant books, *MILLION MAN MARCH* and the bestseller, *WE ARE THE WORLD,* and of having acquired first fiction by Bebe Moore Campbell, Nelson George and Rita Dove.

Adrienne has edited hundreds of books and has also developed projects for Sylvia Woods, the Paul Robeson Foundation, Norma and Carol Darden, *Signature Bride* magazine, Reverend Vashti McKenzie, Ed Gordon, the Thurgood Marshall Scholarship Fund, and Reverend Suzan Johnson Cook.

Adrienne conceived, launched and, for eight years, oversaw the magazine *Black Issues Book Review.* The publication was named one of the "top 10" best new magazines by *Library Journal.* As the associate publisher, Adrienne was responsible for editorial and visual components, plus key advertising and strategic direction.

She has consulted for corporations, including Urban Ministries Inc., the largest African American Christian publisher and Doubleday Direct in the strategic planning of *Black Expressions* Book Club. She has ghosted four titles, each with an author of note or with a co-writer. Adrienne received her B.S. in Economics at Georgetown University. She resides in Harlem. She may be contacted at aingrum@aol.com.

Alicia Marie Rivers

"Be confident. Be sensual. Be powerful. Be fearless! Just be! Believe in your beauty," are the poignant words of Alicia Marie Rivers, Founder and Editor-In-Chief of *Jolie Magazine*. With ten years of publishing experience under her belt, Alicia has held several positions within the media world. Most notably, she spearheaded as the first Black female Editor-In-Chief of two non-ethnic hair & beauty magazines...*101 Hairstyles* and *Shortcuts*.

Alicia has also successfully served as Editor-In-Chief of *Black Hairstyles & Trends, Black Hair & Braids* as well as former beauty editor of lifestyle magazines such as *Black Elegance* and *Belle* (a publication geared to the full-figured woman). Alicia's talents have deservingly been featured in highly watched television programs such as BET, Good Day New York and BCD's *In Style*. Her expertise has also been noted in periodicals like *HealthQuest* and *Seventeen*. In addition, Alicia continued to work her craft as she guided the significant success of several hair, beauty, fashion and celebrity lifestyle magazines including: *Hot Hair, Ultimate Hair, Great Hair Now* and *Be Stylish*.

Alicia has continued to showcase her ability to appeal to the mass market as the former beauty and fashion editor of *Teen Celebrity* and *Sweet 16.com*, as well as the former Editor-In-Chief of *Celebrity Cuts*. A former model, Alicia has always stressed self-acceptance in her publications and has also conducted numerous self-esteem seminars. Alicia was born and raised in Detroit, Michigan. Shea attended New York City's famous Fashion Institute of Technology (FIT). (www.JolieLivePretty.com).

Angela P. Dodson

Angela P. Dodson serves as the Executive Editor of *Black Issues Book Review*. Her perceptive editorials gave readers insight of her favorite recommended books. In the January/ February 2006 publication of *Black Issues Book Review*, before it was acquired by *Target Market News*, a leading African American resource that saw the potential of the publication to excel beyond 50,000 readers per issue, she mentioned how Rosa Parks book, entitled *Rosa Parks* (Penguin) is a book she reads most closely.

Angela signified Rosa's death on October 24, 2005 as the launch of a nationwide crusade for people of color to read all of Rosa's books to discover the truth of her actions in her own words. Her heroic stance won over more readers for the issue in addition to a top list featuring "the Powers Behind Black Books" and quite possibly one of the most historical issues of *Black Issues Book Review* which reminded us of all of the people readers became familiar with as some of the greatest "powers behind Black books.

Angela has been a journalist for more than 25 years, primarily as a newspaper editor and more recently as a free-lance editor, writer, consultant. Angela has also done free-lance work for such publications as *Essence* and *BET Weekend*, as well as consulting for the Maynard Institute for Journalism Education and the *Raleigh News & Observer* job fair.

A former senior editor and Style editor for the *New York Times*, Angela has also worked for the *Charleston Gazette*, the *Huntington Advertiser*, the *Gannett News* Service in Washington, D.C., the *Rochester Times-Union*, the *Washington Star* and the *Louisville Courier-Journal*.

A graduate of Marshall University, Angela is a trustee of the university's Chuck Yeager Scholars Program. She has a master's degree in journalism and public affairs from the American University in Washington, D.C.

Carol Mackey

Carol Mackey is the Editor for *Black Expressions* Book Club. The publication is one of the most beautiful showcases of Black literature reaching over a half million readers, and readily featured with ads in publications like *Essence* Magazine. *Black Expressions* Book Club has also headlined on the famous AALBC.com since its inception.

The books featured in *Black Expressions* Book Club continue to rise up the charts and straight to number one. *Black Expressions* Book Club is a phenomenon and many people may not realize that without it, many new titles would go unnoticed. *Black Expressions* focuses on contemporary and classic African-American fiction plus a wealth of titles in key areas such as heritage & culture, inspiration/religion, health and beauty, relationships, cooking and home, career and personal finance, self-help, kid's books and more!

In continuing with the legacy of the club founded by Juanita James, former vice president of the Literary Guild and Monica Harris, Carol Mackey has helped bring African American Literature to the masses. *Black Expressions* was voted "Book Club of the Year" at the 2004 African American Literary Awards Show held in Harlem, New York.

Carol Rogers & Brenda Piper

Carol Rogers and Brenda Piper are the "Book Ladies of Queens" who began their reign as street vendors and wound up helping many literary artists. They sell their books on the streets, on their popular website, www. CBBooksDistribution.com, at renowned events, fairs and expos like Circle of Sisters and Harlem Book Fair, and at their very own Annual Queens Book Fair.

Carol and Brenda do more than promote authors, they honor and recognized self-published authors, with limited budgets, at the beginning of their literary careers. Many of those authors have gone on to become mainstream and reach "best-selling" status. Carol and Brenda always sent inspirational messages and support to authors. Even when their store front burned down. they were able to recuperate and reopen a stand at the Queens Farm Market with thousands of visitors each day.

A long way from a humble start, many authors who appreciated C& B Book Distribution's sincere efforts to promote authors, have now returned to the annual fair that brings out authors and attendees from all over the country. Carol and Brenda's forte is supporting Urban Fiction. Authors like Cynthia D. Hunter and Shannon Holmes have acquired major book deals, the list goes on. Their PR and Media Relations Director, Phil Andrews, continues to make C& B Book Distribution a visible resource on the net for those seeking African-American literature and diverse books that are favorites in the Black community. (www.Cbbooksdistribution.com)

Carole F. Hall

Carole F. Hall consults with established authors, agents, publishers, and organizations on select book publishing projects. During her twenty-year-plus career as a New York editor and publishing executive, Carole guided hundreds of authors through the creative and business process of trade publishing. Her books were cited for excellence by the American Library Association, the American Book Awards, the New York Times (Notable Books of the Year), the NAACP Image Awards, and Publishers Weekly (Best Books of the Year). Her noted authors included actress Ruby Dee; South African musical legend Miriam Makeba; pioneering African American psychologists and researchers Dr. Gail Elizabeth Wyatt and Dr. A.J. Franklin; Yale psychiatrist and educator Dr. James P. Comer; Hurston/ Wright award-winning biographer Paul Robeson, Jr.; and Metropolitan opera star Shirley Verrett.

At John Wiley & Sons, Inc., Carole established publishing alliances and partnerships with the Dana Foundation, the San Francisco Exploratorium, Amber Books, *Black Enterprise* Magazine, the Schomburg Center for Research in Black Culture of the New York Public Library, the Anacostia Museum and Center for African American History and Culture of the Smithsonian Institution, *Black Issues Book Review, Black Issues in Higher Education*, and many other major publications and institutions.

Carole joined Wiley in 1992 as Associate Publisher, was subsequently named Associate Publisher and Editor-in-Chief, and retired in 2003 as Editor-in-Chief of African American interest books. Previously, she served as Executive Editor of Touchstone Books, Simon & Schuster, Inc. (1987-1992). Beginning her career in the subsidiary rights group at Lippincott & Crowell/Harper& Row (now HarperCollins), Carol rose through the editorial ranks to the position of Senior Editor at New American Library (Plume, Mentor, Signet, and NAL imprints, 1980-1987).

A graduate of Stanford University (BA in English, 1967) and a former educator (certified by the Graduate Internship Program in Education, University of California, Berkeley 1969), Carol served for over a decade on the faculty of the Stanford Professional Publishing Course and on the Humanities and Sciences Council of Stanford University.

Her current memberships include the Women's Media Group of New York City; the Friends of Education of the New York Museum of Modern Art; the Links Incorporated; and the African American Experience Fund of the National Park Foundation, of which she is a Trustee. Carole is married to corporate executive Ira D. Hall. They live in Stamford, Connecticut, and have two adult daughters.

Cherise Davis

Cherise Davis is the Senior Editor of Touchstone/ Fireside/ Simon & Schuster. She edited the bestselling novel, God's Gift to Woman (Touchstone, 2003) by Michael Baisden, who is the author of *Never Satisfied: How & Why Men Cheat, Men Cry in the Dark,* and *The Maintenance Man,* which was a national and *Essence* magazine bestseller.

Cherise is also the creator of "HappilySingle.com" and radio host of the nationally syndicated radio show, "The Michael Baisden Show" on 98.7KissFM. Cherise continues to edit a variety of bestsellers.

Cheryl Woodruff

Cheryl Woodruff founded One World in 1991 with four other African American women at Ballantine in order to help give rise to works by authors of diverse cultures. Cheryl became the associate publisher of One World and vice-president of Ballantine Books. It was there that she edited and published dozens of bestsellers.

Clara Villarosa

In the 1980s, as the first African American to serve on the board of the American Booksellers Association (ABA), Clara Villarosa founded a black booksellers group within the organization. Through her work on the board and in her own bookstore, she has become a pioneer in the black bookselling community over the past two decades.

In 2000, after sixteen years of owning her HueMan Bookstore in Denver, Clara sold her business, retired, and moved to New York to be closer to her two daughters and grandchildren. Initially, Clara had no plans to start another bookstore when she moved, but she couldn't ignore the case for opening one right in the heart of Harlem. "The location chose me," she says, explaining that she was approached by community leaders. She said "yes" even though she was she was retired, because it provided her with an opportunity to put together a bookstore that she felt was possible and could work.

Clara knew that she would need to raise some capital, so she found a way to finance her project with two partners, Rita Ewing, former wife of basketball star Patrick Ewing, and Celeste Johnson, wife of former New York Knick Larry Johnson, both of whom she met through public relations executive Terrie Williams. The three women combined their own money and secured a $475,000 loan from the Upper Manhattan Empowerment

Zone, a program that also provided funding for other businesses in the Harlem USA complex. With nearly a million dollars in capital raised, the partners signed a 10-year lease on the 4,000-square-foot store.

Clara's new Hue-Man Bookstore was hailed as a major development in a revitalized Harlem. Maya Angelou, Stevie Wonder, Wesley Snipes, Ashford and Simpson, Jay-Z, Ruby Dee and Ossie Davis all showed up for the store's opening August 1, 2002. *National Public Radio,* the *New York Daily News,* the *Amsterdam News, Newsday* and *Publisher's Weekly* all covered the store's opening.

In 2005, five years after the successful launch of the HueMan Bookstore in Harlem, Clara announced her retirement from bookselling (this time she's keeping her word). The retired grandmother plans to continue her work with the black booksellers group and the ABA. The annual conference, which features the book publishing industry's leading African American authors and publisher, continues to be held during Book Expo America. (Cited from *Black Issues Book Review)*

Dawn Davis

Dawn Davis is the editor-in-chief of Amistad Books. She is the editor of the Pulitzer Prize winner, *The Known World* by Edward P. Jones (Published by Amistad, 2004). *The Known World* has gone on to reach several bestselling top lists. By March 18, 2006, it reached number 486 on Amazon.com. *The Known World* was also selected as an Oprah Book Club Pick.

Denise Stinson

Denise Stinson is the publisher of Walk Worthy Press, a Christian publisher whose ministry is dedicated to showing, through books, how the Word of God in the Bible can be applied to every area of our daily lives.. She is also a highly successful literary agent who has represented high profile authors such as: Queen Latifah, T.D. Jakes, CeCe Winans, Pearl Cleage, Iyanla Vanzant.

Denise launched Walk Worthy Press in 1997 out of her own desire to read Christian fiction that she could not find elsewhere. She partnered with Warner Books to release Walk Worthy's first novel, Temptation by Victoria Christopher Murray, in 2000. Presenting material on the tough issues that African American Christians face every day, Walk Worthy, based in Michigan, is the No. 1 publisher of Christian novels by African American authors.

Denise, a Cleveland native, also serves as editor-at-large at Warner Books.

Emma Rodgers

Emma Rodgers is the co-owner of Black Images Book Bazaar in Dallas. She has been an instrumental force in the publishing industry, as a bookseller and for the implementation of book club meetings and special events in her store. Emma co-founded "Romance Slam Jam", for which the Emma Award was established. Winners have included many well-known best-selling authors. Emma is also the

co-president for the African American Publishing Industry Conference at Book Expo America.

Faith Childs

Faith Childs is a well notes literary agent who has worked with authors such as Valerie Wilson Wesley, Benilde Little and Ralph Wiley to name a few. She is able to get author's works in front of acquisition editors and specializes in all genres from non-fiction to fiction.

Faye Childs

Faye Childs created a list of top bestselling books by African American authors, based on Black bookstores' sales figures and founded *Blackboard Bestsellers* in 1991. The list soon became a reference for all booksellers and was featured in Essence magazine's book review section. Her work has brought excitement to the literary world and gives authors a forum to present their titles and gain national notoriety.

Faye also co-produces and hosts award shows and plans other special events that involve authors, publishers, book clubs and other book industry professionals. Authors and publishers from around the country aspire to be recipients of BlackBoard Bestsellers annual awards program.

Faye is the co-author of *Going Off: A Guide for Black Women Who've Just About Had Enough,* co-written with her sister Noreen Palmer to help black women channel their anger in a way that will benefit them rather than consume them.

Faye is also the publisher of the BlackBoard National Provider (The BNP), the first African American daily Newspaper in America, which debuted at Book Expo 2006. The BlackBoard WordStar Awards Television Show premiered November 2nd, 2006 in Hollywood, California.

Gwen Richardson

Gwen Richardson is the founder of CushCity.com along with her husband, Willis Richardson. CushCity opened in 1998 and has become one of the leading Black commerce websites offering a variety of items from books and gifts to DVD's and music.

In 2006, the couple organized an "Author of Year" Awards program that attracted literary artists nationwide and received over three thousand votes. The selections were narrowed to twenty with hopes of one author winning a free trip on a Cush City Cruise. Gwen and Willis strive to keep Black products in the forefront, many of which are unavailable or difficult to find in stores. Visitors of CushCity.com can always count on the commerce site for great products.

Heather Elitou

Neshee Publication™ was founded in January 2001 by Aalim and Heather Elitou, a husband and wife team also known as Neshee. Neshee means, "my other self, two, or better half." As each other's better half and other self, Aalim and Heather have placed their love, time and energy into forming a self-publishing company that focuses on the creative works of black writers/poets, helping them to become black voices of authority. Heather realized her vision of her authors emerging into mainstream publishing, when one of them Darshell DuBose Smith, was signed by Amber Books at the 1st YOUnity Guild Awards in New York. The Small Press Company's name has become synonymous with producing quality works. They have won the "Small Press of the Year 2005" award by Marguerite Press, as well as numerous other awards. Heather has groomed her daughter, Tweety, to follow in her footsteps with the release of a new title *Girl Power*. (www.NesheePublication.com).

Janet Hill

Janet Hill is the Vice President and Executive Editor of Doubleday. One of a handful, there are only five blacks holding Vice President status in any mainstream publishing establishment.

Prior to acquiring the position at Doubleday, Janet was the managing editor for the number-two book publisher in the nation. She's worked with books like *The Wedding* by Dorothy West and *How to Marry a Black Man* by Monique Gellerette DeJongh and Cassandra Cato-Louis, whose novel was optioned by Whitney Houston's film—production company. (cited from *Essence* magazine, March 1997).

During the Harlem Book Fair, Janet revealed that she had founded Harlem Moon, which explained why some of the greatest books are published under this imprint from authors like E. Lynn Harris, Connie Briscoe and Marita Golden. Janet's eye for excellence has landed her on magazine covers and major media, but yet she is a silent giant which proves that you don't have to have a loud voice to be one of the most powerful women in the publishing industry. A lady of grace, Janet Hill remains a role model for all literary industry professionals. She's a true mover and shaker who makes it happen.

Kim McLarin

Kim McLarin is a former reporter for the *Philadelphia Inquirer* and *New York Times*. She is the author of the novel *Jump In the Sun*, (William Morrow, Inc., 2006). She has also authored critically acclaimed books such as *Taming It Down, Meeting of the Waters* and has co-authored *Growing Up X* with Illyasah Shabazz.

L. Peggy Hicks

L. Peggy Hicks received her Business Degree from Cardinal Stritch College, in Milwaukee, Wisconsin. Peggy is the President/Owner of TriCom Publicity Inc., a Literary Publicity/Marketing and Internet Design company, which she founded in July 1995. Peggy opened the marketing & publicity division of TriCom in 1996, and has successfully worked with Avalon Publishing Group, Avon Books, Ballantine Books, Black Expressions, Carroll & Graf Publish-  ers, Dafina Books, Dutton Publishing, Fireside Books, Harper Collins, Hilton Publishing, I-Traffic, Judson Press, Kensington Publishing, Kensington-Strapless, Nation Books, New American Library, One World Books, Penguin Putnam, Pinnacle Books, Plume Publishing, Random House Publishing, Time Warner Bookgroup, Touchstone, Simon and Schuster, Inc., St. Martin's Press, St. Martin's-Griffin, St. Martin's-Mino-taur, Strapless Books, Strivers Row, Urban Books, Villard, WalkWorthy Press, William-Morrow Publishing, Zebra Books promoting over 200 authors including mainstream, African-American and Latino.

Winner of the Black Business Owner of the Year in 1996, and the Business Owner of the Year in 2001. Peggy is a technology columnist for the *Rockford Register Star* and a marketing columnist for the nationally syndicated *Black Board Bestsellers* Bi-Weekly. She was recently named one of the "50 Most Successful African-American's in the Publishing Industry, one of the Powers Behind Black Books", and was honored by the Memphis Black Writers Conference & Southern Film Festival receiving the "Best Literary Publicist" Award at the 8th Annual Conference's Award ceremony held in Memphis, TN. TriCom has created award winning web sites for businesses, artists, schools, not-for-profits, and organizations since 1995.

Linda Gill

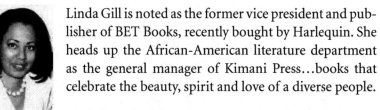

Linda Gill is noted as the former vice president and publisher of BET Books, recently bought by Harlequin. She heads up the African-American literature department as the general manager of Kimani Press…books that celebrate the beauty, spirit and love of a diverse people.

Linda launched the Kimani Press division at Harlequin, as well as its Sepia and New Spirit imprints. She is also responsible for the success of the Arabesque imprint, nationally known as the leading line of African-American romances. An award-winning imprint, Arabesque books are written by beloved African-American authors, many of whom have become bestsellers.

Lottie Gooding

Lottie Gooding is the vice-president of production for Simon & Schuster's Children's Publishing Division, which publishes over 450 children's titles a year. With a staff of ten, she deals with the nuts and bolts of getting a book out. Lottie consults editors and negotiates with bookbinders and printers as far away as Hong Kong and Colombia. The titles are among favorites at Children's Book Fairs and very popular in schools around the nation.

Malaika Adero

Malaika Adero is the Senior Editor of Atria Books/ Simon & Schuster. She's edited works by bestselling authors like Zane, Camille Cosby, Jewell Parker Rhodes, Tananarive Due and Vickie Stinger. Malaika is highly revered in the African—American Community for her work as a co-author of *Speak, So You Can Speak Again: The Life of Zora Neale Hurston* by Lucy Hurston (Doubleday, 2004). She has served on the Harlem Advisory Board and is one of the most influential editors on the market for her extreme professionalism and writing talent.

Malaika has been quoted saying, "You will work hard if you are in the publishing industry." She is a resource for guidance to many aspiring authors and has been featured in many media resources nationwide. Malaika is also, the author of *Up South: Stories, Studies and Letters of This Century's African American Migrations*.

Marie Brown

Marie Brown is a former Senior Editor of Doubleday. A well-regarded veteran in the publishing industry, her longevity is favorably noted, as the agent who opened doors for Black literary artists to gain publishing influence in mainstream publishing houses.

Marie, who is currently the head of Marie Brown & Associates, has represented many notable African American authors including: Susan Taylor, Editorial Director of *Essence* Magazine, Audrey Edwards, Leonard Pitts, Jr. and Michael Cottman.

Marilyn Ducksworth

Marilyn Ducksworth is the vice-president, associate publisher and executive director of publicity for Putnam Publishing Group, the second-largest English-language trade book publisher in the world.

Marilyn is the lady responsible for getting the word out about some 225 adult and children's titles annually. She supervises sixteen people and personally handles media campaigns for celebrities, such as: Bill Cosby, Patti LaBelle and author Tom Clancy.

Niani Colom

As Associate Publisher of Genesis Press Niani Colom with her father, Publisher, Wil Colom successfully carved out a niche for black romance novels when major publishing houses did not dare to venture down this avenue. In 1995 Genesis began publishing African-American romances in trade paperback under the Indigo Romance imprint. One of the first authors under the Indigo imprint was then emerging author, Donna Hill, who went on to publish multiple best-sellers under Genesis Press, Inc., St. Martin's Press, BET and Kensington/Dafina.

In 2004 Kensington Publishing Corporation became the sole distributor for Genesis Press, as part of an agreement that included all backlist Genesis Press titles and the approximately thirty new titles published annually.

Niani is also one of the co-founders (along with Adrienne Ingrum, former Associate Publisher of Black Issues Book Review and Tony Rose, Publisher/CEO of Amber Communications Group, Inc.) of the African American Pavilion at Book Expo America, a leading trade show for the book industry, which is responsible for uniting African American publishers as exhibitors from all over the country.

Oprah Winfrey

Oprah Winfrey is indeed, the "Most Powerful Woman on Earth." "As a supervising producer and host of the top-rated, award-winning *The Oprah Winfrey Show*, she has entertained, enlightened and uplifted millions of viewers for the past two decades. Her accomplishments as a television pioneer, producer, magazine founder, educator and philanthropist have established her as one of the most respected and admired public figures today." Oprah is also the founder and Editorial Director of *O, The Oprah Magazine* (Hearst, 2002), a monthly magazine that has become one of today's leading women's lifestyle publications with a circulation of 2.4 million readers.

Oprah has now marveled the world with a spin off, "O at home", helping to bring a personal style within the home to her readers.

Oprah's company, Harpo Films, has produced top films such as, "Their Eyes Were Watching God", starring Halle Berry and the critically acclaimed *Beloved*, based on the Pulitzer Prize-winning novel by Toni Morrison, which co-starred Oprah Winfrey and Danny Glover. Oprah made her acting debut in 1985 as "Sofia" in Steven Spielberg's *The Color Purple*, for which she received both Academy Award and Golden Globe nominations. She also has been lauded for her performances in the made-for-television movies *Before Women Had Wings* (1997), *There Are No Children Here* (1993), and *The Women of Brewster Place* (1989).

Within its first year, Oprah's Book Club quickly became the largest book club in the world, attracting more than 880,000 members.Oprah.com averages 64 million page views and more than three million users per month and receives approximately 12,000-15,000 emails each week.

Oprah also has developed schools to educate thousands of underserved children internationally and created "The Oprah Winfrey Scholars Program," which gives scholarships to students determined to use their education to give back to their communities in the United States and abroad. The Oprah Winfrey Foundation, she has awarded hundreds of grants to organizations that support the education and empowerment of women, children and families in the United States and around the world. Amongst her various philanthropic contributions, Oprah has donated millions of dollars toward providing a better education for students who have merit, but no means. She also has developed schools to educate thousands of underserved children internationally and created "The Oprah Winfrey Scholars Program," which gives scholarships to students determined to use their education to give back to their communities in the United States and abroad.

To date, Oprah's Angel Network has raised more than $50 million, with 100% of audience donations going to non-profit organizations across the globe. Oprah's Angel Network has helped establish scholarships and schools, support women's shelters and build youth centers and homes—changing the future for people all over the world. Oprah's commitment to children also led her to initiate the National Child Protection Act in 1991, when she testified before the U.S. Senate Judiciary Committee to establish a national database of convicted child abusers. On December 20, 1993, President Clinton signed the national "Oprah Bill" into law.

The Oprah Winfrey Show, consistently ranks second among all U.S. talk shows. Oprah is co-founder of Oxygen Media, which operates a 24-hour cable television network for women that launched in 1998 and is currently available in more than 57 million homes across America.

Twenty years after she made her movie debut as "Sofia" in *The Color Purple,* Oprah made her Broadway debut as a producer for the musical *The Color Purple,* which opened on December 1, 2005, at the Broadway Theatre in New York City. (Cited from www.Oprah.com)

Pamela Yvette Exum

Pamela has been a business consultant for over 10 years and has earned millions of dollars for her clients. She has always been self-employed, even before she earned her college degree. Her undergrad courses focused on Sociology and Nutrition, Consumer Economics, Speech, Computer Technology, Business Marketing, Meal Management, Human Anatomy & Physiology; she was also competitive in Gymnastics and Track.

Pamela developed an expertise in marketing from her entrepreneurial background and interest in the web because "it was fun". She admits that she could not afford to pay the exorbitant fees that many of the web development companies charged so she learned how to do web development herself, and became an expert at internet marketing.

Pamela Yvette Exum is the Founder/ Executive Director of Spirit of Sisterhood, Publisher and Producer of ALAYE' "Men of the Year" Calendar, Founder and Executive Director of GT Express / All American Superstars and Executive Director of the Michael Baisden Foundation.

(www.pyeinc.com).

Rachel Breton

Co-founder and Marketing Director of Jolie magazine, Rachel Breton is a woman who leads with ambition! As an innovative, enthusiastic, and accomplished marketing professional, Rachel Breton has over eight years of extensive corporate experience working for a top Fortune 500 financial services organization.

After earning a Master's of Business Administration degree specializing in Marketing Management, Rachel decided to leave the corporate world and pursue her lifelong dream of entrepreneurship. Rachel brings a wealth of knowledge to the Fabulush, Inc. team, allowing her to successfully leverage the skills and experience she has acquired throughout her career. With an open mind, diligent work ethic, and an ear always to the ground, Rachel is committed to help making Fabulush, Inc. an undeniable success!

Rachael also pens some of the most eloquent articles in the publication that have launched Jolie as the ultimate beauty magazine. (www. JolieLivePretty.com)

Rockelle Henderson

Former marketing director of Harper Collins, Rockelle Henderson, was promoted to the position of Associate Publisher of Amistad, Harper Collins in May 2005. Rochelle had been instrumental in marketing books by these establishments and came up with the idea of creating a video for Karrine Steffan's bestselling memoir, *Confessions of a Video Vixen.* The HarperCollins imprint scored heavy urban radio play, online buzz and bookstore events in conjunction with the Rockelle's Video Vixen marketing campaign.

Shunda Leigh

Shunda Leigh has been an instrumental icon in promoting literary artists. In November 2002, she founded *Booking Matters* magazine with her husband, Jamill, thus igniting a passion and love for literature. As the Editor-in-Chief of *Booking Matters Magazine,* Shunda continues to bring book clubs, bookstores and African American Authors to the forefront. Memphis Black Writers and Southern Film Festival awarded *Booking Matters Magazine* "Best New Literary Magazine" for 2004.

Shunda founded Circle of Friends II Book Club which lead to an appearance on The Oprah Winfrey Show. She hosts monthly events that promote literature. The literary world was so proud of Shunda's sponsored wedding, which was featured on ABC News Primetime in June 2004 and appeared in *Modern Bride Magazine.* She is a member of the DLNA Award forum, and has been featured in *Upscale, the Atlanta-Journal Constitution, Rejoice* and many newspapers, radio programs and media entities. Her warm spirit radiates to her audiences, who have heralded Shunda as a modern day legend of the literary world for her support of authors. (www.BookingMatters.com).

Susan McHenry

A native of Louisville, Kentucky, Susan McHenry earned a bachelor's with honors in American history and literature from Harvard-Radcliffe and a master's degree in literature from Boston University. She was a 1987-88 Knight-Bagehot Fellow in Business and Economics Journalism at Columbia University.

In April 2006, as part of a recent acquisition of *Black Issues Book Review* magazine, by Target Market News, Inc. Susan McHenry returned to her former position as Editorial Director.

Susan, who most recently served the magazine in the position of Editor-at-Large, was founding editor when the publication was launched in 1999. In her new post, she will oversee the development of editorial content for Black Issues Book Review, its Web site, www.bibookreview.com, and future news and information vehicles being planned by the company.

For more than 25 years, veteran journalist Susan McHenry has been a key editor at pioneering magazines and Web sites that have identified and served untapped reader sensibilities among African Americans and among women at large. In addition to heading the editorial team that launched *Black Issues Book Review* in 1999, she helped with the development of BIBR's Web site, bibookreview.com. That same year the publication was named one of the "Ten Best New Magazines" by the American Library Journal.

Susan spent nine years as an editor at *Ms.* magazine (1978-87), where she won a Newswomen's Club of New York Front Page Award for best magazine column for "Sally Hemmings: A Key to Our National Identity."

In 1989, Susan anchored the start-up editorial team of *Emerge* magazine under founder Wilmer Ames and helped build its franchise as a respected monthly magazine of news analysis and commentary from an African American perspective.

She has also been a senior editor at *Working Woman* magazine (1993-95) and executive editor of *The Quarterly Black Review of Books* (1995-96, now known as *QBR*), as well as contributing editor to *women.com*, a Web magazine for women that merged into iVillage.com.

Susan is also a contributing writer to *ESSENCE* magazine, with which she has worked in various capacities since 1997.

Susan, who lives in Brooklyn, New York, is also a member of the National Association of Black Journalists, the Women's Media Group and the American Society of Magazine Editors. Widely interviewed in all media (print, TV, radio and online), she has taught as an adjunct professor at New York University and New York City College of Technology, and currently teaches writing at Brooklyn's Medgar Evers College, CUNY. (Cited from www.bibookreview.com)

Susan Taylor

Susan Taylor, the Editorial Director of *Essence* Magazine, has been the driving force behind one of the most celebrated African American owned business success stories of the past three decades. She rose up through the ranks with the kind of integrity to be admired and respected by many people of diverse cultures. She

Susan oversees the editorial operations of the *Essence* magazine and writes the popular *In the Spirit* column each month. A fourth-generation entrepreneur, Susan was the founder of her own company, Nequai Cosmetics, before becoming *Essence magazine*'s fashion and beauty editor and, in 1981, its editor-in-chief.

She is the author of three books: *In the Spirit: The Inspirational Writings of Susan L. Taylor, Lessons in Living* and *Confirmation: The Spiritual Wisdom That Has Shaped Our Lives*, the latter co-authored with her husband, Khephra Burns. In 1999 Susan became the first African American woman to receive The Henry Johnson Fisher Award from the Magazine Publishers of America, the magazine industry's highest honor.

In 2002, Susan was inducted into the American Society of Magazine Editors' (ASME) Hall of Fame, which celebrates the career-long records of excellence, creativity and impact of a select group of highly influential magazine journalists. She is a member of the National Association of Black Journalists and the American Society of Magazine Editors. Susan is an avid supporter of a host of organizations dedicated to moving the Black community forward, serving as a member of the Commission on Research in Black Education, among others. She is personally committed to serving and empowering the poor and to working with disadvantaged women and teenagers to help them realize their strengths and take charge of their lives.

Susan Taylor is currently co-chair of a capital campaign with Danny Glover to raise money to build housing in the rural areas of South Africa. (Cited from www.Essence.com)

Sybil Wilkes

Sybil Wilkes is one of the most popular ladies on radio. The native Chicagoan attended Northwestern University where she received a B.S. in Political Science and Communication Studies. She began her radio career in 1985 as a production assistant with WKQX-FM, Chicago then eventually went on to news management and reporting jobs. In 1989 Sybil joined WGCI AM/FM in Chicago as a talk show host. A year later, she became a reporter for Chicago's Traffic Network and worked as one of Tom Joyner's sidekicks. As the news anchor of the Tom Joyner Morning Show, she always gives book  "shout outs" to many authors, a gesture which has been instrumental in driving sales of books to a massive audience.

Sybil has received a number of accolades including "The President's Award" from the NAACP Image Awards and an honorary Doctorate Degree from Bennett College in Greensboro, North Carolina.

Tee C. Royal

Tee C. Royal is the founder of one of the largest African-American online book clubs, the "Reading and Writing SISTAZ" (RAWSISTAZ), and their team of reviewers, the "RAWSISTAZ Reviewers" (TRR). Since its inception, the RAWSISTAZ website has become a major resource for readers, writers, and literary enthusiasts with a repository of more than 3000 reviews. The reviewers are highly respected in literary circles and sought out for book reviews and promotion of African American titles. They have reviewed major, small-press, and self-published titles. In addition, RAWSISTAZ has local chapters in major cities across the United States, to include Atlanta, New York, Memphis, and Chicago.

Very active in the literary community, Tee is the Vice-President and Webmistress for "Authors Supporting Authors Positively", a web-mistress for several other literary websites and authors, and a freelance reader, proofreader and reviewer. In addition to leading her own team of 15 reviewers, she reviews professionally for several online and print magazines, is a member of a host of literary organizations, and frequents literary conferences, where she has led or moderated topics on book clubs. She is knowledgeable about the African American literary industry and prides herself on their group motto, *"Keeping you In the Know regarding the African-American Literary community."*

In her former job, Tee was a Captain in the U.S. Air Force, specializing in the field of Software Development and Project Management. She resides in the suburbs of Atlanta with her husband and daughter. To contact Tee, you can reach her via the websites at (Rawsistaz.com and BlackBookReviews.net).

Vivian Stephens

Vivian Stephens is one of the top editors of modern Romance and one of the most powerful forces in the genre. She has edited for Harlequin, Dell (Candlelight Romances), Bantam and other publishers. Often referred to

as "the mother of contemporary romance", Vivian to the genre from the castles of European history to the contemporary American bedroom. It was Vivian who spearheaded the founding of Romance Writer's of Color to help authors write commercial fiction and get their foot in the door to mainstream publishers.

Yvonne Rose

Yvonne Rose is a driving force behind Amber Communications Group, Inc. along with her husband, Tony Rose. With Tony's persistence, she decided to co-write a book on modeling, which received rave reviews. *"Is Modeling for You? The Handbook and Guide for the Young Aspiring Black Model"* by Yvonne Rose and Tony Rose was the flagship book that launched Amber Books and became a "Top Ten National African-American Bookstore Pick" and a national bestseller.

Yvonne who has modeled in the United States and Europe and taught thousands of models how to get their foot in the door of the billion dollar modeling industry, is a silent literary queen who has helped pave the way for many of Amber Communications Group, Inc.'s titles.

Yvonne Rose is the Associate Publisher and Senior Editor of Amber Communications Group, Inc. (ACGI). ACGI's imprints include: Amber, Busta, Colossus, Ambrosia, Amber/Wiley and Amber Books2. AMBER COMMUNICATIONS GROUP, INC. (ACGI) is the nation's largest African-American publisher of self-help books and celebrity biographies.

Yvonne Rose has served as editor and co-editor of more than half of ACGI's catalogue, including: *Urban Suicide: The Enemy We Choose Not to See—Crisis in Black America; 101 Real Money Questions—The African-American Financial Question and Answer Book; Beautiful Black Hair; The*

Afrocentric Bride—A Styling Guide; Born Beautiful—The African-American Teenager's Complete Beauty Guide and *Wake Up and Smell the Dollars! Whose Inner City is This Anyway!*

In her spare time, Yvonne has ghost-written and co-written several top selling non-fiction titles, including: *Fighting for Your Life: The African American Criminal Justice Survival Guide* (Amber Books) by John Elmore, Esq.; *Led by the Spirit: A Sharecropper's Son Tells His Story of Love, Happiness, Success and Survival* (Strickland Books) by Robuster Strickland; and *Let Them Play…The Story of the MGAA* (MGAA Books) by John David

Prior to entering the book publishing industry, Ms. Rose worked as a publicist and fashion and beauty editor for several national magazines, such as: *Sophisticate's Black Hair Care, Unique Hair and Beauty, Black Elegance* and *CLASS*; she is also an award-winning journalist with regular features appearing in *Kip's Business Report, Network Journal* and *Harlem News*.

ACGI's publisher Tony Rose is the recipient of several awards, including: the Chicago Black Book Fair and Conference Independent Publisher/ Press Award and the BlackBoard BestSeller's 2003 African-American Publisher of the Year Award. ACGI is celebrating its eighth year of successful book publishing. In January 2006 Amber Communications Group, Inc.s' publishers were featured in a *Black Issues Book Review* article "The Powers Behind Black Books—Large and In-Charge".

Yvonne is also one of the top requested authors for public speaking appearances. She is the brainchild behind the name "Katrina Literary Collective", which was conceived by Tony Rose when he decided to take charge of the situation following Hurricane Katrina by rallying together thousands of African American book publishers, librarians, bookstores, authors and everday people throughout the United States. Tony Rose, partnered with Black Issues Book Review, Disilgold and several other African Americans in the book industry, as the Katrina Collective and together they raised 70,000 books in a drive to send books to those displaced by the Gulf Coast hurricane.

A big sister to authors and so many literary artists, Yvonne is a living legacy who will go down in history as someone who truly helped to build

a publishing company from the bottom to the very top. She is living proof that "when one believes, one can achieve." Like Iman, Tyra Banks and Naomi Campbell, Yvonne Rose was destined to be a super model, but like Coretta Scott King, stayed by her husband to help build one of the most successful African-American publishing companies in America's history. Yvonne is a giving person who has shown others what it takes to be a success, and that is "Just be you, stay committed, and genuinely support others from the heart."

For further information, contact Ms. Rose at amberbks@aol.com or visit WWW.AMBERBOOKS.COM.

Part Three

Literary Divas Gone Too Soon

Alice Childress

(October 12, 1916—August 14, 1994)

Alice Childress was born to a working-class black family in Charleston, South Carolina. Her Parents separated when Alice was 9, and she moved to Harlem to live with her maternal grandmother, who though not formally educated, encouraged Childress' talent in reading and writing. Childress attended public school in New York City for her middle and high school education, showing significant potential in her literary work and self-expression.

Alice Childress attended Radcliffe Institute and by 1968, she had established herself as a Harvard scholar and writer. Her books include: *Like One of the Family: Conversations from a Domestic's Life* (1956); *A Hero Ain't Nothing But a Sandwich* (1973); *A Short Walk* (1979); *Rainbow Jordan* (1981); and *Many Closets* (1987). By the 1980's, she had written a play based on the life of the black woman comedian Jackie "Moms" Mabley, which was produced in New York City. Her play *Trouble in Mind* won the Obie Award in 1956 as the best original off-Broadway production. Other plays include: *Florence* (one-act play); *Gold Through the Trees; Just a Little; Trouble in Mind; Wedding band; Wine in the Wilderness*; and *When the Rattlesnake Sounds: A Play About Harriet Tubman*. In 1982, her book, *Rainbow Jordan* for young people published.

Alice's legacy will always be her compassionate but realistic portrayal of both blacks and whites—and their relationships—in plays, novels, and shorter prose. Alice was awarded the Paul Robeson Award for Outstanding Contribution to the Arts for her continued work in a multitude of literary mediums. Not only is her work critically acclaimed, it also helped to raise awareness about important issues such as equal rights for minorities, women's opportunities, and the importance of art and storytelling in society. In her later years, Alice lectured at Fisk University and Radcliffe.

Even to the end of her days, Alice was dedicated to literature. When she passed away, she was working on a story about her African great-grandmother, who had been a slave. Alice Childress' literary legacy will be remembered, both on the page and on the stage.

Coretta Scott King

(April 27, 1927-January 31, 2006)

Coretta Scott King, born April 27, 1927, was the wife and backbone of Reverend Dr. Martin Luther King. The world heard about her sudden death, at only 78 years of age, at Santa Monica Hospital, in Baja California, Mexico around 1:00am on January 31, 2006. Coretta's body was respectfully returned to her home in Atlanta to lay side by side with her late husband. Her health had progressively worsened due to a former stroke and heart attack.

Coretta became a symbol of the Civil Rights Movement and advocate of women's rights in South Africa. Dr. Martin Luther King and Coretta Scott King's love for each other was indeed remarkable, but on April 4, 1968, the young reverend who fought for Civil Rights was assassinated. Mrs. King founded the Martin Luther King Jr. Center for Non-Violent Social Change in Atlanta.

She also held the torch to continue the legacy of Dr. Martin Luther King by forming a March that would lead to a national holiday in his commemoration. Congress approved an official federal holiday in honor of Dr. King to be celebrated the third Monday in January, he was born January 15, 1929.

Coretta's autobiography, *My Life With Martin Luther King, Jr.* (Henry Holt & Co, 1993) documents her story in her own words.

Gwendolyn Brooks

(June 7, 1917-December 3, 2003)

Gwendolyn Brooks was born on June 7, 1917 in Topeka, Kansas, and raised in Chicago, Illinois. She attended Hyde Park High, a leading school in the city attended mostly by white students, but soon transferred to Wendell Phillips, an all black school, before transferring to the integrated Englewood High School. Gwendolyn was graduated from Wilson Junior College on 1936.

Before graduating, she had acquired publishing of her very first poem, "Eventide", in *American Childhood Magazine*. This was a grand accomplishment for Gwendolyn, as well as her rich and diversified education, which would be the template of expression for her unique writing style and poetry works that earned her critical acclaim later on. Gwendolyn enjoyed focusing on the plight of urban families living in the south side of Chicago. Her focus and discipline in her craft was intoxicating and attractive to readers of her work.

A courageous writer, Gwendolyn authored more than twenty books of poetry and was inspired by her mentors Langston Hughes and James Weldon Johnson whom she had met in the 1930's. They both encouraged her to read various works of established authors like E. Cummings. She began to write poetry almost daily. By 1934 she had over 100 poems published in her weekly column for the *Chicago Defender*, a triumphant achievement for any poet at the time.

Marriage and having children were calling the avid poet. Gwendolyn married Henry Blakely in 1938, and in 1940, she gave birth to Henry. Jr. Eleven years later, in 1951 she birthed a little girl named Nora.

Her struggle to gain more recognition and support for her poetry led Gwendolyn to join a writing group which launched *Poetry: A Magazine of Verse*. In 1943, she won the Midwestern Writer's Conference Poetry Award. Finally, her dreams came true when in 1945 her first poetry book, *A Street in Bronzeville* was published by Harper and Row. In 1950, Gwendolyn was the first African-American woman to be awarded the Pulitzer Prize for her poetry work, *Annie Allen*.

Gwendolyn's biographical novels include: *Maud Martha* (1953), *Bronzeville Boys and Girls* (1956), and *In the Mecca* (1968). Her work received the American Academy of Arts and Letters award, the Frost Medal, a National Endowment for the Arts award, the Shelley Memorial Award, and fellowships from The Academy of American Poets and the Guggenheim Foundation. One of her greatest honors was receiving a personal invite from President John F. Kennedy to read at an annual Library of Congress poetry festival in 1962.

In 1963, Gwendolyn landed her first teaching job at Columbia College, where she taught poetry. She went on to teach creative writing at Northeastern Illinois University, Clay College of New York, Elmhurst College, Columbia University, and the University of Wisconsin. In 1967, upon attending the Fisk University Second Black Writers' Conference, she decided to get involved in the Black Arts movement. Gwendolyn's poetry had become more aggressive and controversy ensured that her involvement in the Black Arts movement may have caused her to deviate from her usual poetic style. However, she quickly won back the admiration of Chicagoans when she read "The Wall" for an unveiling celebration of the

"Chicago Picasso" in 1967. Gwendolyn's speech was so poignant and riveting, the townspeople invited her to honor a dedication for the entire mural stretch known as "The Wall of Respect."

In 1968 Gwendolyn was named "Poet Laureate" for the state of Illinois. In 1985 to 1986 she was appointed as a poetry consultant for the Library of Congress; and in 1994, she was awarded with a humanities award issued by the Federal government as a selected Jefferson Lecturer of the National Endowment for the Humanities.

To this day, Gwendolyn's work, which includes all forms of poetry, from ballads, sonnets, variations of the Chaucerian style, rhythmical patterns reflecting the Blues & Jazz Era, plus her experimentation with narrative, free verse and lyrical poetry, affirmed the growth of her writing style and reflection of the people from her community in Chicago's south side.

Gwendolyn also loved to write about bold heroes and survival. In 2003, Pam Osbey, the winner of the Gwendolyn Brooks' Estate Award, shared her amazing triumph in front of hundreds of guests at the 1ˢᵗ YOUnity Guild Awards Annual Gala Celebration. As a participant in the Chicago Anthology Project, a 1000 page work featuring many poets influenced by the dynamic poetess, Pam lives on the memory of Gwendolyn Brooks.

Reference Resource
∾ *The Oxford Companion to African-American Literature.* Copyright © 1997 by Oxford University Press.

A Timeline of the Literary Diva's Published Work
∾ 1991—The David Co.1991—Children Coming Home
∾ 1988—Winnie
∾ 1987—To Disembark
∾ 1987—Blacks
∾ 1986—The Near-Johannesburg Boy and Other Poems
∾ 1983—Very Young Poets
∾ 1981—Primer for Blacks
∾ 1981—Black Love
∾ 1981—Young Poet's Primer
∾ 1975—Beckonings

- 1975—A Capsule Course in Black Poetry Writing1972—Aurora
- 1972—Report from Part One: An Autobiography
- 1971—Aloneness
- 1971—Black Steel: Joe Frazier and Muhammad Ali
- 1971—The World of Gwendolyn Brooks
- 1970—Family Pictures
- 1969—Riot
- 1968—In the Mecca
- 1967—The Wall
- 1966—We Real Cool
- 1963—Selected Poems
- 1960—The Bean Eaters1956—Bronzeville Boys and Girls
- 1953—Maud Martha; Novel
- 1949—Annie Allen
- 1945—A Street in Bronzeville

Lorraine Hansberry

(1930-1965)

Lorraine Hansberry was born in Chicago in 1930. She attended the Chicago's Art Institute, the University of Wisconsin, and then went to Guadalajara, Mexico to study art. Lorraine's creativity would be the template for an award-winning play called *Raisin in the Sun*, which she wrote while living in New York. March 11, 1959 *Raisin in the Sun* opened on Broadway, a milestone accomplishment for a play featuring Blacks...the entire production was produced and directed by Blacks with an all Black cast.

Sydney Poitier put his classic touch on *Raisin,* by starring in the movie adaptation. It was then adapted into the musical *Raisin,* and won a Tony Award in 1974. Lorraine managed to produce another Broadway play, *The Sign in Sidney Brustein's Window.* However, fate would take its course during the prime of Lorraine's life when she succumbed to cancer on January 12, 1965 at the age of 35. .

Lorraine's other works include: *To Be Young, Gifted and Black; The Movement; Documentary of a Struggle for Equality;* and *Les Blancs: The Collected Last Plays of Lorraine Hansberry.*

Octavia Butler

(June 22, 1947—February 24, 2006)

Octavia Butler (1947-2006) may have very well been one of the most prolific science fiction writers of our time. She died at 58 after falling and striking her head on a walkway outside her home in Lake Forest Park. She had developed high blood pressure and succumbed to the adverse effects of medications.

Octavia's most popular work is *Kindred*, a time-travel novel in which a black woman is transported back to the violent days of slavery before the Civil War. Her 1979 novel became a must—read in colleges throughout the world. *Kindred* was rejected by numerous publishers; but she remained persistent until she was offered a $5,000 advance for the novel, and the rest is history. Octavia was known to be very reclusive, but did come out for writing conferences.

Octavia also published the *Parable of the Talents*, winner of one of her two Nebula Awards in science fiction. She also received a "Genius Grant" from the John D. and Catherine T. MacArthur Foundation, a quarter million dollar cash prize.

Octavia changed the face of Sci-fi. Her potential for writing more top of the line books came to an end, and leaves daunting memories of someone who was truly the best at her genre.

Rosa Parks

(February 4, 1913—October 24, 2005)

December 1, 1955, a black seamstress by the name of Rosa Parks refused to relinquish her seat to a white man on a city bus in Montgomery, Alabama. She was arrested and convicted of violating the segregation laws, resulting in Black people boycotting the buses in protest of the Jim Crow laws. Rosa's arrest became a factor in resulting actions by Martin Luther King, Jr. who became a civil rights leader.

Many people made up reasons why Rosa did not get up from her seat, but the truth was, she was tired of the humiliation of Black people and their being treated as less than equal human beings. Rosa Parks and her husband became very involved in a local Montgomery N.A.A.C.P. chapter. Later she was described as "the mother of the civil rights movement". Before she was arrested, she had kept herself busy by planning workshops for teenagers.

In her book, Quiet Strength, (ZondervanPublishingHouse, 1994) Rosa stated, "I kept thinking about my mother and my grandparents, and how strong they were. I knew there was a possibility of being mistreated, but an opportunity was being given to me to do what I had asked of others."

After a 381-day Montgomery bus boycott, the Supreme Court ruled in November 1956 that segregation on transportation is unconstitutional.

Many years later, Rosa accepted her honor as the "Mother of the Civil Rights Movement", but insisted that there were others who helped the cause. A gracious and forgiving soul, when she was attacked and robbed by a Black man in 1994 in Detroit, she said, "I pray for this young man and the conditions in our country that have made him this way. Despite the violence and crime in our society, we should not let fear overwhelm us. We must remain strong."

The Rosa and Raymond Parks Institute Family entrusted Swanson Funeral Home, Inc. in Detroit Michigan, to lay to rest Rosa Parks at the McGuire Funeral Home. Her cause was upgraded as "the Mother of the Modern Day Civil Rights." Honorary pallbearers included Muhammad Ali, Senator Hillary Rodham Clinton, Bill Cosby, Ruby Dee, Coretta Scott King, Spike Lee, Cicely Tyson, Oprah Winfrey, The National Association For Advancement of Colored People. Alpha Kappa Alpha Sorority, Inc., the Congressional Black Caucus, and Reverend Jesse Jackson.

Shirley Chisholm

(November 30, 1924-January 3, 2005)

Shirley Chisholm was born in Bedford-Stuyvesant on Nov. 30, 1924. She received her Master's Degree in elementary education at Columbia University. She, then, became a director of the Friends Day Nursery in the Brownsville section of Brooklyn and the Hamilton-Madison Child Care Center in Lower Manhattan. Shirley decided to run for the New York State Assembly in 1964, and was subsequently elected to the U.S. House of Representatives in 1968.

Shirley was an advocate for minority rights. She became the first black woman elected to Congress and later the first black person to seek a major party's nomination for the U.S. presidency. The Reverend Jesse Jackson has been quoted, naming Shirley Chisholm a "woman of great courage."

Shirley died on January 3, 2005. She's had mentioned that she'd like people to say she had guts! (Cited from www. DigitalLiberty.com)

Zora Neale Hurston

(1903—January 28,1960)

Zora Neale Hurston was born in 1903. A maid, who traveled north with a Gilbert and Sullivan company, Zora managed to attend Morgan State, Howard University and Columbia University. She soon met Alain Locke at Howard University and began writing short stories about "opportunity" and

"achieving success". Zora landed a job with Langston Hughes and Wallace Thurman as an editorial assistant for *Fire* Magazine. She had no idea that these days would establish her as Harlem Renaissance icon to be admired in the future.

Zora published *Jonah's Gourd Vine* (1934) and soon afterwards, a novel, *Their Eyes Were Watching God, Mules and Men* (1935), and *Tell My Horse* (1938). *By 1939, she published Moses, Man of the Mountain,* her autobiography; *Dust Tracks on a Road* (1942), and *Seraph on the Swanee* (1948). It would take over 30 years for her autobiography to be considered for reprinting, along with the restoration of several missing pages.

Zora's life was semi—told in the movie depiction of Zora, played by Oscar winner, Halle Berry and produced by Oprah, primarily because no one really understood her lifestyle. By January 28, 1960 when Zora died, it was said that her last days as a Dramatist professor at North Carolina College may have enveloped her final reclusive ways. Today, her story, along with five other works have been restored and reprinted for millions of readers to enjoy. Her work is a much-referred topic for courses in universities.

Bibliography of Suggested Readings & Resources

Books

A Century of Fiction by American Negroes, 1853-1952: A Descriptive Bibliography. Philadelphia: Albert Saifer Publisher, 1969.

African American Writers: A Dictionary. Ed. Shari Dorantes Hatch & Michael Strickland. Santa Barbara, CA: ABC-CLIO, 2000.

Afro American Writers Before the Harlem Renaissance. Ed. Trudier Harris. Detroit: Gale Research Inc., 1986.

Afro American Writers From the Harlem Renaissance to 1940. Ed. Trudier Harris. Detroit: Gale Research Inc., 1987.

Black American Feminisms. A Multidisciplinary Bibliography compiled by Sherri L. Barnes, Associate Librarian at University of California Santa Barbara.

Post Colonial African Writers. Ed. Pushpa Naidu Parekh & Siga Fatima Jagne. Connecticut: Greenwood Press, 1998.

Slavery and the Making of America by James Oliver Horton and Lois E. Horton: Oxford University Press, 2005.

The Collected Poems of Langston Hughes by Arnold Rampersad: Alfred A. Knopf, 2001.

The Disilgold Way: Countdown 101 From Writer to Self-Publisher by Heather Covington: Indiana, AuthorHouse, 2005.

Twentieth-century Caribbean and Black African Writers. First series. Ed. Bernth Lindfors & Reinhard Sander. Detroit: Gale Research Inc., 1992.

Twentieth-century Caribbean and Black African Writers. Second series. Ed. Bernth Lindfors & Reinhard Sander. Detroit: Gale Research Inc., 1993.

Twentieth-century Caribbean and Black African Writers. Third series. Ed. Bernth Lindfors & Reinhard Sander. Detroit: Gale Research Inc., 1996.

Website Resources For Comprehensive Biographies

AALBC.com

About.com

AmberBooks.com

Ask Jeeves.com

Awarenessmagazine.net

AmberBooks.com

BlackExpression2005.com

Book-Remarks.com

BooksthatClick.com

CBBooksdistribution.com

Digital.nypl.org

DistinguishedWomen.com

Gale.com

GoOnGirl.com

imdb.com

Litencyc.com

MosaicBooks.com

QBR.com

Questia. com

TheBlackLibrary.com

Wikepedia.com

About the Author

Heather Covington received her B.A. in Early Childhood Education and dual M.S. as a Certified Reading Specialist in English at Hunter University. A passionate teacher who enjoys facilitating children's reading instruction with her fail-safe techniques and a dash of poetry that teaches integrity and self-respect, she brings her love for books and celebration of historical people to her everyday lessons.

As a youth, she discovered the works of Langston Hughes and Rosa Guy. She was inspired to write poetry and songs daily to escape the harsh realities of her tough urban environment. In the fourth grade, she won an award in history, her favorite subject. The result was a personal trademarked style of poetry entitled PerSOULnalities™ and symbolic of her motto, "In life, everyone must face negativity and knock it down to move on."

Heather Covington is now the author and owner of the *PerSOULnalities*™ Book Series 1, 2 & 3 (2001, Disilgold) *PerSOULnalities:*™ *Poems* for Every Kind of Woman (2002, Author House; Revised 2003), *PerSOULnalities:*™ *Poems For Every Kind of Man* (2003, Author House; Revised 2005), *Li'l PerSOULnalities:*™ *A Children's Book For Parents & Teachers* (2003, Author House; Revised 2005).

She has also authored *The Disilgold Way: Countdown 101 From Writer to Self Publisher* (2003, Author House; Revised 2005), *God's 24 Hour Makeover: 24 Power Moves to Joy* (2006, Disilgold), *Literary Divas:* ™ *The Top 100+ Most Admired Women in African American Literature* (2006, Amber Books), *Literary Dons:*™ *The Top 100+ Most Admired Men in African American Literature* (2006, Amber Books),and hundreds of independent titles distributed and published exclusively by the Disilgold imprint, PerSOULnalities™ Books.

Heather's works have been noted as "Impressive & Intelligent Work!" by Writer's Digest Awards; "The Most original poetry work of our time" by Culture Plus Books; "Undeniable" by Bestselling author, Hope C. Clarke;

"a young and powerful voice that will enlarge the scope of poetry" by Cliff Chandler of WGMN-TV 64 UPN; and a "A star bright personality!" by Dale Benjamin Drakeford, founder of Bronx Poetry Workshop.

Heather's marketing abilities are well known, as a promoter, educator, producer, and editor—in-chief of Disilgold Soul Literary Review. Known as "The HEAT of the Literary World," for her award winning photojournalism, motivational speaking seminars, media coverage of historical events, and poetical activist voice, She is the founder of Disilgold, a Bronx publishing, publicity and awards based business founded in 2001. Disilgold is revered as the number one African-American "Literary & Media Infused Network" and home of the Annual YOUnity Guild "Literary & Media Infusionary™ Awards Gala.

Heather launched www. Disilgold.com 2001, with a mission in mind to provide a promotional literary haven for booklovers and literary artists from multi-faceted industries. She founded Disilgold based on her 5 Principles of Success Formula including: Dedication to one's mission statement; Professionalism; Quality; Integrity; Service to the YOUnity Guild of America.

Heather also debuted the annual anniversary issue of Disilgold Soul Literary Review in print during 2003 with the overwhelming support of sponsors who believed in her mission. The publication, which was forwarded to over friends of the Disilgold network, received rave reviews.

Disilgold Soul, hosted by the Disilgold e-PressReleaseBlaster ™, became the first African-American literary e—publication. Heather launched her "Literary Dish Column", along with a pseudonym name, Heather "The Heat of the Literary World" Covington, which debuted for six months on the famous EURweb.com, QBR.com and the newly formed but very popular, Book Pitch.com.

Heather's live interviews have included, "Tony Rose, Omar Tyree, Terrie Williams, Sonia Sanchez, Nikki Giovanni, Haki Madhubuti, Rosa Guy, Ruby Dee, Donna Hill, Leslie Esdaille Banks, Tee C. Royal, Electa Rome Parks, Cynthia D. Hunter, Lettice Graham, Joe James, Mr. John Rainbow, Margie Gosa Shivers, Denise Campbell, Marc Lacy, Stacy-Deanne and many more renown figures in history.

In 2004, Heather produced the Harlem Book Fair's "Authors On Stage Tour", and had no problem booking top authors from every publishing company. A year later, Heather became Publicity Director of Harlem Book Fair, USA.

Heather has been featured on the Learning Channel, A PBS Documentary, BCATV, Manhattan Neighborhood Cable, 98.7 Kiss FM, 107.5 WBLS, AMAG, and appeared in a candid interview by Nicole Stevenson, which debuted on www. Oprah.com.

She has been written about in *SisterDivas* magazine, *Black Coffee* magazine, *The New York Beacon*, *Carib Life*, *Caribbean News*, *Harlem News*, *The Bronx Times*, *New York Amsterdam News*, Amber Books' *On the Move* newsletter, *QBR: Black Book Review*, *The Daily News*, *Dink Entertainment*, *CineSeven Entertainment*, *Rel Dowdell.com*, *Black Star News*, *Unity First;* and received honorable mentioned in *Black Issues Book Review*. Heather has also been sought by Paramount Studios for show ideas on the "Dr. Phil Show".

Annually, Heather produces the YOUnity Guild Awards, celebrates "August is Reading Marathon Month" to promote literacy, and sponsors a "Back-to-School Fall Jamboree Festival for Youth". She also serves as an advisory member and supporter of Harlem Book Fair, Circle of Sisters Expo, Spirit of Sisters Expo, Book Expo of America, Bronx Book Fair, Divine Literary Tour Queens Book Fair.

Her literary business has received numerous honorary awards and is noted as a Memphis Writer's Conference & Southern Film Festival Hall of Fame Award Recipient; C& B Book Distribution Best Website 2003 and 2004; Poetry Month Spotlight Award Recipient and February Author of the Month. She's also received the Marguerite Press Small Press Advancement Award; Neshee Publication Best Promoter's Award; and the 1st Aspicomm S'Indie Trailblazer Award.

Some of her favorite people are Tony Rose & Yvonne Rose who believed in her work as an author from the inception of her writing career. In 2005, the publishers of Amber Communications Group, Inc. gave Heather her first book deal, and the rest is HISTORY. She continues to write and enjoys every moment.

To learn more about Heather Covington, please visit:
http://authors.aalbc.com/heathercovington.htm.)

Are You Ready for the Literary Divas™ Book Tour?

Heather brings fun and exciting literary baskets full of prizes, books, gift certificates, posters, autographed pictures, and t-shirts to each event. As a celebrated educator and Licensed Reading Specialist, Heather also trains young Literary Divas. If you would like to schedule a booksigning for Heather Covington to visit your bookclub, library, bookstore, college, school, organization, television or radio show, appear as a guest host, emcee, judge, panelist or public speaker for your next event or schedule an interview, contact Heather at Disilgold @aol.com.

All future editions of *Literary Divas*™ will include a comprehensive directory of supporters of this work in the Book Industry from bookstores, libraries and literary services to online sites and businesses. You'll also see ongoing feedback, reviews and contests in search of new Literary Divas for upcoming editions. Coming Soon: *Literary Dons: The Top 100+ Most Admired African American Men in Literature.*

Get the Literary Divas™ Connection. Visit Heather's sites at www.Heather-Covington.com or www.Disilgold.com for her updated photo gallery and online journal and www.LiteraryDiva.com for the latest tour information.

Thank you for supporting Literary Divas around the world. Send your supportive feedback to Disilgold @aol.com or amberbk@aol.com.

See you at Heather Covington's *Literary Divas*™ Book Tour and Self-Publishing Empowerment and Enlightment Seminars™!

International Contest From the Author of Literary Divas ™ and Literary Dons™

Submit your Literary Divas™ Life Story or Literary Dons™ Life Story in less than 1000 words on your journey as a writer, the steps you took to hone your craft and goals for getting your work published or steps you took to get your work published, plus how Literary Divas ™ or Literary Dons ™ inspired you to take this journey. If selected, you may appear in the next volume or updated versions of *Literary Divas*™ or *Literary Dons*™, and be online at www.LiteraryDiva.com.

Include a sample of your work, Timeline of all published works, future projects or literary works, head shot, biographical and contact information. By submitting your life story, it may be published. Do not send originals. Submissions will not be returned. This contest is subject to change at anytime. Be sure to get a copy of the next *Literary Divas*™ or *Literary Dons*™ to find out if your entry was selected or visit www. LiteraryDiva.com.

E-Mail your submission to Amberbk @aol.com or Disilgold@ aol.com.

Inspire a young Literary Diva™ or Literary Don™!

Give this book as a gift!

ORDER FORM

WWW.AMBERBOOKS.COM
African-American Self Help and Career Books

Fax Orders: 480-283-0991
Telephone Orders: 480-460-1660
Online Orders: E-mail: Amberbks@aol.com

Postal Orders: Send Checks & Money Orders to:
Amber Books Publishing
1334 E. Chandler Blvd., Suite 5-D67, Phoenix, AZ 85048

_____ *Literary Divas*
_____ *Beside Every Great Man…Is A Great Woman*
_____ *Beautiful Black Hair: A Step-by-Step Instructional Guide*
_____ *The Afrocentric Bride: A Style Guide*
_____ *The African-American Woman's Guide to Great Sex, Happiness, & Marital Bliss*
_____ *The African-American Music Instruction Guide for Piano*
_____ *The African-American Family's Guide to Tracing Our Roots*
_____ *How to Be an Entrepreneur and Keep Your Sanity*
_____ *The African-American Guide to Real Estate Investing, $30,000 in 30 Days*
_____ *The African-American Writer's Guide to Successful Self-Publishing*
_____ *How to Get Rich When You Ain't Got Nothing*
_____ *Fighting for Your Life*
_____ *Urban Suicide: The Enemy We Choose Not to See*
_____ *The African-American Travel Guide*
_____ *The African-American Teenagers Guide to Personal Growth, Health, Safety, Sex and Survival*
_____ *Langhorn & Mary: A 19th American Century Love Story*
_____ *No Mistakes: The African-American Teen Guide to Growing Up Strong*
_____ *The House that Jack Built*
_____ *The African-American Woman's Guide to Successful Make-up and Skin Care*
_____ *The African-American Job Seeker's Guide to Successful Employment*
_____ *Wake Up and Smell the Dollars! Whose Inner City is This Anyway?*

Name:_____

Company Name:_____

Address:_____

City:_____ State:_____ Zip:_____

Telephone: (_____) _____ E-mail:_____

Literary Divas	$16.95	❏ Check ❏ Money Order ❏ Cashiers Check
Beside Every Great Man	$14.95	❏ Credit Card: ❏ MC ❏ Visa ❏ Amex ❏ Discover
Beautiful Black Hair	$16.95	
The Afrocentric Bride	$16.95	CC#_____
Great Sex	$14.95	
Music Instruction Guide	$14.95	Expiration Date:_____
Tracing Our Roots	$14.95	
How to be an Entrepreneur	$14.95	**Payable to:** Amber Books
Real Estate Investing	$14.95	1334 E. Chandler Blvd., Suite 5-D67
Successful Self-Publishing	$14.95	Phoenix, AZ 85048
How to Get Rich	$14.95	
Fighting for Your Life	$14.95	**Shipping:** $5.00 per book. Allow 7 days for delivery.
Urban Suicide	$14.95	**Sales Tax:** Add 7.05% to books shipped to AZ addresses.
Travel Guide	$14.95	**Total enclosed: $**_____
Teenagers Guide	$19.95	
Langhorn & Mary	$25.95	
No Mistakes	$14.95	For Bulk Rates Call: **480-460-1660**
The House That Jack Built	$16.95	
Successful Make-up	$14.95	## ORDER NOW
Job Seeker's Guide	$14.95	
Wake Up & Smell the Dollars	$18.95	